Developmentalism, Dependency, and the State

CHRISTOPHER HOPE

Developmentalism, Dependency, and the State

Industrial Development and Economic Change in Namibia since 1900

Basler Afrika Bibliographien 2020

©2020 The author
©2020 Basler Afrika Bibliographien

Basler Afrika Bibliographien
Namibia Resource Centre & Southern Africa Library
Klosterberg 23
PO Box
4001 Basel
Switzerland
www.baslerafrika.ch

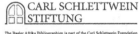

CARL SCHLETTWEIN
STIFTUNG

The Basler Afrika Bibliographien is part of the Carl Schlettwein Foundation

Cover design: James Pryor

ISBN 978-3-906927-21-3

Contents

This book is dedicated to my mother,

to the memory of my father,

and to the memory of Giulio Regeni.

Acknowledgements

This work is a revised version of my doctoral research, undertaken at the University of Cambridge, UK, under the supervision of Dr. Ha-Joon Chang. My immense thanks to Ha-Joon, an excellent and considerate mentor, and to the University, which was a thoroughly engaging place in which to study. The Centre of Development Studies in which I was based was a place of friendly faces and bright ideas. Thanks to the staff of the Centre, especially Doreen Woolfrey. Amongst my fellow students, my gratitude particularly goes to Shachi Amdekar, Lorena Gazzotti, Amir Lebdioui, Paola Velasco, Noura Wahby, Mihiri Warnasuriya, and Kiryl Zach. A word for Giulio Regeni, my friend and fellow student, who was abducted, tortured, and killed whilst conducting field research in Egypt. Giulio directly contributed to this research, pointing me in the direction of several works that proved integral to my argument. Also in Cambridge, I'd like to thank Mahvish Ahmad, Justin Kemp, Alicia Krozer, Marcela Morales, Nina Rismal, Bob Rowthorn, and the institutions and staff of Darwin College, Marshall Library, and the African Studies Library.

Returning to Namibia, where I lived from the ages of four to ten, to conduct research at various points from 2015 to 2017, was a great experience. I am extremely grateful to the Institute for Public Policy Research Namibia for hosting me. Thanks to Martha Nangola, Salmi Shigwedha and, in particular, to Graham Hopwood and Max Weylandt. Thanks also to Klaus Schade of the Economic Association of Namibia, Titus Kamatuka at the Namibia Statistics Agency, and Irene Izaacs and Werner Hillebrecht at the National Archives of Namibia. Thanks, too, to all those who agreed to be interviewed as part of my study, and to those who provided me with welcoming places to stay and personal support: Kauna Ndilula and her family; Nicky Marais, Martin Harris and Helen Harris; Vera and Mike Leech; and Zula and Anvar Muhamedrahimov.

Elsewhere in the world, I am grateful to the staff of the Basler Afrika Bibliographien in Basel and the British Library in London for their help during my time researching in their institutions. Thank you very much to Andrea, Klaus, and Luisa Braig for hosting me in Britzingen, Germany, whilst I conducted my research in Basel.

Thanks to Graham Hopwood, Amir Lebdioui, Bernie Moore, and Kiryl Zach for reading parts of my research and offering constructive feedback. Thanks to Antonia Perelló, who read all of it. Thanks too, to Antonia, for so much more than that. My gratitude also goes to my dear friend James Pryor, who designed the maps in this research and offered advice on its overall layout. I'm very appreciative of the considered comments and guidance that I received from my doctorate examiners, Dr. Shailaja Fennell of the University of Cambridge and Dr. Eka Ikpe of King's College London.

I was very fortunate to have been chosen as the Cambridge Political Economy Society Trust's Scholar for 2014, thereby securing funding for the research. Additional funding for field research was received by the Department of Politics and International Studies in Cambridge and by the Smuts Memorial Fund. Thanks to all these bodies for their financial support.

The final word is for my family. Thanks to my mum, Susan Hope, who has been loving and caring throughout my life and particularly during the writing of this work. My dad, Andrew Hope, died four years before I started my doctorate, but was always in my thoughts as I conducted this research. This work is dedicated to his memory, to my mother, and to the memory of Giulio Regeni.

1 Introduction

This book explores economic development in Namibia from 1900 to present day, with a principal interest in industrial development and the role of the state in facilitating its progression. The main questions which are addressed are 'what industries have been able to develop in Namibia and why?' and 'has the Namibian state played a role in supporting industrial development and what explains its action or inaction?'. The line of enquiry is based on the premise that industrial development and economic diversification were the main (economic) variables that explained why some countries were able to rapidly increase their wealth during the 20th century whilst others could not achieve a level of economic change that would allow for the quality of life of its citizens to decisively improve. If we accept that industrial development and economic diversification are central to the process of economic development, then trying to understand their fates – what has worked, what has gone wrong, why did an economy move in particular ways – becomes a central point on investigation.

The argument of the study is that, whilst industrial development in Namibia has been affected by a host of 'economic' factors (such as a small domestic market, distance to major markets, etc.), progress has been fundamentally constrained by a lack of state support to the sector and by actions from international actors which have thwarted efforts towards structural transformation of the economy. In the colonial era, the state was willing to intervene in the economy to support the economically influential farmers of the country but was unwilling to support its industrialists. The lack of state support exacerbated the issues for the manufacturing sector caused by competition from South African firms who, due to free access to Namibia's market owing to the country's status as a South African colony, were to entirely overrun Namibian firms.

In comparison, the most remarkable feature of industrial development in Namibia since independence is its continuity with the colonial era. Again, one can see how the influence of Namibia's leading economic actors (particularly in the mining and trading sectors) have stood in opposition to structural transformation, and the evident lack of commitment from the state to achieving industrial development. More so in the independence era, the influence of international political economy factors in both shaping the attitude of the Namibian state to industrial policy and in undermining efforts towards industrial policy is stark.

The following study is in part historical: charting the course and causes of industrial and economic development in Namibia over the 20th and 21st centuries, and in part contemporary: studying current issues in industrial and economic development in the country. Both elements of the study can be seen to reflect present trends in economic research. The first is the renewed interest in industrial policy in Africa today and the second is to so-called 'renaissance' of African economic history (discussed later in this chapter).

My hope is that this book can serve as a useful resource for students interested in the study of the Namibian economy providing, as it does, rarely seen data and information, as well as new theories on the country's economy. But before launching into the historical narrative, it is first necessary to outline some of the thinking and previous research which underpins this study.

Industrial development as the driver of economic development

Industrial development, as understood in this research, refers to the structural transformation of the economy that sees increased levels of manufacturing and concurrent technological advancements. Accordingly, when I refer in this research to 'structural transformation' I effectively mean 'the process of the industrialisation of the economy'.

This is a relatively narrow definition of structural transformation. It seems that the term (also sometimes referred to as 'economic transformation' or 'structural change') has come into prominence as an attempt from academics who study economic development to broaden the term 'industrialisation' to incorporate other features of the economy associated with high-income countries and because some view industrial development to no longer be essential for economic development. For an example of the former, a good definition of structural transformation is that it: "involves diversifying the economy away from dependence on a few primary commodities to an economy based on value addition in agroindustry, manufacturing, and knowledge-based services; greater application of technology to upgrade agricultural processes and raise agricultural productivity; and moving from low-value exports to higher-value exports" (Whitfield et al., 2015: 5). My only qualm with this definition is that I do not see why reference is only made to greater application of technology to upgrade agricultural processes and raise agricultural productivity, when, clearly, structural transformation also refers to such upgrading in connection to the manufacturing sector. The definition of 'manufacturing' used throughout this research is that of the UN's Industrial Classification of All Economic Activities (ISIC).[1]

---

[1] The UN ISIC definition of manufacturing is: "the physical or chemical transformation of materials, substances, or components into new products... The materials, substances, or components transformed are raw materials that are products of agriculture, forestry, fishing, mining or quarrying as well as products of other manufacturing activities. Substantial alteration, renovation or reconstruction of goods is generally considered to be manufacturing" (United Nations, 2008: 85). This is the typical international working definition of manufacturing and is used in most (if not

The onset of modern industrial development was the industrial revolution, commencing in Britain in the 18th century before spreading across Western Europe and to North America and then to other parts of the world. It was, as the name suggests, a landmark moment, when "for the first time in human history, the shackles were taken off the productive power of human societies, which henceforth became capable of the constant, rapid, and up to the present limitless multiplication of men, goods and services... By any reckoning this was probably the most important event in world history, at any rate since the invention of agriculture and cities" (Hobsbawm, 1962: 28–29). Furtado (1964: 116) similarly argues that "the advent of an industrialised economy in Europe during the last few decades of the eighteenth century, entailing a disruption of the world economy of the time, involved a qualitative change of the same order as the discovery of fire, of the wheel, or of the experimental method".

The industrial revolution – marked by technological innovation, urbanisation, proletarianisation, and the pervasion of the factory system – saw a massive shift in employment from agriculture to manufacturing, as well as growing efficiency in farming driven by technological advancement (Ashworth, 2017). Its onset was the birth of the modern era and the rapid expansion of gross domestic product (GDP) that has occurred globally since then.

The view that industrial development is the essential driver of economic development has a long history, with academics having pointed to its central role in explaining the expansion of wealth in first Britain, then Western Europe, the United States, the Soviet Union, and eventually East Asia (for an overview, see Reinert, 2007). The typical argument stressing the importance of industrial development to economic development states that manufacturing activities (and certain services) have "growth-inducing or growth-enhancing effects", meaning that the advancement of these sectors is more likely to cause development than the advancement of other sectors of the economy (Tregenna, 2008: 176). These effects include 'learning by doing', dynamic economies of scale, increasing returns, externalities and spillover effects which are most likely to be found in manufacturing activities (Palma, 2008). The expansion of manufacturing activities thus can cause massive economic advancement.

But the view that places prominence on the manufacturing sector is by no means universally accepted. The renowned free-trade advocate Jagdish Bhagwati, for example, has described the focus of some economists and policymakers on industrial development as a

---

all) of the national accounts of governments across the world, and by the likes of UNIDO and the World Bank. It covers the manufacture of a host of products, including food (e.g. dairy products, the processing of meat and fish), beverages, clothes, paper, printing, chemical products (e.g. fertilizers, paints, plastics), fabricated metals (e.g. windows, door frames), electrical equipment (e.g. batteries, domestic appliances, computers), machinery, transport equipment (e.g. ships, plans, motor vehicles), furniture, and jewellery.

"manufacturing fetish", with this 'fetish' seen to have emerged from the erroneous belief that services are technologically stagnant (Bhagwati, 2010). Deindustrialisation in the likes of the UK and the US from the 1960s onwards, 'premature deindustrialisation' in many low-income countries since the 1980s, as well as rising automation in the economy, have added further fuel to the fire of opinion that industrial development is no longer necessary for economic development.

Recent research has, however, continued to stress the importance of industrial development to economic development (see, for example, Szirmai, 2011; Haraguchi et al., 2017; Felipe et al., 2018; Rocha, 2018). If low-income countries are to markedly increase the well-being of their societies, it appears that industrial advancement will still be necessary. The track record, to date, has been disappointing. In the cases of Latin America and Africa, for example, their contributions to global manufacturing value added (MVA) have decreased from 36.2% and 9.2% in 1990 to 13.0% and 4.4% respectively in 2017 (UNIDO, 2017).

The importance of industrial policy

For industrial development to occur the state must typically play a crucial role in inducing its advancement through actively intervening in the economy. In other words, states must successfully execute 'industrial policy'. Industrial policy will be understood in this research as a government strategy "that includes a range of implicit or explicit policy instruments selectively focused on specific industrial sectors for the purpose of shaping structural change in line with a broader national vision and strategy" (Oqubay, 2015: 18).2 In direct contradiction to free-market views of economic development, which envisage a limited role of the government in the economy, industrial policy advocates argue that if countries are to positively restructure their economies, then the state will be required to support firms, build and maintain infrastructure, foster innovation, and manage sectors of the economy (Chang & Andreoni, 2016).

---

[2] Settling on a definition of industrial policy is not straightforward. For example, I initially thought to follow White (2008: 4): industrial policy as "a concerted, focused, conscious effort on the part of a government to encourage and promote a specific industry or sector with an array of policy tools". But what is lacking in this definition, unlike in that of Oqubay, is the link between industrial policy and the ambition of effecting structural change. This is important. For example, I do not consider the targeted support of a pre-established mining industry, such as through generous tax cuts, to be industrial policy, because it is not related to the ambition of altering the economic structure of the country. A potential issue with Oqubay's definition, conversely, emerges precisely from the linking of industrial policy to structural change. Could countries with advanced economies perform industrial policy under Oqubay's definition? Accordingly, his definition may be improved by stating that its purpose is in 'shaping structural change *and economic development more broadly'*.

Economic history provides overwhelming evidence to support the argument that states that have succeeded in achieving economic development have done so through concerted industrial policy (for reviews see Chang, 2003 and Reinert, 2007). As Chang (2003: 125–126) concludes, "[a] consistent pattern emerges, in which all the catching-up economies use activist industrial, trade and technology policies… to promote economic development… The policy tools involved in such promotional efforts may have become more varied, complex and effective… but the general pattern has remained remarkably true to type".

Whilst in the 1950s and 1960s the idea that in order to develop states would have to play an active role in the economy was accepted by most leading development economists, the rise of neoliberal theory in the 1970s and 1980s and a concurrent predominance of free-market arguments from economists and international organisations meant that this belief lost all currency (for an excellent discussion, see Toye, 1993). Industrial policy was, for many years beginning in the mid-1980s, "one of the most toxic phrases in the whole of the economics vocabulary" (Wade, 2014: 1) and research on the subject "lapsed into three decades of ideologically-motivated wilful neglect" (Chang & Andreoni, 2016: 3).

Over recent years, however, industrial policy has "enjoyed something of a renaissance" in the mainstream economic literature, with a host of prominent academics and international organisations now writing expansively on the best ways for states to actively foster economic growth (Wade, 2014: 2). Edited volumes from Cimoli et al. (2009), Stiglitz & Lin (2013), Felipe (2015), and Page & Tarp (2017a), as well as a host of articles and monographs[3] and reports written by the likes of the World Bank[4] and the UN Economic Commission for Africa,[5] have provided ample case-studies of countries' experiences, theoretical insights, and policy prescriptions. Specific to Africa (a region that has garnered particular attention during the renaissance of the literature), Stiglitz et al. (2013a) and Noman & Stiglitz (2016) have compiled continent-specific assessments of industrial policy. Moreover, many governments across the world are now speaking openly about the need to have an industrial policy and are themselves publishing strategy documents. Evidently, industrial policy has returned to the mainstream, both in policy and in academic circles.

This development should be welcomed. The more analytical energy that can be dedicated to industrial policy, the more informed policymakers can be, the greater the expectation will be that countries pursue well-formulated industrial policies, and the less able wealthier countries will be able to pursue trade agreements that reduce industrial policy space in poorer nations.

---

[3]   See, for example, Rodrik (2004); Hausmann & Rodrik (2006); Lin & Chang (2009); Chang (2009); Page (2012); Altenburg & Lütkenhorst, 2015; Chang & Andreoni (2016); Chang et al. (2016).

[4]   See Stiglitz et al. (2013b).

[5]   See UNECA (2014)._

Nevertheless, the mainstream works on industrial policy to have emerged during the renaissance can be criticised for their prescriptive nature. These works typically outline perceived 'correct' policies to achieve structural transformation, such as: improving the business climate and aggressively courting FDI (Page, 2009); depreciating the exchange rate (Greenwald & Stiglitz, 2013; Rodrik, 2014); improving infrastructure (Harrison et al., 2014; Page, 2012; Stiglitz et al., 2013a); making labour markets more flexible (McMillan et al., 2014); and improving firms' access to finance (Harrison et al., 2014). Whilst often valid, they tend to do little more than outline a 'best practice' of industrial policy, thereby implying that all a country needs to structurally transform is to know and emulate the historic or contemporary successful examples of industrial policy (allowing for some variation in method based on a given country's conditions).

Though they do not make the process of structural change sound easy, they do often make it sound formulaic. This can be particularly seen in the works that try to couch their industrial policy analysis in terms of 'market failures' (see, for example, Greenwald & Stiglitz, 2013; Lin & Monga, 2013), which imply that with the correction of a market failures (say, large transaction costs in doing business or a lack of access for firms to finance) well-functioning markets will emerge and thrive.

In reality, the process of successful structural transformation is inherently complex and fraught with difficulties. There is no simple fix, and moreover there is no simple explanation of economic progress. As Hirschman (1958: 28) wrote in making the same point, "[o]ur approach leads us to doubt the existence of a pent-up energy that is held back by villainous obstacles". The suggestion in this research is that, to try to understand processes of structural transformation and industrial policy implementation, it is necessary to look beyond simple policy prescriptions, and to investigate the underlying power dynamics and institutions that drive states' actions. In other words, it is necessary to investigate the *political economy* of industrial policy and development, an aspect which is largely absent from the mainstream industrial policy literature.[6]

---

[6] This is not to suggest that many of these writers do not acknowledge the relevance of political economy to understanding processes of structural change. For example, Rodrik et al. (2016: 35) write that "[i]n Botswana, some of the constraints are as much political economy as technical ones". Page & Tarp (2017b) too, acknowledge the need for states to be committed to industrial policy implementation and to have the capacity necessary to implement it successfully. Nevertheless, political economy analysis is rarely at the forefront of these works.

The study of the political economy of industrial policy and development

The term 'political economy', often bandied around in academia in a host of contexts and with an apparent multitude of unstated meanings, will be understood in this research in the manner put forth by Collinson (2003: 3):

> Political economy analysis is concerned with the interaction of political and eco-
> nomic processes in a society: the distribution of power and wealth between different
> groups and individuals, and the processes that create, sustain and transform these
> relationships over time.[7]

This research assumes that political economy, or the 'politics of economics', is essential to understanding processes of structural transformation. What role do power relations play, what motivates states to pursue industrial policy, why have some states not pursued indus-trial policy at all (or at least not with any real rigour), how do state institutions affect indus-trial policy: these are questions that are taken in this research to be paramount. For most readers this assertion will come as little surprise – states act differently to each other on a whole manner of issues, economic policy notwithstanding, and the causes are in large part political.

Political economy considerations – whether looking at the manner in which trade arrange-ments are determined, who holds influence over states' economic policies, or what institu-tions are in place – has a lengthy and rich history in research on industrial and economic development.[8] Of the post-war development economists (by no means the first 'political economists'), the likes of Hirschman (1958; 1968), Gerschenkron (1962), and Myrdal (1968) included analyses of power relations in their explanations of (a lack of) economic develop-ment.[9] For example, Hirschman (1968: 29) argued that a "prerequisite" for manufacturers in Latin America to push themselves to export was that "the industrialist class must feel reasonably sure that it can control certain crucial fiscal and monetary policies of its govern-ment... only a cohesive, vocal, and highly influential national bourgeoisie is likely to carry in-dustrialization beyond relatively safe import-substitution to the risk export-oriented stage".[10]

---

[7]   My only contention with this definition is that it implies that the economy and polity can be neatly separated (for a critique of such views, see Chang, 2011).

[8]   And in the social sciences in general. For a discussion of the role of interests in shaping economic policy choices of states, see Hall (1997).

[9]   Free-market-advocating development economists have also included the role of interests in their explanations of the failure of states to implement free-market policies: in other words, using the exact same reasoning as those economists cited above, but to explain why states have been un-willing to liberalise their economies, as opposed to why they have not been interventionist (see, for example, Lal, 1983).

[10]   Despite such arguments, analyses of power and institutional arrangements, generally, were not at

Analyses of power were at the forefront of the arguments of the 'dependency' school of writers of the same epoch. Common across this diverse school (which included Baran, 1957; Furtado; 1964; Cardoso & Faletto, 1969; and Sunkel, 1969) was the argument that the global capitalist 'centres' (the wealthy, industrialised nations) exert pressure on its 'peripheries' (poorer, typically commodity producing nations), particularly through alliances with the elites of peripheral economies, to maintain the international economic order, thereby making it difficult for the latter countries to structurally transform and thus entrenching an economic dependence on the centre. Here, industrial policy in the 'periphery', as in the example quoted from Hirschman above, is often seen to be inhibited by the actions of states in the 'centre' and by a lack of commitment from the peripheral states to achieving structural transformation.

The 1980s saw the rise of the 'developmental state' approach to the study of processes of industrial development in the 'East Asian miracle economies', beginning with Johnson (1982) and followed by the likes of Amsden (1989) and Wade (1990). These works did deploy political economy arguments, but generally "were more concerned with establishing that the state had a role to play in late industrialization than with explaining the politics that made state interventions possible and successful" (Whitfield et al., 2015: 6). Subsequent developmental state works delved deeper into political economy considerations of the make-up and origins of such states that could successfully drive forward structural transformation, with Evans (1995) seeking to understand the institutional framework for successful industrial policy, and the likes of Leftwich (1995) and Mkandawire (2001) theorising on the reasons as to why developmental states with the necessary commitment to industrial development have emerged in some countries and not others. The developmental state approach, however, has, in terms of its popularity and prevalence, seen a decline since its heyday of the late 1980s and early 1990s, with Fine (2013: 3) observing "the dilution and marginalisation of [the approach] over the past 20 years".

Much of the developmental state works were particularly focussed on the 'institutions' needed for economic and industrial development, pinpointing how the structure of the state (e.g. its bureaucratic framework) and its relations with society (e.g. how able the state was to fruitfully interact with the private sector) were facilitating successful industrial policy. Indeed, the 1990s and early 2000s was a time when institutions were becoming a main focal point in the study of economic development, with the 'new institutional economics' (NIE) of the likes of North (1990) and Acemoglu et al. (2001; 2004) bringing the study of institu-

---

the forefront of development economists' research in the 1950s and 1960s. As Leftwich (1995: 403) argues, in these works "a major role for the state was announced, but the political and institutional conditions for its effective discharge of that role were never identified".

tions into mainstream economics. With institutions in vogue, political economy works on industrial policy and development dedicated significant energy to their study (see, for example, Burlamaqui et al., 2000; Chang, 2002; Chang & Evans, 2005; Chang, 2007a). But whilst successfully critiquing the NIE approach and demonstrating the political contestation involved in the establishment of institutions, the heterodox institutions school was unable to notably advance its own research agenda on the political economy of industrial policy.

An increasingly prevalent branch of research today on the political economy of industrial policy has sought to explain industrial policy successes or failures based on the balance of power in society, just as the likes of Hirschman and, particularly the dependency school, had tended to do. This has meant the analysis of what has been called by some the 'political equilibrium' of a society (Robinson, 2009) and more frequently the 'political settlement' of a country (Khan, 2010; Gray, 2013; Whitfield & Burr, 2014; Whitfield et al., 2015). For example, Robinson (2009: 9) writes that "[v]ariation in the adoption of industrial policy or in its success or failure has less to do with ideas or economists... and much more to do with the nature of the political equilibrium in society – which interests are mobilized, what their interests are, what are the political institutions, etc.". Meanwhile, the likes of Whitfield et al. (2015: 22) stress that success or failure in industrial policy is dependent on "distribution of power in society". Much of the work within the political settlements approach has been particularly focussed on structural transformation in Africa.

Recent years have also seen the minor re-emergence of the "oft-neglected developmental state literature" approach to understanding industrial policy and development (Thurbon, 2016: 4) in what Thurbon has called the "rebirth of the developmental state" (ibid: 1).[11] Unlike the political settlements approach – which has purposefully distanced itself from the developmental state approach largely because of its supposed misrepresentation (almost idolisation) of the cohesiveness of the East Asian states of the 1970s and 1980s (Whitfield et al., 2015) – analysis of processes of industrial development within the developmental state framework implicitly have as a starting point a conceptualisation akin to something like: 'highly interventionist, dedicated states (i.e. developmental states) have traditionally been the drivers of industrial development – what do they look like, and why have they existed in some places and not others?'.

These approaches typically have a less strict focus on the balance of power in society and are more guided by questions as to the institutional structure of states and, to a lesser extent, on the emergence of a 'developmental mindset' from the state (Thurbon, 2016). Examples of contemporary works in this approach – again, much of which focuses on Africa – in the

---

[11]   Haggard (2018: 72) has also referred to the clear "resurgence of interest" in the approach.

developmental state tradition include: Mkandawire (2010), Ikpe (2013), Williams (2014), Thurbon (2016), Thurbon & Weiss (2016), Mann & Berry (2016), Hsu (2017), Ricz (2017), Behuria (2017), Clapham (2017), Ovadia & Wolf (2017), and Kanyenze et al. (2017). Most of these works offer detailed case studies, with Ricz (2017) and Mann & Berry (2016) proving exemplary in their detailed analyses of the context in which more developmentally-oriented states emerged in Brazil and Rwanda respectively.

There has been a tendency in the industrial policy literature and the developmental states literature to concentrate on successful examples of industrial policy implementation. Noman & Stiglitz's (2016) edited volume on industrial policy and economic transformation in Africa, for example, includes a chapter presenting "lessons from five outstanding cases" (Hosono, 2016), and two other chapters dedicated to industrial sectors in Ethiopia (Abebe & Schaefer, 2016; Shimada, 2016), but no other case studies. Similarly, the edited volume by Newman et al. (2016: 2) on industrial development in Africa and 'emerging' Asia includes eight countries in sub-Saharan Africa, described as "some of the stars of Africa's growth turnaround". As Altenburg (2011: 8) states, "in stark contrast with the... success cases of catch-up development, little is known about the quality and the outcomes of industrial policies in low and lower-middle-income countries" that have seen no substantial rise in industrial development.

The notion that we restrict our analyses of industrial development to the extreme polarity of success is an inattentive proposition. Is there not value in observing more typical cases, and to observe what impediments there have been to success, or to assess what has caused manufacturing development to hold steady? The need to look at unexemplary instances is, moreover, particularly important for matters of political economy (as opposed to, say, determining policy prescriptions). If we are deliberating the determinants of developmentalism and the motivations of states, it is just as important to look at 'unsuccessful' countries as it is to focus analytical attention on the few successes of structural transformation. Whilst the propensity to concentrate on 'success stories' in the industrial policy literature is notably diminishing, it is necessary for this trend to continue. This book seeks to support this objective.

The 'renaissance' of research into African economic history

This book also represents a minor contribution to the recent 'renaissance' of African economic history (for a discussion, see Hopkins, 2009; Austin & Broadberry, 2014). A common field of research in the 1960s and 1970s, the study of African economic history was seen to have waned drastically by the end of the 1990s, but began to re-emerge in the 2000s and is now flourishing, bestowed with "the new generation of economic historians working on Africa" (Austin & Broadberry, 2014: 893). The most famous of whom is the new historians is likely Morten Jerven. (see Jerven, 2015).

Curiously, the renaissance in the literature is typically acknowledged as stemming from a famous and divisive Acemoglu et al. (2001) paper on the colonial origins of comparative development. The literature is consequently, following in the footsteps of Acemoglu and his co-authors, highly focused on an institutional analysis: "[t]he new research programme begins with the hypothesis that institutional variables are more significant than other variables in explaining development" (Hopkins, 2009: 161).

This institutional focus is unsatisfactory as it tends to lead to deterministic analyses trying to explain either of a) underdevelopment: "specialists on Africa have turned to history to try to understand the origins of present-day poverty" (*ibid*: 158) or of b) sudden success: "to look to the past to seek clues about the origins of Africa's current growth boom" (Austin & Broadberry, 2014: 896). The study of history should not, in my view, simply be a case of trying to explain phenomena that we see today (a growth lag, a growth boom, etc.). Such an approach will inevitably fail to show the vicissitudes, complexities and nonlinearity of economic development, as Jerven (2015) and Austin (2008) have argued.

A further problem with the new literature has been a lack of empirical data. Typically, as Jerven (2015: 19) notes, "[i]n African economic histories that have been written using time series data about economic growth, year 1 has been 1960", obviously representing "an artificial starting point". Austin & Broadberry (2014: 900) similarly lament the "unfortunate neglect of long-run economic growth in Africa" within research. There is a need to try to analyse processes of economic development (and in our case, specifically industrial development) in a more long-term perspective, and without diminishing history to a banal variable factor to be included in assessing development prospects and constraints today. Using statistical and qualitative evidence collected from various archives, this book seeks to provide a long-term statistical and political economy analysis of Namibia's industrial and economic development.

Studying Namibian economics, politics, and history

Whilst most readers of this work will be familiar with Namibia, for those who are not, the below lays out a potted history and description of the nation. For a superb general history of the pre-independence era, see Wallace (2011). Melber (2014) provides a good assessment of political developments since independence. Sherbourne (2016) is an exceptionally thorough account of Namibia's economy since independence.

Namibia is located in the south-west of Africa, bordered by the Atlantic coast to the west, South Africa to the south, Botswana to the east, Angola to the north, and, via a relatively small strip of land which juts out from the north-eastern corner of the country, Zambia and Zimbabwe (see Map 1, p. 158). Its population of just 2.5 million people is spread over a large land area, such that it is in fact the third least densely populated country in the world, after Greenland and Mongolia. With two deserts (the Namib and the Kalahari), it has the lowest level of rainfall amongst sub-Saharan Africa countries and much of the country is arid, though the northern parts of the country see more rainfall and are more fertile.

Namibia achieved independence in 1990, having previously been a German colony from 1884 to 1915, and then – following a successful invasion by the South Africans at the behest of the British during the First World War – a South African colony from 1915 to 1989. Officially, from 1920 onwards, Namibia (then known as South West Africa) was a League of Nations Protectorate, with South Africa responsible for its oversight until it was deemed 'ready' for independence.

During the early years of the South African era the emigration of poor white farmers from South Africa to South West Africa (SWA) was encouraged as part of an ambition to expand the South African state and to eventually fully incorporate SWA within its borders. The country was governed by an Administrator who was appointed by South Africa, who sought to create conditions favourable for the prosperity of the white population of Namibia, offering generous support to white farmers. The black population, in contrast, had extremely limited rights, but was viewed as essential labour power for the mining and farming enterprises of the country. The chief productive economic activities of the South African colonial era were livestock raising, mining, and fishing.

In the post-World War II era, with the election of the National Party in 1948, the apartheid era began in South Africa, and apartheid policies were to a large extent mirrored in SWA. At the same time, South Africa officially appealed to the UN (which had replaced the League of Nations) to allow for SWA to be incorporated into South Africa and, although this request was rejected, South Africa increasingly governed the country as if it were part of its own territory, withdrawing responsibilities from SWA's Administration and placing them in the hands of the South African state.

In the late 1950s, independence movements in Namibia began to formulate, the most important of which became the South West African People's Organisation (SWAPO), founded in 1960. From 1966 SWAPO began to fight a war for independence, which occurred mainly in the northern regions of the country, with SWAPO's military bases mostly located in first Zambia and then Angola. Thousands of Namibians fled into exile during this period, and fighting was to continue up until independence.

In 1966 the UN General Assembly took the significant decision of revoking South Africa's Mandate over SWA, stating that "the policies of apartheid and racial discrimination practised by the Government of South Africa in South West Africa [constitute] a crime against humanity" (UN General Assembly, 1966). The three decades prior to independence in 1990 were to first witness South Africa desperately trying to maintain its grip on power, before eventually realising that such efforts were in vain, and from the late 1970s onwards beginning to dismantle the apartheid system in SWA (e.g. by removing rules on segregation) and slowly preparing for the transition of power to an independent Namibian state.

In May 1988 negotiations began towards the implementation of UN Security Council *Resolution 435*, which had been passed in 1978, calling for a ceasefire and for UN-supervised elections to take place. Namibian exiles began to return *en masse*, including the leading figures within SWAPO. SWAPO won the first elections held for independent Namibia in 1989 and accordingly SWAPO's leader throughout the independence struggle, Sam Nujoma, was sworn in as President of Namibia on the 21st of March 1990, the day which marked the official independence of the country. During most of the pre-independence era SWAPO had adopted strongly socialist rhetoric, but by independence there was a consensus within SWAPO over maintaining a free-market system, and as such the economic system in Namibia has remained similar to that of the pre-independence era (i.e. the private sector has been able to operate without significant interference from the state).

Independent Namibia has been characterised by political and economic stability. SWAPO has remained in power to this day, winning the six presidential elections for independent Namibia handsomely. Sam Nujoma stepped down as President in 2005, replaced by Hifikepunye Pohamba, who served until 2015, before Hage Geingob assumed the Presidency. The country performs very strongly by sub-Saharan African standards in measures of good governance, corruption, rule of law, and the like.[12]

Much of the population lives in the northern regions of the country, particularly the regions of Omusati, Oshana, Ohangwena, and Oshikoto, which in 2011 together accounted for 41% of the population (Republic of Namibia, 2013). Another 30% of the population live in the central regions of Otjozondjupa, Erongo, and Khomas. The latter region, Khomas, includes Namibia's capital city, Windhoek, which had an official population of 326,000 in 2011. It is currently the only town in the country with a population over 100,000, though 43% of the total national population is based in urban areas. In terms of ethnic groups, the

---

[12]   In 2017 it ranked 5th of 47 countries in the region in Transparency International's Corruption Perception Index; 8th in the Cato Institute's Human Freedom Index 2017 (which includes consideration of the likes of rule of law, freedom of association, freedom of expression); 7th in the Economist's Democracy Index 2017, and 2nd in Reporters Without Borders' World Press Freedom Index 2018.

largest by some distance is Ovambo (50% of the total population), followed by Kavango (9%), Herero (7%), Damara (7%), Nama (5%), Afrikaans-Namibian (4%), and German-Namibian (2%).

Namibia is relatively wealthy in comparison to other countries in sub-Saharan Africa: in 2016 it was the 7th richest country in the region (data available for 44 countries) in terms of GDP per capita.[13] The economy is dominated by mining, most notably of diamonds and uranium; fishing; cattle ranching; the services sector (financial and business services, real estate, and wholesale and retail trade); as well as by significant government expenditure and employment. Exports are dominated by minerals (diamonds, uranium, copper, zinc) and to a much smaller extent fish.

Namibia's comparatively strong performance in GDP per capita terms is in part explained by its rich mineral wealth coupled with its small population. The statistic masks Namibia's extreme levels of inequality, ranking as it does as one of the most unequal countries in the world according to the Gini-coefficient. High levels of poverty and unemployment persist, with wealth concentrated in the hands in a small proportion of the population.

Whilst there is a wealth of historical research on Namibia (see, for example, Goldblatt, 1971; Wood, 1988; du Pisani, 1989; Wallace, 2011), there has been very little in the way of a presentation of a 'history of economic development' (though the above cited works include good economic data). The Marxist historical account of capitalist development in Namibia offered by Kaakunga (1990) in his PhD research and the descriptive overview from Herrigel (1971) in his PhD research are useful exceptions, and there have also been histories of specific sub-sectors of the economy during the 20th century, such as for the fishing industry (Moorsom, 1984), agriculture (Moorsom, 1982; Lau & Reiner, 1993), the meat industry (Rawlinson, 1994), the diamond industry (Schneider, 2009), traders (specifically in the north of the country) (Dobler, 2014), and the beer industry (van der Hoog, 2016). A history of industrial development in Namibia has never been written.

Academic interest in Namibia was likely at its peak during the 1970s and 1980s, when Namibia was one of the few remaining colonies in Africa and international attention was keenly focused on the actions of the South African apartheid state. See Eriksen & Moorsom (1989) for an incredible bibliography, including almost every piece of research on Namibia ever written up to that point. Economic research was conducted by researchers from the United States and Europe sympathetic to Namibia's independence struggle (Sutcliffe, 1967; Gervasi, 1967; Rijneveld, 1977; Green, 1979; 1986; Green & Kiljunen, 1981; Innes, 1981; Sparks & Murray, 1985; Moorsom, 1990), Namibians in exile (Mbuende, 1986; Kaakunga,

---

[13] Its rank globally in terms of GDP per capita for 2016 was 131st out of 237 countries for whom data was available.

1990); and by some South African academics (most notably Thomas, 1978). Though the first two groups of authors were often forced to be somewhat speculative in their economic assessments, given the lack of data made available by South Africa state, a lot of useful analysis was provided. Some research was conducted on industrial policy and development in the 1980s and early 1990s (UNIDO, 1984; 1990; 1994; Thomas, 1985; Zinn, 1985; Curry & Stoneman, 1993), but for the most part the topic of industrial development was rarely addressed.

Regarding the analysis of economic and industrial development in the post-independence era, several academics have conducted highly useful studies. The Guide to the Namibian Economy written by Sherbourne (2016), now in its fourth edition, is an excellent source of information. Jauch (2001; 2007), as well as in co-authored works (Jauch & Tjirera, 2017) is perhaps the leading Namibian researcher on economic matters. In the 1990s and early 2000s there was also a large body of work on the Namibian economy produced by the Namibian Economic Policy Research Unit (NEPRU). These include Hansohm (1998); Hansohm & Mupotola-Sibongo (1998); and Melber (2000). The NEPRU reports tended to be quite short but provided a good overview. There are also good works on Namibian politics (e.g. Melber, 2007a; 2011; 2014, Hopwood, 2007; Cooper, 2012).

As far as overviews of the manufacturing sector are concerned, Hansohm (2000), Kadhikwa & Ndalikokule (2007), and a chapter within Sherbourne (2016) are the most detailed. Siboleka et al. (2014) analyse the relationship between growth of the agriculture and manufacturing sectors of the Namibian economy. One industry within the manufacturing sector which has received particular analytical attention has been the textile industry (Jauch, 2006; Winterfeldt, 2007). Concerning industrial policy, Rosendahl (2010) and Melber (2015) are the only published academic works on the subject, whilst in her master's research Kamhulu (2014) specifically assesses the usage of infant industry protection in the pasta and dairy industries.

Whilst there has been a reasonable amount of literature on the Namibian economy and the country's politics over the past fifty years, there have been very few attempts to chart the long-term progress of the economy, and this study is the first to traverse both the colonial and independence eras of the country in detail. That it does so through a political economy analysis, assessing power relations and the actions of the state over the course of more than a century, is a novel approach to examining the Namibian economy. The contemporary analysis, too, is original in the depth of its detail on industrial development and in its theories as to the constraints on industrial development.

Methodology

This research is a study of political economy and accordingly the approach used is qualitative and required extensive field research. Field research in Namibia was conducted for six months from December 2015 to May 2016, with a one-month follow-up research trip taking place in May and June 2017.

The main objective of the research trips was to conduct interviews, and over the course of this study close to 100 interviews were conducted. There were three main groups of persons interviewed: government officials, relevant members of civil society, and the private sector (mainly manufacturing firms), with each group of interviewees serving to elucidate different queries within my research.

Of the first group, most interviews were conducted with staff of the Ministry of Industrialization, Trade, and SME development (MITSMED), though interviews were also conducted with the likes of the Minister of Finance, the acting Managing Director of the Namibia Development Corporation, Governor of the Bank of Namibia, and the Director-General of the National Planning Commission. The primary objective of interviews with the bureaucrats of MITSMED was to obtain a sense of the type of work that the Ministry was presently doing (including its successes and failures), the working environment of the Ministry, and the kind of direction that staff were receiving. Interviews with senior officials within MITSMED and other high-ranking officials within the Government were more intended to understand the attitude of Namibia's political elites towards industrial policy and economic policy in general. Interviews were semi-structured and tailored, depending on the position of the interviewee. Though I was unable to meet with some members of the Government who I would have liked to speak with, overall state officials were extremely willing to meet and openly discuss their work and concerns.

Members of civil society were interviewed largely to obtain a clearer picture of the Namibian state, accounts of its recent policies, assessments of the drivers of policy, and the functioning of the Namibian system of accumulation. Interviewees included the editor-in-chief of the leading national newspaper, the head of the Economic Association of Namibia, an economist at the University of Namibia, a researcher at the Metal and Allied Namibian Workers Union, and other leading economists and political scientists. I was also able to take advantage of my being based in the IPPR office in Windhoek, Namibia's capital city, to attend numerous meetings, discussions, and workshops on politics and economics in Namibia, and thereby learn significant amounts about the major players in public policy and their diverging opinions.

In the private sector, the major group that was interviewed was manufacturing firms (39 firms were interviewed, as well as the head of the Namibian Manufacturers Association), in order to learn more about the companies, in particular their major markets, their challenges, the extent of government support, and the reasons that they have been able to succeed. Most of the largest manufacturing firms in Namibia were interviewed, but effort was also made to interview smaller firms, particularly those that have garnered a good reputation, or those in sectors in which the Government has expressed an interest. Tours of various factories were also undertaken to better understand the industrial processes involved in firm activities.

Firms from other sectors of the economy were also interviewed, to achieve a broader understanding of government policy and the economy in general, as well as to observe linkages between other sectors and the manufacturing sector. Interviews were conducted with the Managing Director of a leading commercial bank, the resident director for the *De Beers* diamond mining company in Namibia, and with the managing director of one of the largest holding companies in the country. A further ambition of these interviews was to better understand the ideologies of leading economic actors within Namibia.

Whilst interviews served me well in learning about independence-era Namibia, interviews would be of far less use in charting the trajectory of structural transformation during the colonial era (though interviews were, for example, held with the likes of the former Chairman of the colonial-era First National Development Corporation). Here, archival research had to be my primary research tool. Over July and August 2015 one month was spent at the Basler Afrika Bibliographien in Basel, Switzerland, an archive dedicated to Namibia. Much of my time in Namibia was also spent in the National Archives in Windhoek and after returning to the UK several weeks were spent in the British Library in London. There were two aims within the archival research: to document empirically processes of structural transformation and industrial development; and to uncover political economy elements relating to the trajectory of Namibia's economic progress.

Whilst for many countries the former objective would perhaps not be necessary, given the limited amount of research on the history of Namibian economic development (and the total absence of an historical account of industrial development), it was necessary to first establish and document the economic facts myself, before presenting a political economy analysis. In this regard much time was spent trawling over economic and industrial censuses, company reports, and early 20th century account of economic progress. But effort was also made to undertake research to inform my political economy assessments of the colonial era. This was inevitably far more challenging for the colonial than the independence era, but was never the less achievable, via the perusal of government reports (which set out the ambitions of the state), government annual assessments (which outlined the major developments and issues of the country at the time), and newspapers and annuals from the 1920s through to the 1980s (to uncover debates related to economic policy), as well as the reading of all relevant literature (reviewed at the start of Part II of this research).

An issue which presented itself with regards to the archival research conducted was my inability to speak German or Afrikaans. Fortunately, this proved to only be a minor impediment. Assessments of the German-era (1884 to 1915) were conducted at the time by British and South African sources (with the South African works also written in English) and those documents written in German identified as being of great importance were translated via a computer software and then verified by a German-speaking friend. Concerning Afrikaans, all documents from the Namibian colonial government were written in English up until the 1960s. From then until the early 1980s Afrikaans became the primary language used by the colonial state, making this roughly twenty-year period the hardest for me to research. Again, key documents were translated via computer software but some important documents, particularly those pertaining to the First National Development Corporation, were unable to form part of my analysis. Fortunately, this period was also that which had the largest amount of secondary material (e.g. academic publications) addressing it.

My collection of statistical material was not only limited to the colonial era. Indeed, much time was dedicated to a detailed study of the changes in Namibia's GDP and exports (sourced from the National Accounts), as well as to the uncovering of all available data on Namibian manufacturing. Data features heavily in this research for principally two reasons: because much of the data had yet to be published anywhere; and because I personally have been frustrated by political economy accounts of development that seem too far removed from the economic realities of the subject they are purportedly analysing. Solid statistical data thereby serves both to inform the reader and to contextualise the political economy discussion. Whilst questions can be rightly raised about the quality of data in Namibia, the Namibia Statistics Agency is well-staffed and diligent in its commitment to ensuring the publication of valid data. There are more issues related to the absence of industrial censuses in the independence era (and the seeming lack of comparability between the scant censuses), which did make the piecing together of information difficult at times.

Prior to presenting my research I would also like to reflect on my position as a researcher on the Namibian economy. Though I spent most of my childhood up to the age of ten living in Namibia, I am not a Namibian, and this large-scale, ambitious project to chart developments in the country over more than a century is written, like many studies of African economies in the past, by a white, male, foreigner. And whilst my research does not *directly* concern matters of race, in a research on the politics and economics of a country that experienced colonisation by a white settler minority which saw the systematic and violent subjugation of the black population for well over a century, the subject of the relationship between the white and black population of Namibia of course features, and in this regard my position as a white researcher is important.[14]

Chapter outline

In what follows, the study of Namibian economic and industrial development is divided into three time periods (1900 to 1945; 1946 to 1989; and 1990 to present day), within which are presented detailed analyses of the politics of industrial development and economic change. 1990 is the year that Namibia achieved independence from South Africa, so serves as a natural point of demarcation, whilst it was chosen to split the colonial era at the culmination of the Second World War because the post-war era saw a significant change in the colonial strategy of South Africa which had profound ramifications for Namibia, including its economic and industrial development.

Chapter 2 addresses the early colonial era in Namibia from 1900 to 1945, arguing that the state was instrumental in achieving the limited diversification that did occur in the economy and, through a comparison with the experience of neighbouring Southern Rhodesia (modern day Zimbabwe), argues that the reason that greater industrial development did not occur in Namibia was due to the economic influence of South Africa and the disinterest from the state in achieving industrial development.

Chapter 3 discusses the post-war economic boom era and subsequent unravelling of the colonial state from 1946 to 1989, assessing the scant industrial policy efforts that took place, and arguing that these efforts were mainly born either out of an attempt to support the country's farmers, or to try to legitimise the colonial state's actions.

Chapter 4 discusses industrial development and policy in the independence era, from 1990 to present day, arguing that, despite the strong rhetorical commitment to industrial policy from the state, industrial development has been decidedly lacking, and concurrently so has the advancement of manufacturing.

Chapter 5 provides a political economy analysis of contemporary constraints on Namibian industrial policy. It shows how the 'system of accumulation' in the country serves to undermine both the state's commitment to industrial policy and any efforts it actually does

---

[14] On the subject of race and ethnicity, after deliberation I have decided that where necessary in this study to use the terms 'white' and 'black' to refer to, respectively, people of European ancestry and people of African ancestry. This is problematic for a host of reasons. For example, the term 'black' homogenises several ethnic groups in Namibia. Elsewhere, the likes of Wallace (2011), have chosen to use the terms 'white' and 'African', though I feel this to be unsuitable as white Namibians are surely also African.

make to support industrial development. The role that international developments play in maintaining the system of accumulation is particularly emphasised.

Chapter 6 offers a conclusion to the research, reiterating its central arguments and assessing the consequences of these conclusions for our understanding of the political economy of industrial policy and development in Namibia.

A final comment before starting the investigation of the political economy of industrial policy and development. In my personal reading of studies on economic development, I have often found an issue to be that as the reader I have become lost in the author's narrative due to a lack of clarity. A stray term loosely defined, an unintelligible acronym, assumed knowledge on the part of the author, a meandering structure, or the sacrifice of plain explanation at the altar of intellectual sophistication (not to mention unnecessary rhetorical flourishes), can wholly disrupt narrative flow and thereby lose the attention of the reader. This is a great shame, given that in many instances the author and the reader will consider the subject to be engaging, and the lack of clarity can needlessly sever the bond between reader and writer through which knowledge and critical engagement can flow. I like the remark of Wallace (2005: 115, emphasis in original), in his tirade against academic writing, that "it is when a scholar's vanity/insecurity leads him to write primarily to communicate and reinforce his own status as an Intellectual that his English is deformed by pleonasm and pretentious diction (whose function is to signal the writer's erudition) and by opaque abstraction (whose function is to keep anybody from pinning the writer down to a definite assertion that can maybe be refuted or shown to be silly)". Wallace also quotes George Orwell's assessment of academic writing as a "mixture of vagueness and sheer incompetence" in which "it is normal to come across long passages which are almost completely lacking in meaning" (quoted in Wallace, 2005: 114–115).

With this in mind, I will attempt within this research to navigate all of these prospective pitfalls, and to present an analysis which is intelligible to readers with both no prior knowledge of Namibia and no prior knowledge of the study of economic and industrial development.

2 Economic and industrial development in Namibia, 1900 to 1945: the establishment of a settler colony

Introduction

This chapter covers the final fifteen years of German colonial rule in Namibia (1900 to 1915) and the first thirty years of South African rule in the country (1915 to 1945). As will be shown, despite the difficult economic conditions of the period – particularly in the late 1920s and early 1930s – the economy experienced significant diversification in the years up to 1945, due largely to the enormous sums invested by the SWA Administration to establish agricultural industries for the white farmers of the country. Two industries in particular, the production of butter and karakul (a type of sheep) pelts, were to develop notably over this period.

In manufacturing, aside from the onset of industrial dairy production, development was very limited, with only some other food and beverage industries (e.g. meat, beer, fish) as well as industries related to the construction sector (e.g. joineries, saw mills) emerging. The argument made, particularly through a comparison with industrial development in Southern Rhodesia (Zimbabwe), is that the reason that industry failed to develop was because of competition from South African manufacturers and because of the failure of the SWA Administration to support manufacturing firms. The Administration, whilst wholly committed to the establishment of a pastoral economy, took no interest in industrial development, aside from in food processing, which was seen to be to the benefit of the white farmers of the country.

The Namibian economy in the final years of German rule, 1900 to 1915

Although Namibia officially became a German colony in 1884, progress in colonisation was slow, with small levels of immigration from Germany during the 1880s and most of the 1890s. Colonialism was initially dominated by the German military and a few colonial companies, who, particularly from the 1890s onwards, sought to purchase large tracts of land from the people of southern and central Namibia. These companies, supported by generous concessions from the German state, were responsible for the expansion of rail and road networks in the country, and undertook limited farming and mining activities (Goldblatt, 1971). Germany established a 'Police Zone' within Namibia, covering the central and southern parts of the country (see map 2, p. 159), which was the area within which the colonial state sought to establish white settlement, with the northern region of the country (known as Ovamboland and the Caprivi) initially experiencing far less interference (Wallace, 2011).

Germany hoped to create in SWA a "white man's country", replicating the settler-model of British colonies such as Australia, New Zealand and Canada (Gann, 1975: 219). As such, the primary ambition of the German colonial state was "the development of an export economy out of a farming industry" (Goldblatt, 1971: 198). But "[p]rogress along these lines... was slow. Conditions were hard, water was scarce, distances were great, transport was difficult, and finances were low" (*ibid.*: 198).

Conflict between the German colonial state and the population of southern and central Namibia was rife, with the state seeking to appropriate more and more land from the various ethnic groups and to place them under greater state control.[1] The expansion of a German colonial state eventually caused out-and-out military conflict between the colonisers and the people of south and central Namibia, leading to what became known as the Namibian War 1904–1908 and the genocide of an enormous proportion of the population of these regions of the country.

The colonial economy was to boom with the discovery of diamonds near Lüderitz in the south in 1908. Table 2.1 shows the enormous increase in exports from German SWA from 1909 onwards, with this growth "entirely due to the mining of diamonds and copper" (Union of South Africa, 1915). In 1909 the value of diamond exports was 15.4 million marks and by 1913 this had increased to 58.9 million. Over the same period the export of copper increased from 4.7 million marks to 7.9 million.[2] From 1909 and 1913 the combined total of diamonds and copper accounted for between 91 and 95 percent of the total exports of the territory per annum, with most destined to Germany (*ibid.*). SWA was also exporting reasonably large quantities of lead and tin ore, as well as smaller quantities of goat and sheep hides, meat, wool, and live goats (*ibid.*).[3]

The wealth generated during the 'diamond rush' allowed the German SWA state to invest more money in infrastructure and support for settler farmers to achieve its ambition of establishing an agricultural export economy. The colony also continued to receive "lavish" financial support from Germany (Dundas, 1946: 33), contributing £3.4 million to the revenues of SWA from 1910 to 1915 (38% of the colony's total revenues) (Union of South Africa, 1915). Large sums were spent on the construction of railways, harbours, buildings, water boring, and irrigation schemes (Dundas, 1946).

A host of other direct measures were also used by the state to support settler farms. The most common farming activity was the raising of livestock, and to support this the state

---

[1]   For a discussion, see Wallace (2011), chapters 4 to 7.
[2]   The mining of copper took off following the formation of the *Otavi Mine and Railway Company*, mining the copper deposits of Tsumeb from 1902 onwards.
[3]   Of the 4.9% of 'other' exports for 1913, the largest sub-sections were 're-exports' (1.2%), 'tin ore' (1.0%), 'hides, goats and sheep skins' (0.7%), 'meat' (0.2%), 'small stock' (mainly goats) (0.2%), and 'wool' (0.2%) (Union of South Africa, 1915).

imported a wide variety of types of cattle for breeding and established its own stud farm to undertake selective breeding (Union of South Africa, 1915). Farmers were often given direct financial grants to aid with activities such as the eradication of pests (Union of South Africa, 1915). With increasing support for settlers, the number of migrants from Germany had begun to grow rapidly.[4]

	Total Exports	Total Imports	Trade Balance
1900	0.9	6.9	-6.0
1901	1.2	10.1	-8.9
1902	2.2	8.6	-6.4
1903	3.4	8.0	-4.6
1904	0.3	10.1	-9.8
1905	0.2	23.6	-23.4
1906	0.4	68.6	-68.2
1907	1.6	32.4	-30.8
1908	7.8	33.2	-25.4
1909	22.1	34.7	-12.6
1910	34.7	44.3	-9.7
1911	28.6	45.3	-16.7
1912	39.0	32.5	6.5
1913	70.3	43.4	26.9

Table 2.1: Exports and imports of German SWA (Deutsche Mark, millions), 1900–1912. Sources: For 1900 to 1908, Goldblatt (1971); for 1909 to 1913, Union of South Africa (1915). The low export quantities for 1904 to 1907 are a consequence of the Namibian War. Numbers do not always add up due to rounding up.

The state was also keen for the settler farmers to develop industries beyond the raising of livestock because Germany wanted a colony that could provide it with imports and thereby make it less reliant on other countries and empires (Lau & Reiner, 1993). A Department of Agriculture was established, which included agricultural experts to support farmers in the development of crops (Union of South Africa, 1915). Ten 'experimental farms' (including the aforementioned stud farm) were established across the Police Zone from 1902 to 1912 and, led by the agricultural experts, many of these trialled the cultivation of various vegetables and

---

[4]   In 1896 the white population of Namibia was just 2,000, by 1903 it was 4,700, and by 1913 it was 14,800 (Goldblatt, 1971; Wallace, 2011). In 1913 the black population of the Police Zone was 78,800. The most populous towns in the Police Zone at the time were Windhoek, Rehoboth, Lüderitz, Keetmanshoop, and Grootfontein.

fruits (Gann, 1975). The state also undertook research into the establishment of coffee, cotton, rubber, tobacco and leather industries, and attempted breeding of sheep and goats for wool production, of horses, pigs, camels, ostriches, and poultry (Lau & Reiner, 1993). Increasing production of crops meant that at the time of the onset of World War I farming production was "on the verge of overtaking demand and the question of finding markets for the surplus stock was being carefully investigated when hostilities broke out" (Union of South Africa, 1935: 5).

The colony was in dire need of workers as a consequence of the flourishing diamond mines, increasing number of farms, and the genocide (Wallace, 2011). The ambition of the German colonial state was "to transform the Africans into a landless proletariat, destroy their political organisation and culture, and force them to work in a disciplined and orderly manner for white employers" (*ibid.*: 184). After 1907 the state tried to make it "impossible for Africans to earn an independent living" through legislation that, amongst other things, banned the black population from owning cattle or horses without special permission, and the confiscation of their land (*ibid.*: 185).[5] Migrant workers were also brought in from the north of the country.

Unsurprisingly, the extent of manufacturing in Namibia at this time was limited. It was written in 1915 that "[p]ractically all the necessaries of life, except slaughter stock, are imported... There is, generally speaking, nothing manufactured" (Union of South Africa, 1915: 53). A further report at the time concurred that there was no significant manufacturing in the Police Zone, with the urban population "dependent on the mines, the activities of the Government and commerce generally for their means of livelihood" (Collie, 1915: 11).

Nevertheless, the German era did see "the first feeble beginnings of a secondary industry" in Namibia (Gann, 1975: 251). Manufacturing was limited to small ventures in meat and dairy production, bakeries, the production of beer and other alcoholic beverages, and only a few non-food and beverage processing manufacturing industries. The dairy industry "remained in its infancy", but there was some production of butter and cheese for the domestic market (Lau & Reiner, 1993: 15). Meat was produced by local butchers and in abattoirs, almost exclusively for the domestic market. Very small quantities were exported: £29,000 worth in 1912, just 0.07% of total exports (Union of South Africa, 1915). One butcher sought to establish a meat canning plant in Okahandja in 1914, but his efforts were interrupted by the onset of the war (Rawlinson, 1994).[6]

Beer production was the sole manufacturing success of the German era, and it was written in 1915 that "there are flourishing breweries in Windhuk [German spelling] and Swa-

---

5   For a detailed discussion, see Silvester (1998).
6   Gann (1975) states that there was a cannery in existence in Namibia in 1914, and it is not clear if he is referring to the same facility as Rawlinson.

kopmund, in which towns imported beer has been driven out of the market" (Union of South Africa, 1915: 63). The first brewery had been established in Swakopmund in 1900, with Windhoek and Omaruru soon following suit (van der Hoog, 2016). By 1912 the recently-expanded 'Felsenkeller' brewery in Windhoek was "the largest industrial site in the colony" (*ibid.*: 49). There was also a nascent wine and spirits industry and an ice-making factory in SWA at the time (Gann, 1975; Lau & Reiner, 1993).

In non-food and beverage manufacturing, there was some production of leather, with two tanneries in operation in 1914, and in 1912 £19,000 worth of leather goods exported (Union of South Africa, 1915; Gann, 1975). One firm constructed wagons, whilst "there were numerous small workshops belonging to individual artisans" (Gann, 1975: 251). A printing and publishing firm, *John Meinert Ltd*, was established in Windhoek in 1912.

The production of cigarettes and cigars was seriously considered by the German colonial state and likely would have soon been undertaken on an industrial scale, were it not for the outbreak of World War I (Lau & Reiner, 1993). Tobacco was a reasonably well-cultivated crop in the early 1900s in Namibia, and in the final years of German rule several tobacco farmers tried to produce cigarettes and cigars, but their endeavours proved unsuccessful because their individual production levels were too small (*ibid.*). To resolve this, tobacco growers concluded that large "centralised factories" were necessary for cigarette production to be viable (*ibid.*: 40). The colonial state agreed, and in 1914 it signed a contract with a German tobacco firm which obliged it to establish a tobacco factory in the colony in exchange for a monopoly on tobacco marketing and certain tax incentives (*ibid.*). The factory was never constructed however, as Namibia was to fall under the rule of South Africa.

The extent of manufacturing in the regions of Namibia outside of the Police Zone was also limited but had a much lengthier history than the manufacturing activities of the settler population. The Ovambo population produced baskets made of palm leaf; axes and hoes were manufactured out of smelted iron for agricultural purposes, as well as weapons (bows, arrows, spears, and knives); jewellery was made of iron; and clay pots and dishes were also produced.[7]

On the eve of World War I, German SWA was economically booming. A sturdy transport infrastructure had been established, including a rail network of 2,100 km, and the settler farms appeared to be advancing impressively (Lau & Reiner, 1993; Wallace, 2011). As the first South African Administrator of SWA commented in 1917, the German colonial state

---

[7]   NAN NAO 71 32/9, Native Customs and Practices: Manufacturing and Sale of Basket Ware. 20/8/1947 – 3/11/1954, letter to Native Commissioner titled 'Purchase and Sale of Native Curious and Handicraft. Pots, dishes, and baskets were made by most Ovambo women, whilst the production of goods from iron has made by specific trained blacksmiths who made up a small proportion of the population.

had "laid the foundations of a progressive administration... [SWA is] exceptionally well equipped for a country so sparsely settled [to develop] its vast unexploited and to a great extent unexplored resources" (quoted in Swanson, 1967: 649).

Agricultural and economic development under South African rule, 1915 to 1945

Political background

Following the onset of World War I, South Africa, at the behest of the British, declared war on German SWA, and following the swift defeat of the German army, took control of the country. South Africa governed by military rule until 1919, when at the Treaty of Versailles South Africa was awarded a mandate to govern the country, and in 1920 the period of South Africa's civilian rule over Namibia officially begun (du Pisani, 1989).

The League of Nations mandate gave South Africa "full power of administration and legislation over the Territory", but South Africa was required to write annual reports to the League on the country (quoted in Dundas, 1946: 26). Though the wording of the mandate suggested that the duty of South Africa was to help prepare SWA for its own independence, this was seen by the League as unlikely to happen for a very long time, if at all. In any case, this was never the intention of South Africa, which hoped to incorporate SWA into its own nation (Swanson, 1967). To South Africa, SWA represented land well-suited to the resettlement of poor white farmers from South Africa that was, moreover, richly endowed with mineral reserves, and a natural extension of what it hoped would eventually become a "greater Union" in Southern Africa, encompassing modern-day South Africa, Namibia, Botswana, Lesotho, Swaziland, Zimbabwe, and Zambia (*ibid.*: 633).

In 1920 a civilian Administrator was appointed to govern SWA. The Administrator had the authority to proclaim laws, which were often replications or close approximations of Acts of the South African parliament and there was an assimilation of the laws of SWA to those of South Africa during the 1920s. A large proportion of the German population was repatriated to Germany at the end of World War I (though many chose to stay in SWA), and large numbers of white South African farmers migrated into the country (Silvester, 1998).

Political arrangements in the early 1920s were consistently criticised by the white population of SWA, with the Administrator and the staff of his Administration viewed as incompetent and as only serving the interests of South Africa, thereby stifling economic development (Swanson, 1967). As was written in the *Windhoek Advertiser* in 1924 by its editor, "[w]e are of the opinion that no real development can take place under Union [South African] rule as at present constituted. It is imperative that responsible government of some kind be conferred upon South West Africa, after which its people will be in a better position to decide what steps can be taken for the betterment of existing conditions" (Lardner-Burke, 1924: 2). In a letter to the Prime Minister of South Africa, the Windhoek Chamber of Commerce (1924: 3) similarly argued that for economic development to occur an Administration more attentive to the needs of the white farming community was necessary: "[w]e... beg to emphasize that an early and fundamental change of the existing form of Government constitutes the most important of all economic questions of this country". In response to the criticisms, SWA was given a Legislative Assembly by South Africa in 1925, though it evidently had rather limited powers, with most authority remaining with the Administrator and, by extension, South Africa.[8]

The SWA colonial state maintained the existence and practice of the Police Zone. Treatment of the black population closely mirrored that of German SWA, with the black population viewed as a source of labour for SWA's 'formal' economy (Wallace, 2011). Men living north of the Police Zone were encouraged to migrate to work in the mines and farms (though this was not always easy to achieve[9]), and within the Police Zone racial segregation was enshrined through the creation of 'reserves' for the black population which were, like the area of the country north of the Police Zone, to serve as pools of labour (Swanson, 1967; Wallace, 2011).[10]

State-led efforts to create an agricultural export economy

Whilst the German colonial state had been cut short in its ambitions of developing an agricultural export economy in Namibia, the South African colonial state was to largely follow in its footsteps, envisaging the establishment of an economy centred around large-scale farming by white settlers, particularly the raising of livestock. As the Administration wrote of its own ambitions, "[t]he country would appear eminently suitable for stock-raising... [one can] look forward with confidence to South-West Africa taking its place in the foremost ranks of the meat-producing countries of the world" (Report of the Administrator, 1921: 6).

---

[8] The Legislative Assembly had no authority to legislate on the following matters: mines and minerals; railways and harbours; public service; constitution, jurisdiction and court procedure; posts, telegraphs, telephones; military organisation; movement and operations of the Defence Force of South Africa; immigration; customs and excise; and currency and banking. A host of other areas (including the police, the education system, and management of the state's Land and Agricultural Bank) were to possibly be transferred to the Legislative Assembly after three years, but never were (Dundas, 1946; Bunting, 1972).

[9] For example, in his report for the year 1925, the Administrator wrote that "there has been an acute shortage of native labour which has hampered both mining and farming development", with the issue aggravated "by the prosperity that the natives have enjoyed during the year" outside of the Police Zone, following good harvests in Ovamboland and Okavango (Report of the Administrator, 1925: 9).

[10] In the mid-1920s the white population of the Police Zone was 25,000, the black population of the Police Zone was 93,500, and the combined population of the northern regions (Ovamboland, Kaokoveld and Okavango) was estimated to be 154,000 (Report of the Administrator, 1927).

Accordingly, "heavy expenditures were devoted to the settlement of South African farmers and other measures to encourage development of a pastoral export economy in order to reduce its dependence upon the apparently wasting resource of metals and diamonds" (Swanson, 1967: 663). The Administration invested in boring, irrigation, experimental farms, infrastructure development, export facilities, the technical education of farmers, and bringing in overseas expertise to aid the industry, as will be discussed below.

To encourage the migration of South African farmers to Namibia, "generous terms [were] provided for white settlers" (Silvester, 1998: 106). A Land Settlement Act was passed in 1920, under which loans could be granted to help settlers establish homes on farmland, and advances could also be made for the construction of reservoirs, wind pumps, and homes, as well as for the purchasing of livestock (ibid.). A Land Bank was established in 1921 to provide loans to farmers, and it was to become the major mechanism through which white settlement was supported (Report of the Administrator, 1920). The Administration up to the end of 1925 had advanced £225,000 to farmers for the purpose of breeding stock and purchasing implements, and the Land Bank at the time controlled investments amounting to over £650,000 (the equivalent of 13% of SWA's GDP) (Report of the Administrator, 1925). From 1926 to 1933 the bank advanced on average £79,000 per annum to settlers (Hirsekorn, 1935). The heavy expenditure dedicated to the support of settlers from South Africa was having the intended effect, with the Administration reporting that "people are rapidly coming into the Territory... the country is becoming better known and... confidence in it is growing" (Report of the Administrator, 1925: 9).

Throughout the 1920s and 1930s the Administration spent heavily on boring to improve water access for farms: boring accounted for 13% of the Administration's extraordinary expenditure from 1920 to 1933 (Union of South Africa, 1935). Whilst there were only thirteen boring machines in the country in 1921, the number increased to 66 by the end of 1925 (Report of the Administrator, 1925), and between 1922 and 1927 a total of 1,051 boreholes were sunk (Rawlinson, 1994).

A number of the experimental farms established by the German colonial state were taken over by the new Administration and were used to enhance the quality of livestock, particularly cattle and karakul sheep, with "first-class" livestock imported from overseas in large quantities (Report of the Administrator, 1929: 35). Over the course of 1918 to 1938 officially a total of 4,763 cattle were imported into SWA (Rawlinson, 1994). By the end of 1925, 433 pure-bred karakuls had been sold to farmers, and it is likely that this number increased dramatically over the following two decades (Report of the Administrator, 1925). The high-quality livestock reared at the Administration's farms were then sold to farmers at generous rates. In 1926 an agricultural school was set up near to Windhoek to train young white men in farming practices such as animal husbandry, masonry, and wood and iron work (Report of the Administrator, 1926).[11] In 1930 the Administration passed the Cattle Improvement Ordinance, which meant that SWA was "the first country in Africa to enact legislation to bring about the improvement its cattle population by voluntary annual inspection of its bulls" (Rawlinson, 1994: 60). The white farmers of Namibia were also strongly supported through the creation of laws that were biased against the black farmers of the reserves within the Police Zone and those living north of the zone. Farmers in these areas saw their access to markets in the Police Zone heavily restricted, and furthermore "traders buying stock from Africans were generally able to fix prices at well below the market rate" (Wallace, 2011: 235-236).

A key element of the Administration's ambitions was to aid the farmers of the country to become export competitive. Accordingly, in 1921 the colonial state repealed an export tax on slaughter stock, removed customs duties on all produce exported to South Africa, and reduced railway rates (Report of the Administrator, 1922). Most importantly, to be able to export agricultural products it was essential for the country to construct cold storage facilities (i.e. large-scale refrigeration) so as to be able to store produce at the coast before they were shipped overseas. For many previous settler colonies, the establishment of such facilities had been a crucial precursor to economic development. For example, cold storage facilities constructed in New Zealand, Australia and Canada were "[e]xceedingly important both in their social and economic effects" and "proved to be the beginnings of industrial enterprises" in the colonies by allowing them to export agricultural products to Europe (Knowles, 1924: 19).

The Administration was desperate to find a company to construct the facilities at the Namibian coast, and in 1922 it offered the *Imperial Cold Storage Company* generous incentives to construct them, including agreeing to expand the harbour facilities at Walvis Bay, aiding in the construction of the premises, constructing a water pipeline for the site, and granting the company the sole right to export livestock overseas for three years and meat for fifteen years (Rawlinson, 1994; Dieckmann, 2013). The facilities were finished in 1927, and with it the country was now able to begin exporting fish, meat and dairy products overseas in significant quantities for the first time.

In response to the severe negative economic consequences of the world depression and a major drought in Namibia, the Administration introduced additional policies to support struggling farmers in the 1930s. Farmers were given highly discounted rail rates to trans-

---

[11] Shorter courses in specific subject areas, such as wool production, were also available (Report of the Administrator, 1926). The principal course of the agricultural school lasted two years, only after which would a student be considered as a potential recipient of a farm (Report of the Administrator, 1929). The school was permanently closed during World War II (Agricultural Policy Commission, 1949).

port their livestock to the few strips of land in the country where rain fell, with the Government's boring machines working twenty-four hours a day in these areas (Report of the Administrator, 1930). Proclamations were also made to allow for delayed repayments to the Land Bank, to create farmer co-operatives, and to launch 'relief work' projects (such as the construction of roads) for unemployed farmers (*ibid.*). In the 1930s marketing boards for the major agricultural products produced in the country were introduced (Wallace, 2011), and in 1932 export subsidies were introduced for wool, meat, butter, slaughter stock, lobster, and hides and skins (Report of the Administrator, 1931).[12]

The record of efforts towards agricultural and economic development

The ambition of the colonial state in SWA was to drive forward the creation of an agriculture-based export economy, reducing the colony's reliance on the export of diamonds and copper to advance the wellbeing of its white citizens. The following section presents the colony's record on economic and agricultural development up to 1945, demonstrating that, whilst the colony experienced significant economic difficulties during the interwar period, it still proved exceptionally successful in the reorientation of the economy towards agricultural production.

The national economy of Namibia from 1915 to 1945 went through four distinct periods. The first was one economic uncertainty and depression from 1915 to 1924, caused by an outflow of German capital from the country, stagnation of the diamond sector, and a severe slump in livestock trade due to drought and the oversaturation of the South African market in the early 1920s (Report of the Administrator, 1922; Swanson, 1967). The second period was one of "rapid advance" from 1925 to 1929 due to increased production in the agricultural sector and the resumption of large-scale diamond mining (Swanson, 1967: 647).

The third period saw the positive mood of the colonial state at this time to spectacularly fall away in the wake of the world depression which, coupled with severe drought in Namibia (the longest on record), led to "economic stagnation, financial and political crisis" (*ibid.*: 647). The drop in the value of minerals led to the near-total cessation of mining activity in the country – mining's contribution to total GDP went from 40% in 1929 to contributing 0% of GDP in both 1933 and 1934 (Krogh, 1960). Exports of diamonds, which valued £1.55 million in 1929 (44% of total exports) was in 1933 just £10,100 (0.7% of total exports) (Report of the Administrator, 1931; 1937).

Meanwhile, for farmers the drought meant that cows were yielding no milk, livestock was in an unsaleable condition, and sheep were not producing sellable wool. And, irrespec-

---

[12] The rates for 1932 were: 25% for wool and mohair; 20% for meat; and 10% for butter, slaughter stock, lobster, and hides and skins (Report of the Administrator, 1931).

tive of drought, the world depression had led to the complete drop in the value of farm produce (Union of South Africa, 1935). Merchants, too, were hard hit, and the number of insolvencies and liquidations in the country increased markedly, whilst the Administration also began to accrue massive debts owed to the South African state (Report of the Administrator, 1931). In 1933 SWA owed South Africa £2.07 million (112% of GDP) (Union of South Africa, 1935) and by 1934 over 50% of its revenues were spent servicing debt to South Africa (Swanson, 1967). Remarkably, by 1933 GDP had fallen to under 30% of what it had been in 1929 (Krogh 1960).

The final period, from 1935 to 1945, was one of very strong economic recovery, driven by rapid growth in the agricultural sector, and well supported by the resumption of diamond and copper mining in the late 1930s. During World War II growth was particularly impressive, and it was observed that the country began to experience "remarkable change… the war years have been the most prosperous in South-West Africa's history" (Dundas, 1946: 36). The steady growth experienced from 1935 onwards meant that by 1946 the GDP per capita (constant prices) of Namibia was almost double what it had been in 1921.[13] The below figures, presenting data on GDP and trade for SWA from 1921 to 1945, well illustrate the above-described trends in economic performance.

A common misconception in previous work on this period is that the interwar years did not see any marked change in the economic structure of the SWA colony. For example, Innes (1981: 66) wrote that "between the world wars the Namibian economy was characterized by stagnation and limited diversification and the country was in a state of chronic underdevelopment". In reality, this period witnessed a significant reorientation of the economy away from mining and towards agriculture, including in some related manufacturing activities.

For example, whereas in 1921 mineral exports accounted for 78.3% of total exports, by 1945 they had fallen to just 16.3%, and mining's contribution to GDP had reduced from 35.2% to 12.9%. Mining's declining significance was principally due to the growth of new sectors of the economy, most particularly the production of wool, butter, preserved fish and above all the enormous rise in the production of karakul sheep pelts. These four industries, virtually non-existent in 1924 (between them they contributed just £92,000 of SWA's exports of £2.9 million for that year), contributed an extraordinary £5.3 million of SWA's total exports of £8.2 million in 1945. From 1920 to 1945 the contribution of agriculture and fishing to GDP increased from 12.9% to 45.8%. The economic structure of SWA had been dramatically transformed.

---

[13] GDP data comes from SWA Department of Finance (1988); population data from Republic of Namibia (2013).

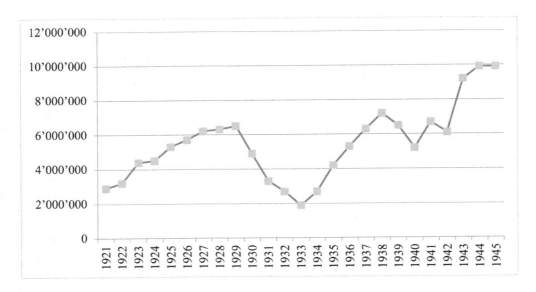

Figure 2.1: GDP of SWA (£), 1920–1945. Source: Krogh (1960).[14] GDP is shown at current prices.

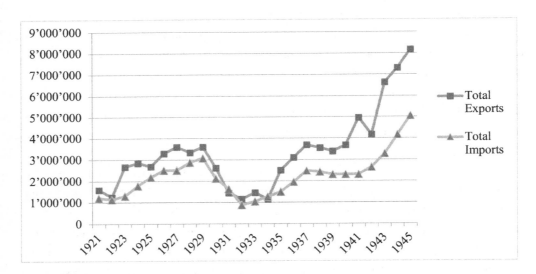

Figure 2.2: SWA total exports and imports (£), 1921–1945. Sources: Report of the Administrator (1937; 1939); Union of South Africa, Department of Customs and Excise (various years).

---

[14] The study of the history of the Namibian economy is well-aided by the work of Krogh (1960) of the University of Pretoria, who constructed GDP data for Namibia from 1920 to 1956. Krogh's major sources in determining GDP estimates were the trade statistics and the reports of the Administrators which I have frequently cited. He states that given "the considerable amount of available data" his estimates have "a high degree of reliability... at least for the post-Great Depression years" (ibid: 5).

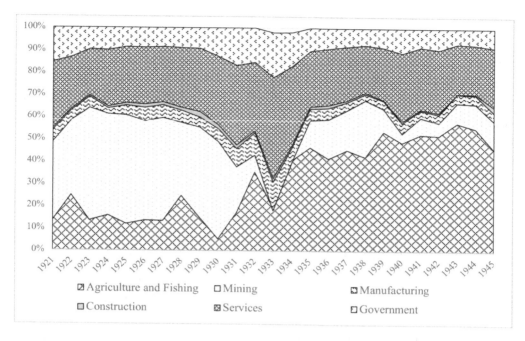

Figure 2.3: Change in SWA GDP by sector (%), 1921–1945. Source: Krogh (1960).

	1924	1931	1938	1945
Diamonds	49.0%	15.8%	22.4%	14.6%
Base metals	26.4%	24.9%	14.9%	1.6%
Live cattle, sheep, and goats	15.6%	13.0%	9.1%	11.3%
Karakul pelts	0.3%	4.7%	27.3%	52.8%
Wool	0.2%	3.0%	4.6%	2.4%
Butter	2.1%	7.3%	11.6%	6.6%
Fish, preserved	0.6%	7.2%	1.6%	3.1%
Other (including re-exports)	5.8%	24.1%	8.5%	7.6%
Total	100.0%	100.0%	100.0%	100.0%

Table 2.2: SWA exports (%), 1924–1945. Sources: Report of the Administrator (1929; 1935; 1939), Union of South Africa, Department of Customs and Excise (1946). Highlighted indicates sectors of sizeable growth in contribution to total exports.

The meteoric rise of karakul production

Evidently, then, it was the growth of agriculture, purposefully supported by the colonial state, that was driving the impressive economic recovery and expansion in the SWA colony in the years after the world depression. Most importantly, this occurred through the meteoric rise of the karakul sheep pelt industry. I have already outlined the extensive general measures through which the Administration was supporting white farmers, but I will now present the essential support measures that it offered directly to the karakul industry. Support that, in large part, explains the industry's great success.

The pelts of karakul sheep (a breed of sheep which originated in central Asia) became an important international commodity in the early and mid-20th century, with the soft pelts of new-born karakul prized material to produce luxury coats and other clothing items. The extent of the industry's growth in Namibia cannot be overstated. The industry was miniscule even in the mid-1920s but was to become the largest contributor to SWA exports by 1937, and by 1945 it remarkably contributed over 50% of total exports. In that year SWA was exporting some 2.5 million karakul pelts per year, making it one of the leading exporters of karakul in the world, along with Russia (1–2 million), Afghanistan (2–3 million), and China (2.5 million) and the country could "claim to have outstripped the homelands of the karakul in methods of breeding and in registration of pedigrees and to equal them in quality of pelt produced" (Agricultural Policy Commission, 1949: 45). The industry was of huge benefit to the SWA economy, "practically by itself responsible for the territory's gradual and stable economic development" after the world depression (Krogh, 1955: 113).

Karakul sheep first appeared in Namibia during the German era of colonial rule in 1907 when the state – after lobbying from a local German entrepreneur – ordered a consignment of karakul breeding stock from Uzbekistan (Agricultural Policy Commission, 1949; Rawlinson, 1994). But the number of farmers producing karakul pelts remained very small, partly because of "the need for scientific experimentation in the cross-breeding of the Karakul" to improve pelt quality before production could become profitable, and mainly because of "the well known reluctance of farmers to adopt new, even if, more remunerative farming practices" (Krogh, 1955, 103). The latter factor was "of particular importance" in explaining the lack of initial success, with farmers associating karakul pelt production with irregular demand due to changes in luxury fashion styles and preferences (*ibid.*: 103).

It was the state that was needed to induce private farmers to undertake the large-scale production of karakul pelts, and it did this principally by a) single-handedly increasing the quality of pelts to world-class levels through experimentation in cross-breeding, and b) by actively seeking to halt the establishment of a karakul industry in South Africa.

On the former, the Administration had inherited the German colonial state's karakul flock, with the six hundred karakul sheep constituting "the nuclei of the karakul population of S.W. Africa" in the early 1920s (Agricultural Policy Commission, 1949: 42). Within the flock, experiments in breeding karakuls were undertaken "with a view to determining the grades or crosses which are necessary for the purpose of producing high-class skins" (Report of the Administrator, 1919: 12). After much labour the Administration proved successful in its aims, and a world-renowned type of karakul pelt (known as 'Swakara') was developed. As Rawlinson (1994: 82) states, the Administration's experimental farm was "directly responsible for the fact that the most sought-after Karakul pelts produced in the world originated form the Territory of South West Africa" (*ibid.*: 82).

On the latter, the Administration also actively protected the SWA karakul industry. From 1929 onwards, the state introduced the control of the export of karakul sheep capable of breeding "with the object of protecting the karakul sheep farming industry", and during the 1930s this control "developed into total prohibition of export" (Agricultural Policy Commission, 1949: 45). The ban on exports included to South Africa, with farmers in Namibia consistently (and successfully) opposing suggestions to revoke the ban to allow South Africa to freely import Namibian karakul (*ibid.*).

Evidently, the Administration was keenly involved in the emergence of the karakul industry, investing time and capital into the development of quality pelts and seeking to stop the emergence of competitors in other countries, particularly South Africa. Perhaps most tellingly, farmers within the colony had themselves been reluctant to undertake karakul production, based on the perceived risks of this new type of farming, and it took investment from the state to make this economic activity viable. The karakul industry became the defining feature of Namibia's economy, almost entirely due to the efforts of the state.

Industrial development

Overview

What development occurred in Namibia's industrial sector during this period of profound state-driven economic restructuring? Did the state prove as willing to foster industrial development as it had agricultural development? No research has ever been undertaken to ascertain the development of Namibian manufacturing in the first thirty years of South African rule, and this section is the first attempt to do so.[15]

---

[15] An exception is Bewersdorf (1939) who wrote his research on the industrialisation of South Africa and South West Africa. The work is heavily concentrated on South Africa. In a footnote, Lau

As reported in an industrial census for the financial year 1920/21, at the onset of civilian South African rule of Namibia there were 96 manufacturing firms in the country, employing 800 people, the equivalent of just 0.7% of the total population of the Police Zone.[16] From this humble starting position, manufacturing in Namibia experienced only minor progression in the years up to 1945, with the development that did occur almost entirely driven by the emergence of three food processing export industries – dairy production, fish processing, and to a lesser extent meat processing. As will be shown in the following sections, the state played an essential role in the establishment of the dairy industry and was also heavily involved in the less successful meat processing industry, but otherwise showed scant interest in industrial progress.

Food and beverage production was easily the largest manufacturing sub-sector in Namibia prior to 1945, accounting for 40 of the 96 firms in Namibia in 1920/21, including abattoirs, dairy factories, meat producers, aerated water factories, breweries,[17] bakeries, and grain mills. There were also a number of other firms in construction-related activities (e.g. sawmills, joinery works, lime works, and tile manufacturing) supporting the expansion of towns, farms and mines. In other sub-sectors, there were firms making leather shoes and apparel, a small number of firms making tobacco products, a major local printer and publisher,[18] one firm building wooden fishing boats,[19] and some firms building wagons.[20] One or two firms were also produc-

---

& Reiner (1993) refer to their own intention to write a volume on the history of manufacturing in Namibia in the colonial era, but this never came to fruition.

[16] NAN SWAA 0277 A29/2, Industrial Census, 1920/21. The industrial census actually states that there were 112 firms employing 949 people. However, I have deemed one of these sectors, 'Building and Contracting', to not be part of the manufacturing sector. Industrial censuses were also conducted for 1919/1920, and every year up until 1926, though no record of the results of the later surveys could be found. In 1926 the conducting of industrial censuses in SWA was cancelled, with the director of Census and Statistics, Pretoria, informing the SWA Administration that "[i]n view of the comparatively small number of Industrial establishments in your Territory, an Annual Census is perhaps not justified" (NAN SWAA 0277 A29/2, Letter from South Africa Director of Census and Statistics to the Secretary for South West Africa, 17th August 1927).

[17] In 1920, the four breweries remaining from the German era (a number had shut down during World War I) were merged by *Ohlthaver & List* to form *South West Breweries* in Windhoek (van der Hoog, 2016). In 1922 a further brewery, *Union Brewery*, was established in Windhoek, and a third brewery called *Hansa Brewery* was established in Swakopmund in 1928. Small levels of exports to South Africa started in 1928, and increased gradually throughout the 1930s, stalling somewhat during World War II due to a difficulty in importing inputs, but began expanding again towards the end of the war (Union of South Africa, Department of Customs and Excise, various years).

[18] This firm was the aforementioned *John Meinert Ltd*. The company expanded during the 1920s, buying the *Swakopmunder Buchhandlung* in July 1924 and also taking over the *Windhuker Druckerei and Buchhandlung* in the same year (NAN SWAA 0277 A29/2, Letter from John Meinert Ltd to SWA Police, 8 December 1924).

[19] *Nieswandt Boat Yard* was established in Lüderitz in the mid-1920s by Fritz Nieswandt, who had learnt shipbuilding in Hamburg (Kraatz Engineering, n.d.).

[20] Interestingly, *Pupkewitz & Sons*, was founded in 1925 as a wagon building firm in Okahandja

---

ing guano fertiliser at the Namibian coast (Bewersdorf, 1939). As is the case today, the largest industrial town in terms of number of firms was Windhoek (27 firms in 1927), with nearby Okahandja likely the location of the second largest number of firms (13 firms in 1925).[21]

There appears to be little evidence of significant manufacturing related to mining activities in Namibia during this era, with the country's minerals being exported unprocessed. There were upstream linkages between mining and the manufacturing sector, with many of the construction-related industries servicing the mines (though most inputs for construction were imported). Moreover, mines, as large employers in remote areas, often required food processing and beverage facilities onsite. For example, the diamond mine in Lüderitz run by the *Consolidated Diamond Mines Company* had refrigerating works, soda water works, and its own butchery constructed (NAN SWAA 0277 A29/2, Letter from Post Commander, SWA Police, Lüderitz, to the Magistrate, Lüderitz, 21 May 1926).

In the more populated areas of Namibia north of the Police Zone, small-scale industrial activity declined in the years prior to 1945, in part because so much of the population was working as migrant labourers in the Police Zone, and in part because manufacturing activities were "slowly dying out" in the face of increased competition from imported products (Dobler, 2014: 76). Writing in 1948, the Native Commissioner for Ovamboland observed that "the blacksmiths... are fast disappearing; they cannot compete with similar articles of European manufacturer which nowadays are more easily and cheaper acquired at the local shops".[22] There were, however, at least three small industrial schools in Ovamboland founded in the 1920s set up by missionaries, which taught the manufacturing of hoes, buckets, deck chairs, tables, chairs, and shirts which were sold locally, and baskets, which were exported to South Africa (Report of the Administrator, 1930; Dobler, 2014).[23] Dobler (2014), however, concludes that there is no evidence that any professional craftspeople emerged from the schools.

---

and went on to be one of the largest trading companies in Namibia today (interview with Marcel Lamprecht, Managing Director, *Pupkewitz Megabuild*. 30.3.2016).

[21] NAN SWAA 0277 A29/2, Industrial Censuses, 1919–1926. In Windhoek in 1926 there were 27 firms, including a brewery; slaughterhouse; several bakeries; a sausage making facility; a blacksmith and wagon builder; cement works; building & constructing; carpentry & joinery; boot manufacturing; and gun-smithing. In 1925 in Okahandja there were 13 manufacturing firms – the *Liebig's Extract of Meat Company* was registered both for its meat factory and for its fertilizer works; along with two other slaughterhouses and a creamery; three tobacco manufacturers; two lime works; a boot and shoes manufacture; a blacksmith and wagon builder; and a motor car and cycle repairman.

[22] NAN NAO 78 32/9, Letter Rodent Inspector to Native Commissioner, 12 July 1948.

[23] In Ongwediva, Engela, and Oshigambo. Toivo Ya Toivo, one of Namibia's most iconic leaders of the independence movement, attended the Ongwediva industrial school from 1939 to 1942, where he was trained as a carpenter (Nembwaya & Shivute, 2014).

Manufacturing value added as a percentage of GDP (MVA/GDP) failed to present an upward trend from 1920 to 1945, aside from during the years of the great depression, at which point the sector experienced a dramatic spike in its relative contribution to the economy due solely to the complete collapse of the mining sector, as shown in figure 2.4. Indeed, MVA/GDP was in fact on average higher from 1920 to 1929 (4.6%) than it was from 1936 to 1945 (3.9%), pointing to the limited growth of the sector in relative terms. In constant prices manufacturing output doubled between 1921 and 1945, though it did not grow as fast as the overall economy (SWA Department of Finance, 1988).

The interwar years did, however, see the establishment of the first meaningful manufacturing export industries in the country's history: dairy, fish and meat processing. Accordingly, from contributing only 2% of total exports in 1921, manufacturing exports went on to average 19% of total exports from 1928 to 1945. In current prices, manufacturing exports in 1945 were thirty-five times higher than they had been in 1921, increasing from £31,000 to £1.07 million. The impressive growth meant that the export of dairy and prepared and preserved fish became established as important parts of the Namibian economy.

Beyond these two food processing industries (and to a lesser extent, meat processing), however, manufacturing exports did not increase markedly from their tiny base in 1921 during the interwar years. That said, an interesting development was the increase in the export of non-food and beverage manufacturing products during World War II. Non-food and beverage exports (such as furniture, wagons, apparel, leather goods, whale oil and prepared

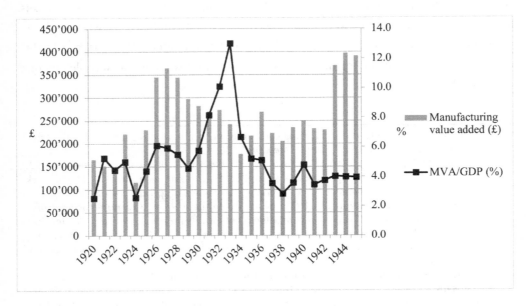

Figure 2.4: Manufacturing's contribution to GDP (£ and %), 1920–1945. Source: Krogh (1960).

furs to South Africa) first emerged in the late 1920s and had averaged just £21,000 from 1931 to 1938. During the war, however, exports in this category increased sizeably, reaching £109,000 by 1945, thereby doubling their contribution to total exports, even though total exports were themselves soaring at this point (Union of South Africa, Department of Customs and Excise, various years).

Almost all non-food and beverage manufactured products exported during World War II were destined for South Africa. The onset of war had caused the large-scale reduction of industrial imports from Europe, leading to shortages but also an enormous surge in industrial activity in South Africa (Feinstein, 2005). It appears that these shortages in South Africa caused the increase in manufacturing exports by Namibia. Again, the extent of this growth, should not, however, be overstated, and it was the above-mentioned food processing industries that were the sole major development in Namibia's manufacturing prior to 1945. The evolution of these food processing export industries will be outlined in the following two sections.

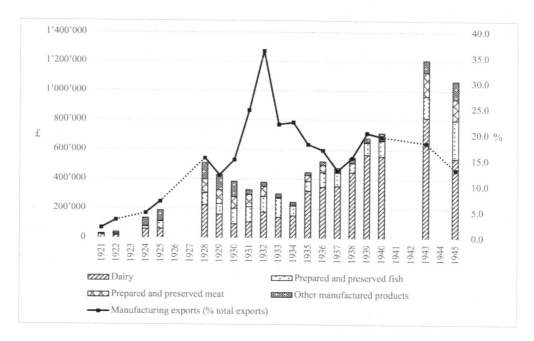

Figure 2.5: Manufacturing exports (£ and % of total exports), 1921–1945. Source: Union of South Africa, Department of Customs and Excise (various years). Dotted lines indicate missing data. Data missing for 1923, 1926, 1927, 1941, 1942, and 1944. Note it has been decided to include 'fresh meat' within the 'prepared and preserved meat' category, but to exclude 'fresh fish' from the 'prepared and preserved fish' category, on the grounds that a) this appears to be the current method used in Namibia's national accounts so it is a useful demarcation on the grounds of continuity, and b) because fresh meat requires some preparation, whereas fresh fish does not.

The emergence of a dairy export industry

The largest manufacturing sector to emerge in Namibia in the pre-1945 era was the dairy industry, particularly butter production. Contributing less than 2% of total exports in 1921, butter production grew such that between 1932 and 1944 it consistently contributed between 10% and 16% of total exports for the country. From exporting just 331,000 lbs. of butter in 1921, Namibia was exporting nearly 10.5 million lbs. by 1943, principally to South Africa (Agricultural Policy Commission, 1949).

Dairy production first emerged in earnest in Namibia in the mid-1920s, with farmers producing milk 'on the side' of their meat cattle ranching activities as an additional source of income (Rawlinson, 1994). As such, by the end of the 1920s there were thirteen creameries processing the milk of farms into butter in Namibia, with some of these also producing cheese, and an outright cheese factory was also established in Okahandja during the 1920s (Lau & Reiner, 1993). The number of creameries had consolidated down to six by 1949, at which point there were also three cheese factories, which were supplied by most farmers in the centre and north of Namibia (Agricultural Policy Commission, 1949; Lau & Reiner, 1993).

It is commonly argued that the industry was not supported by the SWA Administration during its emergence. Rawlinson (1994: 63) writes that "[t]he authorities did not encourage dairy ranching. They in fact repeatedly warned farmers against the over milking of cows". Lau & Reiner (1993: 18) state that "the profitable dairy industry was allowed to exist rather than actively supported from South Africa" and that within SWA "official enquiries [into dairying] were either on a minute scale; or haphazard".

But whilst it is true that the Administration was wary of the consequences of farmers using the same herd of cattle for slaughter-stock and dairy products, this does *not* mean that the Administration did not want to develop a dairy industry. Rather, the approach of the Administration was to encourage the existence of separate dairy herds within farms, and, in this respect, it was extremely supportive of the nascent industry.

For example, the Administration imported dairy cows from overseas and reared them at its experimental farms, so as to "be an example for the farmers, to show how a dairy herd should be looked after and fed. The progeny of this herd will be sold to farmers to improve their herds", with dairy cows sold to farmers at below market prices (Report of the Administrator, 1925: 39). As the Administration made clear, it was "doing all in its power to break [the practice of using the same herd for both industries] by increasing its own herd of pure-bred dairy cattle with a view to placing itself in a position to supply dairy bulls at low prices to farmers" (Report of the Administrator, 1926: 10), and it noted positively that because of its actions dairy "has increased very considerably throughout the Territory. The practice of farmers milking the ranching cows is on the wane and strenuous efforts are being made to secure dairy cows" (*ibid.*: 44).

The Administration also took efforts to improve the quality of the output of the industry. In 1926 the Administration passed the Dairy Industries Ordinance, which established a system for the protection for the growing butter industry (such as, for example, "prohibiting the processing of imported cream into Namibian butter" (Lau & Reiner, 1993: 11)), imposed uniform standards of cleanliness on producers, and gave the Administration increased power to inspect the industry (Report of the Administrator, 1926). In 1929 it appointed a specific dairy expert, whose role was to improve the quality of butter for export through advising on methods of preparation and packaging, and by improving the hygiene standards of producers (Report of the Administrator, 1929).

The passing of the 1926 Ordinance directly led to an increase in exports of butter from Namibia (Lau & Reiner, 1993). Due to the high quality-standards of the sector, "Namibian butter was making a name for itself on the London market" (*ibid.*: 16), and the Administration observed that "[t]he strict and consistent standard of grading and inspection exercised by the Dairy Inspectors at Walvis Bay has again elicited very favourable comment from the trade experts in London, both in regard to butter and cheese exported to that centre" (Report of the Administrator, 1939: 69).

Beyond protection and strict hygiene regulation, the colonial state also offered financial incentives for exporters of butter during the 1930s. In 1931 a Dairy Industry Control Ordinance was passed to aid dairy producers to find a market for their products through the provision of generous export incentives (Report of the Administrator, 1931). All dairy farmers were required to pay a levy on the production of butter and cheese, and out of this fund substantial export bounties were paid on dairy exported overseas. Farmers benefitted generously from this scheme – in 1931 Namibian producers contributed £17,000 in levies but received £57,000 in bounties (Union of South Africa, 1935). The South African state would go as far as to say that "[t]he dairy industry of South West Africa is dependent not only for its success but for its existence on the bounty which is paid to the producers" (*ibid.*: 19).

Despite the tensions that were present between dairy and meat production throughout this era, the above has shown the active role that the SWA Administration played in the establishment of the dairy industry in the country, the first major manufacturing industry in the country's history. And this, it should be remembered, excludes all the financial incentives and other support measures that were being afforded to white farmers in general, most of which were involved in dairy.

Fish processing and abortive attempts at large-scale meat processing

Although the major boom in fish processing in Namibia was to occur in the years after 1945, the sector already became important in the interwar years.

At Lüderitz, in the mid-1920s lobster canning became a large part of the local economy and was the second most important economic activity for the town after diamond mining. There were three lobster canning factories employing some 450 people in total at the height of the canning season, and an additional factory processing the waste of these factories into animal feed and fertilizer (Report of the Administrator, 1927; Bewersdorf, 1939). Lobster canning continued throughout the 1930s and experienced a sharp surge in exports to both Britain and South Africa during World War II.

At Walvis Bay, the expansion of the harbour in the mid-1920s led to the commencement of large-scale fishing operations. It was hoped that canning factories would concurrently emerge, but no factories were established, at least until World War II. Fishmeal, however, was manufactured at Walvis Bay, reportedly in a "large quantity" and was exported (Report of the Administrator, 1927: 15). Whale oil was also produced during the 1920s: between 1924 and 1930 it was the largest export from the country after diamonds, base metals, slaughter animals, hides, and butter (Report of the Administrator, various years), though price drops during the depression coupled with overproduction caused the industry to shut down permanently in 1930 (Bewersdorf, 1939). There is limited record of the colonial state actively supporting the development of fish processing in this era, though it did greatly facilitate the recruitment of labour to the canning firms.

There is, however, ample evidence of the state support for the meat processing export industry, although these efforts proved largely unsuccessful. The export of meat only became possible with the establishment of cold storage facilities. The *Imperial Cold Storage (ICS) Company* had been awarded a fifteen-year monopoly on meat exports from Namibia in the mid-1920s and, beyond the generous measures offered by the colonial state to encourage the ICS to build cold storage facilities already discussed, the state also offered export incentives for the firm, including rebates (Rawlinson, 1994). In 1927 ICS began exporting to Europe, but exports paused from 1933 to 1934 because of an outbreak of foot and mouth disease, and production remained extremely low throughout the remainder of the 1930s (*ibid.*). Fresh meat exports from ICS suddenly surged during World War II due to increased demand from South Africa, but this proved short-lived. ICS laboured on for some time more, but eventually the plant was shut down in 1958 (*ibid.*).

There were also attempts at the export of canned meat (as opposed to frozen fresh meat) in the 1920s and 1930s. Already in the early 1920s there were small canning or extract facilities in four towns in Namibia, largely serving the local market but occasionally exporting in small quantities (*ibid.*). The Administration was keen for large-scale meat canning to commence because this was the most profitable way to sell lower-quality meat, and it had initially approached ICS to incentivise it to undertaking canning operations, and though a deal had been reached, the factory was never built (*ibid.*). Large scale meat processing did commence in 1925, however, when the *Liebig's Extract of Meat Company* set up a meat extract factory in Okahandja, with the meat extract then exported to Europe for further processing (Report of the Administrator, 1925). The factory, however, was shut down in 1931 during the world depression, and though it was reported that it was briefly reopened again in 1936, there is no record of the company having exported meat products after 1930 (Rawlinson, 1994).

Conclusion

Despite the emergence of the dairy, fish processing, and meat processing export industries in the pre-1945 era, in 1945 manufacturing played an extremely limited role in the Namibian economy. Its contribution to GDP and to total exports were just 4% and 11% respectively, and the sector had remained technologically unsophisticated, with next-to-no quantities of what Lall (2000) classified as 'medium technology manufactures' and 'high technology manufactures' being exported, and the sector continuing to be dominated by food processing and beverages.[24]

Why was industrial development so limited in Namibia at this time? Was its meagre progression an inevitability, or could things have developed differently? The general perception of the colonial Government, at least, was that industrial development would be next-to-impossible to achieve in Namibia due to the country's characteristics. As the Administration wrote in 1946:

> Having regard to the arid and semi-arid climatic conditions in South West Africa, its agriculture is mainly pastoral in nature. Since the production of minerals is also, with the possible exception of diamonds, on a limited scale and as it has a small population, thinly scattered over a wide area, it has not any secondary industries, nor is there, in view of the circumstances stated above, any prospect of such industries being established on a paying basis (Report of the Administrator, 1946: 11).[25]

Similarly, Dundas (1946: 40) saw the limited industrial development of Namibia to be because of the lack of natural fuel supply, the arid climate, and the small domestic market, which meant that "there are no secondary industries, neither does it seem probable that

---

[24] The only exports from Namibia that would fall under Lall's 'medium technology manufacturing' classification would be the small quantity of soap that was exported, and the occasional wagons and boats exported to South Africa.

[25] The motivations of the Administration in writing this edition of the report must be questioned. The tone of the report is far more pessimistic than previous editions, and the reasons for this may be political, given that it was at this point that South Africa was appealing to the United Nations to permit the incorporation of Namibia into South Africa. It is possible that they were painting a deliberately gloomy picture to stress the dependence of the country on South Africa.

there will be development in manufacture... it is to be assumed that South-West Africa will always be an importer of manufactures".

Rather than subscribe to the narrative that industrial underdevelopment was inevitable due to characteristics of the country, the following section will outline the way industrial development (and economic diversification more broadly) in Namibia from 1915 to 1945 was hindered by the nature of colonial rule in South Africa, coupled with the actions and ambitions of the ruling elites within Namibia.

Constraints on economic diversification and industrial development

This chapter has outlined the profound change in the structure of the SWA economy that occurred between 1915 and 1945, characterised by the emergence of a pastoral practices centred on the export of karakul pelts, butter, and wool. By 1945 the economy was booming, and, in "a period of unprecedented prosperity", the colonial Administration was well satisfied with the progress being made (Dundas, 1946: 46).

Nevertheless, as this section will seek to argue, Namibia's economy was less developed than it could have been, and industrial development had been stunted due to free trade relations between South Africa and Namibia and because of the lack of action taken by the SWA colonial state to support manufacturing firms. As will be shown, free trade relations caused many manufacturing and agricultural industries in Namibia to be overrun by South African competition, leading to their stagnation or decline, and thereby limiting economic diversification.

Moreover, the view taken here is that even if the SWA colony had had independence from South Africa in the pre-1945 era, it would still likely not have pursued industrial development with vigour, and would not have sought to amend free trade relations with South Africa in a manner that would have been conducive to economic diversification. In other words, the state and its leading economic actors were not committed to achieving industrial development. In making this argument, I compare Namibia's experience with that of neighbouring Southern Rhodesia which, unlike Namibia, experienced significant industrial development in the years up to 1945.

Trade relations with South Africa

In 1910, one month after the formation of the Union of South Africa, a trade agreement was signed by South Africa, Basutoland (Lesotho), Bechuanaland (Botswana) and Swaziland, with the latter three at the time British 'High Commission Territories' (HCTs) (Gibb, 2006). The trade agreement was the Southern African Customs Union (SACU), and it created a free trade area between the four states and established a common external tariff on imports and exports. SACU was entirely dominated by South Africa, who had the "right to determine unilaterally all issues relating to the Custom Union's common external tariff" and, moreover, "South Africa's own institutions, for example the Treasury and the Board of Trade of Industry, assumed responsibility for running the Customs Union" (ibid.: 589).

With the onset of civilian colonial rule in Namibia and following the passing of the Customs and Excise Duties Amendment Act in South Africa in 1921, the SWA state "was regarded as being part of [South Africa]. It thus became a member of the Customs Union of South Africa and other territories" (Union of South Africa, 1935: 7). This meant that, like the HCT territories, Namibia had free trade with South Africa and its external tariff set by South Africa.

Whilst in 1921 SACU tariffs were quite low this situation completely changed in 1925. Following elections in South Africa in 1924, a coalition of the National Party and the Labour Party formed government and "immediately introduced a policy designed to promote industrial development" (Feinstein, 2005: 117). This led to the passing of a new Customs Tariff Act in 1925 which imposed large import tariffs on a host of manufactured products, and which meant that firms in Namibia and the HCT were compelled to source greater volumes of manufactured goods from South Africa (Gibb, 2006). Thus, Namibia's membership of SACU led to a massive increase in the import of manufactured and agricultural goods from South Africa and the reduction in imports from overseas.

The import of goods from South Africa was deliberately aided by the South African state through the South African state railway company – now also governing rail systems in Namibia – whose policies were "based on the sole principal of facilitating the trade with South West Africa of [South African] producers, manufacturers and importers to the utmost extent" (Hirsekorn, 1935: 117). It did this by offering extremely low rates for the transport of goods from South Africa to Namibia, effectively subsidising exports, without which they "could not compete" (ibid.: 117), much to the frustration of the SWA colonial administration which, despite consistent requests, was not permitted to have representatives on the board of the railway company (Union of South Africa, 1935).

The impact of free trade and subsidised exports from South Africa to Namibia was that several industries saw progress thwarted. In manufacturing, according to prominent local businessman Dr. Hirsekorn, "on account of the facilitated competition of Union surplus stocks, local industries were either destroyed or have not been developed", adding that "furniture, farm gates and other implements, soap, leather, boots and shoes, wire screen netting and perhaps other articles, may be manufactured at reasonable prices in South West Africa, as pointed out by witnesses connected with the trade", but had been unable to develop due to South African subsidised imports (Hirsekorn, 1935: 100). Similarly, the production of liquor from locally produced fruits and vegetables "was destroyed within a few years" of the onset of South African rule (Lau & Reiner, 1993: 9), whilst a host of other industries have also been cited as struggling due to South African competition, including the manufacture of sieves for mining purposes and the manufacture of tobacco products (Union of South Africa, 1935; Lau & Reiner, 1993).

In the case of furniture production, the industry had existed at least from the early 1920s onwards and had even been exporting products to South Africa in reasonable quantities in the late 1920s. However, in 1935 it was reported that "the small industry has been crushed by the cheap furniture manufactured in the Union" (Union of South Africa, 1935: 21). An industrialist in Namibia had been willing to "erect a [furniture] factory equipped with up-to-date machinery" within the country were a tariff to be imposed on imports from South Africa, but his request was rejected by the South African state (Union of South Africa, 1935: 21).

Tobacco manufacturing, which appeared to be on the cusp of large-scale advancement at the end of the German colonial era, struggled greatly under South African rule. In the 1920s three small tobacco manufacturers (producing cigarettes and cigars) were operating in Okahandja, but the market was becoming overrun with South African products, and the situation worsened in the 1930s, when South African producers began using a loophole to import their tobacco products at a reduced rail rate, threatening to entirely destroy the tobacco manufacturing and tobacco farming industries (Union of South Africa, 1935).[26] Although tobacco production was able to limp on in Namibia, by the 1940s there was only one firm producing cigarettes in the country, at levels of production a far cry from the large-scale tobacco products industry that was deemed plausible in 1913 (Lau & Reiner, 1993).

It was not just in manufacturing, but also in agricultural industries, including a promising maize industry, that development was stunted by trade relations with South Africa (Lau & Reiner, 1993). There were strong calls within Namibia for increased protection of agricultural products, with Hirsekorn (1935: 100) arguing that "[a] certain quantity of the local requirements of vegetables, potatoes and tobacco can be grown under irrigation in the country. I am convinced that South West Africa would produce more of these articles if some protection were given to encourage and promote agriculture".

Hirsekorn, and some other important figures in Namibian society, were, in the 1930s, increasingly critical of the customs arrangements between South Africa and Namibia. Ac-

---

[26] The loophole was that South African tobacco manufactures began exporting tobacco to SWA under the title of 'lick and dip' tobacco. This tobacco, which was supposed to only be used as animal feed or agricultural spraying, could be imported at a particularly low railway tariff and then sold for human consumption (Union of South Africa, 1935).

cordingly, the establishment of a new customs agreement that would give greater autonomy to SWA was being "contemplated" by the Administration (*ibid.*: 100). South Africa, however, proved unwilling to yield, with a commission established to investigate the economic relationship between the two countries concluding that "no alteration should be made in the Customs tariff or railway rate" (Union of South Africa, 1935: 61). No new customs arrangements were ever formed, and the SWA colony was forced to accept the continuation of trade relations which seriously thwarted the expansion of industry and agriculture in the country.

The interests of the Namibian elite

The trade relations imposed by South Africa on SWA clearly impeded industrial and agricultural diversification, and greater protection would have permitted their expansion. But, importantly, to say as much is not to suggest that were the SWA colony to have had increased license to protect nascent manufacturing industries that it would necessarily have done so. Indeed, my argument is that within the relations that existed between the SWA Administration and the South African state there *was* more scope to support industrial development than the Administration chose to deploy.

As stressed throughout this chapter, the SWA Administration had a clear vision of the economic structure that it wanted to create in Namibia, with its vision encapsulated in the following remark: "[t]he country is settling down to work. The farmers have been making money. The mines have been busy and the traders have benefited from the general prosperity" (Report of the Administrator, 1919: 14). Industrial development was not part of this economic model. As the Administration later wrote, "[a]part from mining potentialities there is no prospect of building up considerable industry in the near future except farming, for the population is small and the country at present produces little in the way of raw material" (Report of the Administrator, 1927: 24).

Consequently, whilst the Administration was more than willing to intervene in the economy to encourage the establishment of agricultural industries, it was unwilling to do so for most manufacturing industries. The intention of economic policy was, first and foremost, to support Namibia's white farming population. Thus, whereas the Administration decided, for example, to impose a ban on the export of karakul sheep to protect the industry or to establish an export subsidy for wool producers, at no point in the pre-1945 era did it demonstrate a willingness to foster broad industrial development.

Indeed, whilst the Administration was critical of Namibia's de facto membership of SACU, this criticism was not borne out of concern for industrial development. Rather, the reason that the Administration was opposed to SACU was because its high external tariffs after 1925 meant that Namibian firms and consumers had to spend greater sums of money on South Africa's more expensive products than they had had done previously when purchasing goods on the world market (Union of South Africa, 1935). Also, because imports were now predominantly coming from South Africa, the Administration was receiving far less revenue (in the form of import tariffs) than it had done previously. The Administration even pointedly observed that the very reason for the SACU tariffs was to develop local industries, which was of no use to the colony, because "South West Africa has practically no industries to benefit by such a policy" (*ibid.*: 13). Evidently, the Administration's thoughts were not with its struggling industrialists.

The apathy toward industry from the Administration was shared by the economic elites of Namibia (principally farmers, miners, and traders). For example, in a letter written in 1933, the Windhoek Chamber of Commerce argued in favour of free trade between the countries, stating that "a differentiation of customs tariffs does not appear desirable", and again the chamber's only criticisms of Namibia's de facto SACU membership were the increased costs of living and the loss of revenue for the Administration (quoted in Union of South Africa, 1935: 71).

Simply put, irrespective of the fact that the SWA Administration was operating in an extremely constricted policy environment, the Administration and the economic elites of Namibia at no point in the pre-1945 era expressed an interest in promoting industrial development and did not choose to use the policy space available to them to advance manufacturing.

It is important to bear in mind that these two factors (South African trade relations and the attitude of the Administration) were not separate issues occurring in isolation from each other. Rather, they were interrelated, with the absence of industrial development due to trade relations with South Africa making the Administration less interested in pursuing industrial development, and the disinterest from the Administration further making industrial development less likely. To demonstrate the symbiotic relationship between these factors, below is a depiction of Southern Rhodesia's industrial development during the first part of the 20th century. Unlike Namibia, Southern Rhodesia was to experience rapid industrialisation in the 1930s and 1940s, establishing itself as the second largest industrial nation in Africa, after South Africa. As will be shown, Southern Rhodesia's success in industrial development was largely determined by its relative protection from South African competition and the shifting attitude of the state towards the need for manufacturing development.

Changing trade relations with South Africa and shifting attitudes from the state: industrialisation in Southern Rhodesia

Southern Rhodesia's industrial development in the first part of the 20th century took place in a similar context to Namibia's – the neighbouring countries were both settler colonies with relatively small populations,[27] in similar geological settings, with established practices of importing manufactured goods, and both were located well within South Africa's sphere of influence.[28]

As such, early industrial development in Southern Rhodesia took on similar patterns to Namibia, with a brewery established in 1899, creameries first emerging in 1909, and grain mills, saw mills, bakeries, as well as firms producing fertiliser, furniture, processed meat, leather products, soaps, and the like during the 1910s and early 1920s (Phimister, 2000a). In the mid-1920s Southern Rhodesia's manufacturing sector was likely four to five times larger than Namibia's in terms of total value, though in very similar sub-sectors, and around the same size in per capita terms (Krogh, 1960; Phimister, 2000a).[29]

But from a similar standing in the mid-1920s, the countries were to experience extremely different trajectories of industrial development over the next thirty years, as is indicated below in table 2.3, with Namibian manufacturing increasing by 2.5 times between 1926 and 1951 and Southern Rhodesia's growing to an incredible 33 times its previous size.

	1926	1938	1945	1951
Southern Rhodesia	£1,560,000	£5,107,000	£14,045,000	£50,812,000
	13.0%	24.7%	–	20.0%
Namibia	£345,000	£205,000	£391,000	£902,000
	6.1%	2.8%	4.0%	2.3%

Table 2.3: Comparison of manufacturing's contribution to GDP in Southern Rhodesia and Namibia (£ and %), 1926–1951. Sources: For Namibia, all figures are from Krogh (1960). For Southern Rhodesia, 1926 is an estimate calculated from Phimister (2000a: 11) stating that "manufacturing contributed about 13 percent of Southern Rhodesia's estimated £12 million gross national income in 1926". Manufacturing outputs for 1938, 1945, and 1951 are from Phimister (2000a; 2000b). Total economic output for 1938 is from Phimister (1988), and MVA/GDP for 1951 is from Kamarck (1952).

Not only was Southern Rhodesia's manufacturing sector to increase at a much greater rate than Namibia's, but it was also able to notably diversify production away from food processing and beverages. From accounting for 47% of total manufacturing exports in 1939, food

---

[27] Southern Rhodesia's population was larger: 899,000 in 1921, compared to Namibia's 229,000 (Phimister, 2000a; Republic of Namibia, 2013).

[28] Phimister (2000a; 2000b) has provided a superb account of industrial development in Southern Rhodesia over the period 1894 to 1965.

[29] In 1926 13% of Southern Rhodesia's national income came from the manufacturing sector, in the same year manufacturing contributed 6% of Namibia's GDP (Phimister, 2000a; Krogh, 1960). The overall economy was also larger in Southern Rhodesia than Namibia at this point: Namibia's GDP in 1926 was £5.2 million; whereas in Southern Rhodesia national income was £12.0 million (Report of the Administrator, 1927; Phimister, 1988).

processing and beverages' contribution dropped to just 17% in 1953, with large quantities of textiles, apparel, chemicals, metal products, electrical machinery, and transport equipment now being exported (Phimister, 2000b). By contrast, in Namibia food and beverage exports still accounted for 97% of total manufacturing exports in 1939 and 83% in 1953 (Union of South Africa, Department of Customs and Excise, various years).

Why did these two similar countries experience such contrasting levels of industrial development? Like Namibia, "the growth of local secondary industry was crucially conditioned by the interwar pattern of Southern Rhodesia's trade relations with South Africa" (Phimister, 2000a: 9). Essentially, the greater protection that Southern Rhodesian firms were awarded from South African manufacturers (and the level of protection varied greatly in an era of frequently reworked trade agreements between the countries) the greater was industrial development. And like Namibia, the colonial Government of Southern Rhodesia initially presented an indifference to industrial development, with leading agriculturalists and miners in the country opposed to any form of protection. The colonial Government was keen to support its farmers and miners and to therefore promote free trade, with the Premier of Southern Rhodesia stating unequivocally in 1930 that "[t]he country as a whole has not asked for a policy of Protection" (quoted in Phimister, 2000a: 17).

But despite the ambivalence of the colonial state towards industrial development, through moments of good fortune, and through the Southern Rhodesian Government seeking to satisfy other agendas to support its agriculture and mining sectors, Southern Rhodesia's manufacturers were afforded significantly more protection than their Namibian counterparts. For example, in response to the South African Tariff Act of 1925, Southern Rhodesia "was obliged to take defensive action", and whilst its aim through the renegotiation of trade relations had been to ensure continued trade with the British, it did also afford some further protection to local industries (Phimister, 2000a: 27).

Additional effective protection was also inadvertently obtained through other means. South Africa's decision to delink from the British Pound in 1931, for example, caused rapid currency appreciation such that South Africa imports into Southern Rhodesia were "in effect subjected to a disability or tax of 20%" (Controller of Customs in Southern Rhodesia, quoted in Phimister, 2000a: 18), giving further space for industries to grow as "[l]ocal industrialists rushed to take advantage of the new situation" (Phimister, 2000a: 18).

With South Africa reversing its decision and 'relinking' its currency to the British Pond a few years later South African manufacturers came back strongly into Southern Rhodesia. The growing industrial sector in Southern Rhodesia subsequently lobbied the Government for increased protection through a reworking of customs arrangements with South Africa. The appeals of industry "might well have gone unheeded", but fortunately for them agricultural and financial interests were also unhappy with the existing customs agreement, and as such Southern Rhodesia terminated the existing agreement and renegotiations began in 1935 (*ibid.*: 19). The subsequent Customs and Excise Tariff Act of 1937, whilst having the interests of Southern Rhodesian commerce and agricultural industries in mind and offering only limited protection to secondary industries "was nonetheless greater than anything which had previously applied to manufactured imports from South Africa" (*ibid.*: 22). South African firms now only had equally favourable access to the Southern Rhodesia market as British manufacturers and, consequently, many South African firms moved to set up factories in the country itself, leading to "a marked upsurge in industrial expansion" in the late 1930s (*ibid.*: 22).

Despite progress, the manufacturing sector was still relatively small and unsophisticated in the late 1930s, struggling in the face of foreign competition. World War II, however, caused imports from overseas to be slashed, and left the colonial state with little choice but to support local industry to fill the void in industrial goods:

> Propelled by force of circumstance rather than its own volition, the Southern Rhodesian Government soon realised that drastic action was needed to overcome supply bottlenecks which threatened to stifle both the Colony's war effort and its broader industrial expansion (Phimister, 2000b: 31).

Several measures were adopted to support industry, such as the establishment of an Industrial Development Agency in 1940 and the nationalisation of iron and steel works in 1942. Manufacturing subsequently boomed from 1943 onwards and its output markedly diversified.

To conclude, the key reason as to why manufacturing developed more robustly in Southern Rhodesia than in Namibia during the 1930s and 1940s was that trade relations between Southern Rhodesia and South Africa were more favourable to Southern Rhodesian manufacturers than they were to their Namibian counterparts because Southern Rhodesia, as a non-South African colony, had greater autonomy to negotiate trade deals with South Africa.[30] Moreover, this independence meant that, for example, Southern Rhodesia industry could benefit from South Africa's currency appreciation of the early 1930s, a luxury not afforded to Namibia. And whilst in Namibia the manufacturing sector remained an insignificant part of the economy from the perspective of the Administration, in Southern Rhodesia the sectors reasonable growth increased the state's willingness to support its development,

---

[30] There were, of course, other factors. For example, whilst the Southern Rhodesian economy was to suffer greatly during the great depression, with national income falling from £13.9 million in 1929 to £8.7 million in 1931 (Phimister, 1988), the countercyclical nature of the value of gold, mined in Southern Rhodesia but not to any serious extent in Namibia, helped Southern Rhodesia to recover quickly from the depression. The reasonable economic recovery meant that domestic demand for manufactured goods was restored (and in fact increased) far more quickly and robustly than in Namibia.

and ultimately the onset of World War II forced the colonial state to increase support measures. Whilst World War II also saw growth in Namibia's manufacturing sector, lack of protection afforded to the industry in the 1920s and 1930s meant that its scope for expansion was much smaller than that of Southern Rhodesia's.

Conclusion

This chapter has outlined the progression of manufacturing in Namibia from the turn of the 20th century until the end of World War II. It is the first work ever to have attempted this exercise. It is also one of only a handful of works addressing Namibia's economic history for this period, and the first which has been able to utilise detailed trade statistics from the era to understand processes of economic change.

In a period that saw successful state-led efforts to establish an economy centred on the raising of livestock, manufacturing remained at a very small-scale. That said, two food processing export industries were to emerge strongly from the 1920s onwards, with dairy production and fish processing becoming major components of the colonial economy. In the case of the dairy industry, as well as in the less successful meat processing industry, the state was instrumental in driving forward their progression. Some relatively minor growth was also perceivable in non-food and beverage sectors of the economy during World War II.

Nevertheless, the period saw industrial development fundamentally obstructed by trade relations between Namibia's and its colonial ruler, South Africa, with free trade meaning that nascent firms in Namibia were overrun and ultimately unable to compete. Manufacturing's development was further undermined by the inaction of the Administration which, whilst willing to intervene in the economy and counter the interests of South Africa to foster agricultural development, was uninterested in doing so for the sake of industrial development, aside from those food processing industries of benefit to farmers. What we can witness in this era is a system of accumulation established to serve the economic and political interests of South Africa and the agricultural elite of the country.

In the years after World War II the political and economic situation in Namibia was to be profoundly reformed. South Africa became increasingly marginalised in international affairs as outrage over its system of racial segregation grew, a war of independence that would define Namibia's landscape in the late 20th century was launched, and eventually a transition towards independence was orchestrated. The following chapter will assess the state of industrial development in this tumultuous context.

3 Industrial development from 1946 to 1989: boom, stagnation, and the near total absence of industrial policy

Introduction

This chapter charts Namibia's industrial development from 1946 through to the final year of colonial rule. As in chapter 2, the era covered has been subdivided in two, with analysis first concentrated on the economic boom years of 1946 to 1963, and then addressing the final twenty-five years of colonial rule, a period characterised by the onset of a new South African economic policy for its colony, episodes of economic stagnation, political turmoil, and the Namibian war of independence.

Whilst industrial development was to flourish in the 1940s, 1950s and 1960s, the final decades of colonial rule saw progress in industrial development stall. The dairy industry, a vibrant part of the economy from the 1930s through to the 1960s, was to collapse entirely, and the hugely important fish processing industry, having grown enormously in the postwar years, was to fall to a fraction of its former size during the 1970s. Whilst the manufacturing sector did see some diversification – with large firms emerging in the production of maize, plastic packaging, paint, soap, chemical cleaning products, copper smelting, and meat processing – ultimately, the final era of South African rule saw only limited advancement, meaning that at the onset of independence Namibia's industrial sector was small and undiversified. The argument made is that the main reason for the sector's slow progress was, as in the pre-war years, the lack of state support for industrial development and the competition firms faced from South Africa's comparatively enormous industrial sector.

Political change and rapid economic growth in the post-World War II era

The years after the Second World War were ones of political, social, and economic change in Namibia, marked by increased efforts from South Africa to officially incorporate Namibia into its own nation, the gradual entrenchment of apartheid policies, and massive economic growth.

During the 1940s there were heightened calls from Namibia's white population for the country to become part of South Africa, with the Legislative Assembly in 1943 unanimously passing "a motion calling upon the local Administrator to request the Union Government to annex South West Africa... and to terminate the Mandate Agreement" (du Pisani, 1989: 30). This desire was shared by the South African state, and in 1946 it formally approached the newly formed UN to request the full incorporation of Namibia into South Africa (Wallace, 2011). A highly contentious referendum of the black population of Namibia, which purportedly showed overwhelming support for independence, was presented as supporting evidence, but an unconvinced UN rejected the request. Two years later, however, the election of the far-right National Party in South Africa, which was "eager to foster a closer relationship with Afrikaans-speaking whites in Namibia", led to renewed efforts to incorporate Namibia (*ibid.:* 245). In 1949 The South West Africa Affairs Amendment Act No. 23 was passed in South Africa, giving white Namibian citizens the opportunity to elect officials to the South African parliament, and in the same year South Africa abolished the practice of submitting annual reports on Namibia to the UN (*ibid.*). With these developments, Namibia had "effectively, if not legally, moved towards becoming South Africa's fifth province" (*ibid.:* 245). In 1950 the National Party of SWA won a large majority in the Legislative Assembly, claiming 15 of the 18 seats available. Under its leadership and as part of a "new emphasis on ethnic segregation", laws were passed to further limit the rights of Namibia's black population (*ibid.:* 253). These included the Native (Urban Areas) Proclamation of 1951 (which imposed controls on the movement of black Namibians), the Industrial Conciliation Ordinance of 1952 (which banned black Namibians from joining trade unions), and the Prohibition of Mixed Marriages Ordinance of 1953.

The strong economic growth experienced by Namibia during World War II had buoyed the local white population, with one local magazine writing that "there are good reasons for believing that the country has at last emerged from the pioneering period, and that in the years to come, though it may not be able to maintain present flourishing conditions, its financial stability will be firmly based" (South West Africa Annual, 1946: 81). In the late 1940s and early 1950s, the Namibian economy was to more than surpass these expectations, experiencing a period of "unparalleled prosperity", the likes of which have never been seen again (Union of South Africa, 1952: 8).

From 1946 to 1951 GDP growth (constant prices) was an extraordinary 18.0% per annum, with GDP growth averaging 10.7% per annum from 1946 to 1963 (SWA Department of Finance, 1988) and GDP per capita increasing at a rate of 5.4% per annum from R110 in 1946 to R255 in 1962 (Republic of South Africa, 1964). Its GDP growth rate was nearly double that of South Africa (itself experiencing an economic boom), with the South African state commenting that Namibia's growth from 1946 to 1956 was "surpassed by few countries in the world" (*ibid.:* 325). Namibia's total exports were exploding in value: from £8.2 million in 1945 they were worth £55.2 million in 1956 and the country began recording enormous annual trade balances (Union of South Africa, Department of Customs and Excise, various years; Sutcliffe, 1967). By 1965 Namibia's GDP per capita was higher than South Africa's, likely for the first time in the country's history (Thomas, 1978).

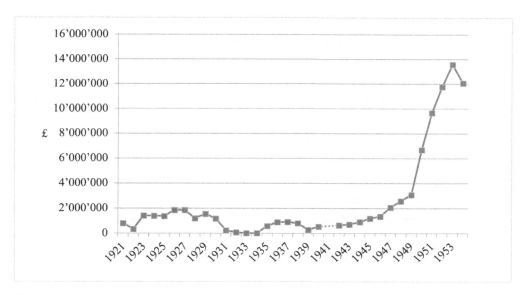

Figure 3.1: Diamond exports (£), 1921–1954. Source: Union of South Africa, Department of Customs and Excise (various years). Dotted lines indicate missing data. Data missing for 1941.

Whilst growth was broad based, the economic boom was mainly driven by the re-establishment of mining, particularly diamond mining, as the major economic activity of the country. From contributing 12.9% to GDP in 1945, by 1956 the sector accounted for 43.4% (Krogh, 1960), and over the same time period the total value added of the sector extraordinarily increased from R28 million to R269 million in constant prices (SWA Department of Finance, 1988). Mining exports increased from 16.5% of total exports in 1945 to 63.0% in 1952, with their value increasing from £1.3 million to £22.0 million (Union of South Africa, Department of Customs and Excise, 1945; 1952). Almost entirely controlled by *De Beers' Consolidated Diamond Mines*, diamond mining had been forced to nearly cease production entirely during the world depression and continued to struggle during the Second World War (Cleveland, 2014). But *De Beers* emerged from the war "determined to reenergize sales" globally and successfully reinvigorated the global diamond industry (*ibid.*: 89). The post-war period consequently "saw the beginning of permanent substantial mining by Consolidated Diamonds Mines" in Namibia and exports soared (Green, 1979: 11).

Base-metal production also grew markedly in the post-war years. In 1947 the Tsumeb mine was sold by the state (who had taken it over during the war) to the *Tsumeb Corporation Limited* (Innes, 1981).[1] The mine proved a success in a time of favourable world

---

[1] A consortium of American, British, and South African companies which included *Newmont Mining Corporation, American Metal Company,* and the *O'okiep Copper Company* (Jones & Mackey, 2015).

prices. Lead ore exports, which had valued zero in 1946, were worth £750,000 in 1947 and £7,700,000 in 1952. Between them, *De Beers' Consolidated Diamond Mines* and the *Tsumeb Corporation Limited* were to play an enormous role in the Namibian economy, producing "about 90% of the mining industry's output during the 1950s and 1960s. They were responsible for almost one-third of Namibian GDP and contributed almost 50% of exports" (Innes, 1981: 70).

The export of fish and fish products – largely pilchards, but also anchovies and lobster – was also to experience "phenomenal" grow in the post-war era (United Nations, 1957: 12), increasing from an average of £98,000 per annum between 1936 and 1940 (2.8% of total exports) to £5.1 million in 1954 (13.7% of total exports). The enormous growth in fishing and mining activities in the country and some growth in meat processing, added to the previous boom in karakul pelt, wool and dairy production, meant that by the mid-1950s Namibia had a large and relatively diversified export basket.

	Value (£)	% of Total
Diamonds	12,100,000	32.5
Lead Ore	6,900,000	18.6
Fish and fish products	5,100,000	13.8
Karakul Pelts	3,900,000	10.5
Cattle	3,000,000	8.0
Wool	1,100,000	3.0
Butter	1,000,000	2.6
Meat and meat products	950,000	2.5
Other	4,100,000	8.5
Total	37,100,000	100.0

Table 3.1 Namibia exports (£ and %), 1954. Source: Union of South Africa, Department of Customs and Excise (1954). Values do not add up exactly to total value due to rounding up.

The boom years of industrial development, 1946 to 1963

The decades following the end of World War II, continuing from the steady industrial growth in Namibia from 1935 onwards, far and away represent the high-water mark of industrial progress in the country. At no other point in Namibia's history was manufacturing output to increase so rapidly. From 1946 to 1963 manufacturing's growth rate was

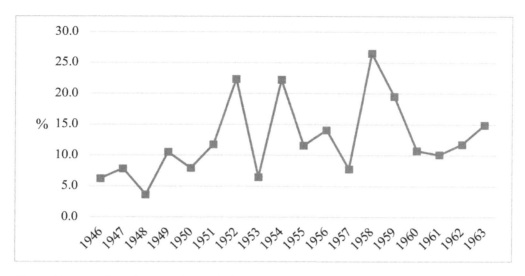

Figure 3.2: Manufacturing growth rate (%), 1946–1963. Source: SWA Department of Finance, 1988. Constant 1980 prices.

12.6%, even higher than GDP growth at the time (SWA Department of Finance, 1988).[2] MVA/GDP, which was just 2.8% in 1948, increased to 9.0% in 1960 (Krogh, 1960; Thomas, 1978).

Trade data is only available up to the year 1954 (at which point South Africa stopped publishing trade statistics for Namibia), but this too demonstrated the rapid advancement of manufacturing: the sector's contribution to total exports increased from 9.9% in 1946 to 20.2% in 1954 and in value from £940,000 to £7.5 million. As figure 3.3 shows, the growth in manufacturing exports during the late 1940s and early 1950s was mainly due to increased production of prepared and preserved fish, though the period also saw the increased export of prepared and preserved meat, as well as 'other manufactured products' (mainly the export of wagons, apparel, beer, and leather and leather manufactures), whilst dairy production slightly declined. Exports of fish and meat products found markets in Europe and the United States, as well as South Africa, whereas dairy was largely exported to South

---

[2]   The statistics on manufacturing growth rates in Namibia at this time are compromised because manufacturing statistics from the SWA Department of Finance (1988) deliberately exclude fish processing – the single largest contributor to manufacturing in Namibia over this period. The SWA Department of Finance data for the years 1920 to 1956 is based on the earlier assessments of Krogh (1960), but Krogh's work was adjusted later by the Department of Finance to exclude Walvis Bay – which by the 1980s was (cynically) considered an enclave of South Africa rather than part of the Namibian colony. As the SWA Department of Finance explained, the adjustment "basically entailed the elimination of the estimated value added resulting from fish processing activities in that area" (Hartmann, 1988: 9).

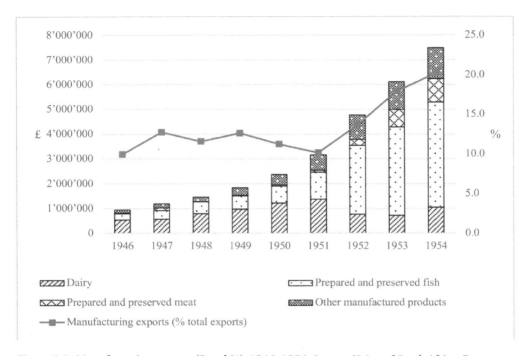

Figure 3.3: Manufacturing exports (£ and %), 1946–1954. Source: Union of South Africa, Department of Customs and Excise (various years).

Africa, and almost all the other manufacturing exports went solely to South Africa (though some apparel found small markets in Northern and Southern Rhodesia).

Namibia was not unique on the African continent in experiencing significant manufacturing growth over this period, with the 1950s witnessing "a spurt in the growth of manufacturing across British and French Africa" primarily because of growing consumer demand "underpinned by expanded earnings from agriculture" (Austin et al., 2017: 354). Across Africa, the major manufacturing industries were in food processing and high-volume goods for the local market, including "food and beverages, cigarettes, cotton textiles, footwear, furniture, soap, and perfume" (*ibid.:* 354). Beyond these, there was some "export processing of cash crops... ore smelting, sawmilling, and cement production", but outside of South Africa and Southern Rhodesia "there were only very limited developments in iron and steel, engineering, machinery, transport equipment, and chemical sectors" and "there was little production of intermediate products and virtually none of capital equipment" (*ibid.:* 254–255). As will be shown in the following sections, this general trend was largely replicated in Namibia.

The export of food products: thriving fish processing, well-developed meat processing, and diversified dairy output

The undeniable leader during this period of strong industrial growth in Namibia was fish processing. The late 1940s and early 1950s saw a flurry of investment in fish processing in Namibia by South African companies, part of a global expansion of fish processing due to heightened demand for cheap, durable sources of protein (Troadec et al., 1980). In Walvis Bay, fishmeal and canning facilities were set up by six South African companies[3] between 1948 and 1954, and exports of processed fish from the town increased from £200,000 in 1947 to £1.7 million in 1954, whilst fishmeal exports increased from £20,000 to £1.7 million over the same period (Republic of South Africa, 1964; Union of South Africa, Department of Customs and Excise, 1948; 1954). Walvis Bay was now being described as a "boom town", with its factories "working under full pressure to cope with the flow of fish" from the near-seventy fishing boats that operated from the port (Davis, 1953: 57). In Lüderitz lobsters were the main fishing catch, and the export of preserved lobster was also increasing: from £121,000 in 1947 to £900,000 in 1954. By the early 1960s there were two major rock lobster factories in the town, *Lurie's Canning Factory* and *Table Mountain Canning Company*. Two other canneries, *Lüderitz Bay Canner* and *African Canning Co.*, owned by the company that owned *Lurie's*, were closed to consolidate activities (Republic of South Africa, 1964).

The 1950s saw a conservative approach to fishing from the Administration, keen, despite pressure from the fishing companies, to limit fishing volumes to safeguard the longevity of the industry (Moorsom, 1984). Accordingly, several regulations were introduced, including the banning of the establishment of further processing companies, limiting the number of ships operating in the region and their total permitted catches, and setting individual quotas for each facility on the amount of total fish that could be processed (*ibid.*).

The disgruntled companies were thus forced to improve efficiency to maximise profits, which led to the purchase of new machinery and an increased focus on producing canned fish (the most valuable form of processing). Processed fish exports continued to grow significantly throughout the 1950s and early 1960s, and by the late 1950s employment in the fish processing industry at Walvis Bay had reached 4,000 people (*ibid.*). It was clear in the early 1960s that "[t]he most valuable processing industries in South West Africa are based on fish" (Republic of South Africa, 1964: 345)

The flourishing fish processing industry spawned a degree of upstream diversification. The most momentous development came in 1956, when a tin can production factory was

---

[3]   *Walvis Bay Canning Co., West Coast Fisheries, Tuna Corporation of Africa, Oceana Fishing Co. Ltd., New Western Fishing Industries Ltd., Namib Visserye* (Republic of South Africa, 1964).

established to manufacture the cans in which fish were exported, and which was "[o]ne of the most important manufacturing industries in South West Africa" at the time (*ibid.:* 353). The factory, established by the *Metal Box Company of South Africa*, was, in scale, unlike anything else in the manufacturing industry up to that point, with the company registering an enormous initial capital of £3.5 million – at the time the largest investment in Namibia in the post-war era, and the third largest investment in the country from 1945 to at least 1968 (BL OGS.270 No. 1278, Official Gazette of South West Africa, 1947–1968). The magnitude of the investment can be appreciated by noting that the *entire* capital invested by new companies registered in Namibia in 1955 (of which there were 91) was £2.4 million. In 1959 *Metal Box* increased its capital yet further to £4.5 million, and again in 1968 to R16 million (£8 million). The factory was a large employer and, by 1973, according to a worker in the factory, *Metal Box* paid "the highest salary in the whole of Walvis Bay" (quoted in Cronje & Cronje, 1979: 43). This period also saw other upstream firms emerge, such as one producing jute bags for the transportation of fish products (Republic of South Africa, 1964).

Meat processing for export, unsuccessful in the interwar years, was to establish itself as an important part of the Namibian economy during the late 1940s and 1950s. The export of canned meat was attempted in earnest for the first time in the early 1950s by *Damara Meat Packers* (owned by a collective of farmers), which was established in Windhoek in 1953 and exported its products to Europe (Rawlinson, 1994).[4] A smaller canning company, based in Okahandja, was also established in the early 1950s, and was exporting products in low quantities to Britain and to some southern African countries (*ibid.*). From close to zero exports in 1949, largely between these two firms, meat exports were worth nearly £1 million in 1954 (Union of South Africa, Customs and Excise, 1949; 1954).[5]

Though well-established in the country by the mid-1950s, the Administration had much greater ambitions for the industry, and it consequently formulated a national 'meat scheme' which would involve the construction of processing facilities across the country to allow for large-scale export (Rawlinson, 1994). The wheels were in motion, but progress stalled when the Meat Board of South Africa, dissatisfied with the productivity of South Africa's cattle farming, revised its own meat scheme in 1956. It was unclear how these policy changes would affect producers in Namibia, and as such the decision was taken by the Administration to delay its scheme, first temporarily, but eventually "for an indefinite period of time" (*ibid.:* 152).

---

[4]   *Damara Meat Packers* was run by a group of local farmers, who had taken over the canning facility from two local businessmen, De Jong and Isenberg, which had been established in 1948 (Rawlinson, 1994).

[5]   It appears that other firms were also exporting fresh meat (as opposed to canned). *Imperial Cold Storage* was still in operation until 1958, and smaller firms likely also exported in some quantity.

Despite the confusion caused by the cancellation of Namibia's meat scheme, *Damara Meat Packers* established a new, larger plant towards the end of the 1950s (*ibid.*). By 1962 63,000 cattle per annum were being slaughtered nationally for canning purposes, and in the same year a third canning facility was constructed in Otavi (Republic of South Africa, 1964). In 1964 it was stated that, behind the karakul pelt industry, the meat industry now "occupies the second position in the agricultural economy of South West Africa" (Republic of South Africa, 1964: 273).

The dairy industry continued to perform relatively well in the late 1940s and 1950s, with butter exports still presenting an upward trend up to 1954, though at a less impressive and more erratic manner than during the pre-1945 era. Exports increased from £540,000 in 1944 to £970,000 in 1954 but had been as high as £1.2 million in 1951 (Union of South Africa, Department of Customs and Excise, various years). In the mid-1950s there were five creameries in the country (in Omaruru, Rietfontein, Okahandja, Gobabis, and Otjiwarongo) and four cheese factories (in Outjo, Windhoek, Otavi, and Kalkfeld) (DICB, 1956). Total butter production declined slightly from 1954 to 1958, and in hindsight it is clear that this era marked the beginning of the end of the once flourishing industry, even if in 1964 dairying was still "an important part of the agricultural economy of the Territory" (*ibid.*: 279).

There was evident diversification of production activity within the dairy sector during the 1950s, in line with the ambitions of the national Dairy Industry Control Board (DICB), established in 1951. In the early 1950s, four of the five creameries in the country began producing buttermilk for export to South Africa, and two of the four cheese factories produced powdered milk (DICB, 1956). In 1956 a casein factory was established in Walvis Bay, which could produce 1 million lbs. of casein annually for export to Europe (DICB, 1956; Republic of South Africa, 1964). The industry was seen in the late 1950s as "extremely diversified and sophisticated" (Lau & Reiner, 1993: 13).

The state of manufacturing in 1963

The industrial growth of Namibia during the 1950s had seen MVA/GDP increase nearly fourfold in just over a decade and manufacturing exports (chiefly of processed fish) were at their highest point to date.[6] In 1963/64 the sector employed some 8,400 people, over ten times its level in 1921, and manufacturing employment as a percentage of Namibia's population was four times larger.

---

[6] Trade data is unavailable for Namibia from 1955 to 1979, meaning that it is hard to know for sure. But Innes (1981) has estimated that fish exports accounted for nearly 25% of all Namibian exports during the 1960s and given that this percentage is alone larger than total manufacturing exports contribution to total exports in 1954, it stands to reason that manufacturing exports must have been higher than 25%.

The sector was, however, still overwhelmingly dominated by food processing, as shown in table 3.2. In 1963/64, of the 212 manufacturing firms, 56 were involved in food processing, accounting for 70% of manufacturing employment and 74% of total output. Beyond the dominant fish, meat, and dairy industries, other food producers included a grain mill, firms producing prepared feeds for animals, and several bakeries (Republic of South Africa, 1964). In beverages, the two major breweries (*Hansa Breweries* in Swakopmund and *South West Breweries* in Windhoek), continued to operate (van der Hoog, 2016). There were six major carbonated drinks and mineral water producers.[7]

	Number of firms	Number of employees	Value of output (R'000)
Fish and allied products	10	4,107	10,636
Canned and preserved meat	4	970	1,525
Bakeries	26	348	478
Butter and cheese	5	216	351
Other food products	11	217	344
All food products	*56*	*5,858*	*13,334*
Metal products	16	724	1,478
Beverages	19	333	847
Transport equipment	15	254	490
Printing and publishing	13	189	483
Non-metallic mineral products	16	418	359
Furniture and fixtures	20	129	216
Machinery (excl. electrical machinery)	5	73	166
Wood products (excl. furniture)	18	158	165
Clothing and footwear	18	66	92
Electrical machinery, apparatus and appliances	5	61	81
All other products	11	123	372
Total	*212*	*8,386*	*18,083*

Table 3.2: Industrial census for Namibia, 1963/64. Source: Republic of South Africa (1967).

---

[7] *Paradise Beverages (SWA) Pty Ltd* in Windhoek, *Pelican Minerals* at Walvis Bay, and four others in Grootfontein, Karibib, Okahandja, and Omaruru.

Construction-related manufacturing did, however, experience strong growth during the 1950s due to the hive of construction activity at the time, such that in the early 1960s there were "a considerable number of... carpenters, furniture makers, plumbers, electrical firms, manufacturers of steel windows and doors, and welders" (Republic of South Africa, 1964: 353). There were also manufacturers of wooden doors, windows, and their frames; saw-mills; brick and tile producers; marble works; and firms producing sheet metal, metal ca-bles, and fencing wire (Republic of South Africa, 1964). The manufacture of metal products was by far the largest sector outside of food and beverage production in the early 1960s and a number of new construction-related manufacturing activities appeared during the late 1940s and 1950s, including the production of paint,[8] bevelled and silvered glass, and oxygen and acetylene (*ibid.*).[9]

In other manufacturing activities, the situation was similar to that of the interwar years, with small-scale printing and bookbinding, the manufacture of jewellery, manufacture of plastic products and advertising signs, the manufacture of candles, one tannery, and the manufacture of transport equipment (wooden boats and wagons) focused on servicing the local market (*ibid.*). Soap had been exported in tiny volumes since the 1920s. In 1956, the *Elephant Soap Company* (still in operation, and today known as *Elso Holdings*) was estab-lished, and was likely the largest soap operation in the country up to that point.

An industry of interest was the production of apparel. In the late 1940s there was a mas-sive boom in the export of apparel (mainly shirts) to South Africa, increasing in value from £28,000 in 1947 to £220,000 in 1951. This was likely a consequence of the establishment of *Windhoek Clothing Manufacturers* in Windhoek in 1948.[10] The firm, about which little is known, had a sizeable initial capital investment, but it appears that at some point in the 1950s or early 1960s it was forced to shut down. The apparel industry was very small by the early 1960s, employing less than 70 people (Republic of South Africa, 1967).

As in the pre-1945 era, there was little value addition to Namibia's mineral resources. The boom in diamond production in the late 1940s and early 1950s did lead to serious efforts within Namibia to establish a diamond cutting industry in the 1950s, with the Ad-

---

8   Paint-producing companies included the *Walvis Bay Paint Factory* and *Neo Paints Factory*. *Neo Paints*, still in operation today, was established by German immigrants that had arrived in the country following the end of World War II (Interview with Erich Muinjo, Manager: Material Requirement Planning & Projects, *Neo Paints Factory Pty Ltd*, 8.2.2016).

9   *African Oxygen & Acetylene*, a South African company, set up a subsidiary in Namibia in 1949. The subsidiary in Windhoek produced oxygen and dissolved acetylene, principally servicing the mining sector, but also general construction work (South West Africa Annual, 1951).

10   BL OGS.270 No. 1278, Official Gazette of South West Africa, 1947–1968. In 1950 a further com-pany called *S.W.A. Textiles* was registered with a small amount of capital in Windhoek, and the following year *Namib Textiles* was registered in Swakopmund.

ministration keen to develop the industry to generate employment, but such plans were categorically rejected by *De Beers*, and consequently no such industry was established. In 1950 a South African entrepreneur, M.E. Kahan, approached the Diamond Board of SWA requesting permission to establish a diamond cutting facility. The Diamond Board rejected this request on the grounds that processed diamonds, unlike unprocessed ones, were not subject to an export levy, and thus there were concerns that the establishment of a diamond cutting industry would reduce government revenues. Kahan reapplied in 1956, stating that capital of £100,000 would be available for the immediate establishment of a factory. This time the Administration expressed greater interest and approached *De Beers* about the possibility of the company selling diamonds to Kahan. A meeting took place between *De Beers* and the Administration in August 1957, with Sir Ernest Oppenheimer, head of *De Beers* since 1927, in attendance, just three months before his death. Minutes from the meeting reveal how the Namibian Administration was chastised by Oppenheimer for even suggesting the possibility that diamond cutting could happen in the country and how *De Beers* point-blank refused to supply Kahan with diamonds for cutting (NAN Correspondence IMW 62 A44/1/3/19, Establishment of a Diamond Cutting Industry in S.W.A. 1950–57).

Most industrial activities continued to be concentrated in the centre of the country – principally in Windhoek and at the coast in Walvis Bay, and to a lesser extent in Okahandja. Within the Police Zone in 1963/64 there were 9,500 people working in manufacturing (Republic of South Africa, 1967).

North of the Police Zone, manufacturing remained limited. There were some unsuccessful attempts to establish manufacturing activities here. In 1953 a firm applied to the Native Commission to establish a hides and skins tannery in Kaokoveld. Whilst their proposal was met with enthusiasm by the Commission, the enterprise never commenced activity. Effort was also made to establish a carpet making project amongst Ovambo women, but the Native Commission was unwilling to fund the project (NAN NAO 103 68/3 (v3), Industries Ovamboland. Carpet making). In 1954 a company applied to set up a meat canning factory, but their application was rejected by the Native Commission for being "impracticable" and unrealistic, stating that "[t]here is no reason to suppose the Ovambos will sell their stock in any quantity to any meat canning factory" (NAN NAO 103 68/3 (v1), Industries Ovamboland. Meat canning). There were probably more applications to establish manufacturing enterprises after 1954, but because "Native Affairs in Ovamboland came under the control of the South African Ministry of Native Affairs in 1954, the archival situation becomes more difficult" (Dobler, 2014: xxv).

As demonstrated in table 3.3, in 1960 Namibia likely had one of the largest relative manufacturing sectors in Africa, with the sixth largest share of manufacturing in total GDP

	MVA/GDP	Manufacturing output per capita (US$)	Income per capita (US$)	Population (million)
South Africa	20.2	83.7	435	17.4
Zimbabwe	16.0	33.4	206	3.6
Democratic Republic of Congo	14.0	9.0	58	14.1
Kenya	9.5	7.5	79	8.1
Senegal	9.5	20.8	218	3.1
Namibia	9.0	29.6	343	0.6
Uganda	6.5	5.7	87	6.7
Ghana	6.3	13.9	222	6.8
Sierra Leone	6.3	8.7	133	2.3
Gabon	6.1	20.0	294	0.4
Ethiopia	6.0	3.0	49	20.7
Cameroon	6.0	6.5	109	4.7
Zambia	5.5	8.8	155	3.2
Ivory Coast	5.3	9.7	181	3.2
Sudan	4.8	3.7	77	11.8
Nigeria	4.5	3.9	88	40.0
Angola	4.3	6.5	151	4.8
Togo	4.1	3.9	92	1.6
Tanzania	3.0	2.1	67	9.6
Benin	2.6	1.9	74	2.4

Table 3.3: MVA/GDP, manufacturing output, income per capita, and population in selected African countries, 1960. Sources: For South Africa, World Bank (2018). For Namibia, Thomas (1978). For all other countries, Kilby (1975). The figures for per capita income for South Africa and Namibia are in fact GDP per capita (current US$), though the GDP per capita figures presented in World Bank (2018) and Thomas (1978) for other African countries are very close to the per capita income figures presented by Kilby (1975), which has made me consider the figures comparable. Figures for Togo, Benin, and Sierra Leone are for 1965, not 1960. Namibia's manufacturing output was converted into US$ from South African Rand based on the fact that in 1960 Rand was exchanged at a ratio of 2 to 1 with the British Pound, and the Pound was exchanged with the Dollar at 1 to 2.8

and the third largest manufacturing output per capita out of the twenty African countries for whom data is available. Indeed, excluding Zimbabwe and South Africa, Namibia's manufacturing output per capita was close to four times the average of the other seventeen countries. Nevertheless, the structure of Namibian manufacturing (a predominance of food processing activities and a lack of more advanced manufacturing) was still far more like African countries other than South Africa and Southern Rhodesia, which exhibited more technologically complex manufacturing activities (Ewing, 1968; Kilby, 1975).

We can thus state that in 1963 Namibia had a reasonably well-advanced manufacturing sector, dominated by fish processing. Meat processing had also made advances, and construction-related manufacturing activities had grown in line with economic expansion. The manufacturing sector had experienced enormous rates of economic growth in the 1950s, with increasing prosperity having increased local demand for manufactured goods. Nevertheless, the sector was failing to diversify significantly into non-food processing activities in the way that the sectors of neighbouring South Africa and Southern Rhodesia were doing, with, for example, attempts at large-scale textile production in the early 1950s proving unsuccessful.

Despite the relatively positive state of Namibia's manufacturing in 1963, however, over the next twenty-five years of momentous economic, political and social change – culminating in Namibian independence in 1990 – the sector was to largely struggle and, to an extent, regress. This period will now be addressed.

War, political uncertainty, and economic crises: the final years of colonial rule, 1964 to 1989

The mid-1960s was an important point in Namibian history, defined by concerted efforts from South Africa to reorganise the country's society and politics and the gathering of momentum towards Namibia's independence.

On the former, in 1964 South Africa published its infamous "Report of the Commission of Enquiry into South West Africa Affairs 1962–1963", known as the *Odendaal Report*, which had been commissioned to put forward recommendations for the development and reorganisation of Namibia, with a focus on the black population (Republic of South Africa, 1964). *Odendaal*, mirroring policy developments in South Africa, proposed the creation of eleven 'ethnic homelands' for the various groups of the country, that were in theory to exist as mini, independent states (see map 2, p. 159). As part of attempts by South Africa to legitimise its actions, *Odendaal* also articulated a thorough strategy to launch economic development in the new, 'independent' states, which led to a host of large-scale infrastructure projects that were financed via huge investments from South Africa (Thomas, 1978; du Pisani, 1989; Wallace, 2011). The recommendations of *Odendaal* also reduced the power of the SWA Legislative Assembly, with the South-West Africa Constitution Act of 1968 and the South-West Africa Affairs Act revoking its ability to legislate on a host of matters, giving South Africa more power to control its colony (du Pisani, 1989; Wallace, 2011). The Administrator remained the "chief executive officer" of the country and had the authority to determine government policy (Republic of South Africa, 1968: 1).

On the latter, in 1966 a war of independence broke out, with the liberation movement led by the South West Africa People's Organisation (SWAPO), founded in 1960. Moreover, international condemnation of South Africa's rule in Namibia was growing. In 1966 the United Nations formally revoked South Africa's mandate over Namibia, stating that "the policies of apartheid and racial discrimination practised by the Government of South Africa in South West Africa [constitute] a crime against humanity" (UN General Assembly, 1966). In 1973 the UN General Assembly remarkably identified SWAPO as the "sole and authentic representative of the people of Namibia" (du Pisani, 1989: 32).

Despite military conflict and sanctions against South Africa, strong economic growth in Namibia was to continue during the latter half of the 1960s and most of the 1970s. Average annual growth from 1964 to 1977 was 4.2%, which, whilst far less than that from 1946 to 1963, was nevertheless impressive (SWA Department of Finance, 1988). In GDP per capita terms, Godana & Odada (2008: 245) estimate average annual growth between 1960 and 1979 to have been 4.5%, "a respectable growth rate even by international standards". Growth was driven by mining, fish processing, and agriculture, with Godana & Odada (*ibid.:* 245) noting the "high investment rate, favorable terms of trade, and reasonably good climatic conditions" at the time.

The late 1970s and early 1980s were, however, to see the "disintegration of the economy" of Namibia (Green, 1986: 3), caused principally by the global shocks following the second oil crisis in 1979, massive drought from 1977 to 1984, and steep decline in the output of the fishing sector (Wallace, 2011). Increasing uncertainty over the country's constitutional future, coupled with escalating conflict in the war of independence, also contributed to a state of paralysis in the economy. GDP growth (constant prices) was negative for six of the eight years from 1978 to 1985, and levels of unemployment began to grow greatly for the first time (SWA Department of Finance, 1988; Wallace, 2011).

A host of factors, including military deadlock, the costs of war for the South African state, growing international condemnation and internal resistance to the apartheid state, and the economic difficulty meant that by the late 1970s the South African state was arriving at the conclusion that Namibian independence was an inevitability. This led to significant changes within the country. Constitutional reform during the late 1970s meant that "most of the powers for the direct rule of Namibia that had been taken by the South African government since the Second World War were returned to Windhoek" (Wallace, 2011: 287). South Africa also set about trying to win the hearts and minds of the Namibian population to try to secure a favourable post-independence arrangement. From the early 1970s, many forms of apartheid legislation were repealed, with this tendency escalated in the late 1970s when the Administration abolished legislation outlawing interracial sexual relations and marriage and introduced equal pay for all races (*ibid.*).

There were also efforts to build up an "African petty bourgeoisie" through increased state employment of black Namibians (Mbuende, 1986: 97). Kaakunga (1990: 138) noted that "[a]n indigenous bureaucratic segment of the Namibian capitalist class has emerged into the open since the late seventies and the beginning of the eighties. In addition, a high-income group of an estimated 50,000 households has been created during the 1980s". Following constitutional reform in the late 1970s, the idea of entirely separate ethnic nations proposed in *Odendaal* was replaced by a new three-tiered system of government: the central government (the white Administration); eleven ethnic administrations forming a second tier; followed by a third tier of local and municipal authorities, and concurrently the size of government employment and expenditure increased dramatically. This great "proliferation of government" was seen as a "clumsy and extravagant political solution", with the second-tier governments spending heavily under limited financial control, and numerous instances of corruption and mismanagement were attested to (Wallace, 2011: 300–301). A government commission in 1983 stated that the expansion of government jobs had placed an "unbearable burden" on the already struggling Namibian economy (quoted in Wallace, 2011: 301).

Whilst moves towards independence further advanced in the late 1980s, the economy too was recovering, with reasonable growth rates achieved from 1986 onwards. As such, in economic terms, the final twenty-five years of South African rule can be characterised by extremely large levels of investment from South Africa in the Namibian economy and a period of initially strong growth driven principally by mining and fish processing, followed by serious economic crisis in the late 1970s and early 1980s, before a slight uptick as independence approached. At the end of colonial rule, Namibia's GDP per capita was the 6th highest in sub-Saharan Africa.

The sluggish growth of manufacturing over the final years of colonialism

The final twenty-five years of colonial rule failed to see significant degrees of industrial development in Namibia. Unlike from 1946 to 1963, the sector was unable to sizeably increase its relative contribution to the economy, and only achieved modest diversification. Moreover, two important manufacturing sectors – fish processing and dairy production – were to suffer enormously, with the latter almost entirely wiped out.

In contrast to the 1900 to 1963 period, there has already been a reasonable amount of research which discusses industrial development in the final years of colonial rule, all of which was written at the time. Importantly, however, most analyses suffered from a consistent and significant underestimation of the size of the manufacturing sector in Namibia, which greatly coloured analysis. Indeed, most authors state that Namibia's MVA/GDP over this period was around 4% to 5.5%, whereas the reality was that MVA/GDP was consistently double this figure. This is important, because it can lead to inaccurate conclusions. For example, Kaakunga (1990: 118) states that Namibia's MVA/GDP is "much lower than for neighbouring countries" and Curry & Stoneman (1993: 42) write that "manufacturing industry generates only about 5 per cent of GDP, one of the lowest anywhere".

There were two main reasons for this underestimation. Firstly, particularly in the 1970s, when the South African state jealously guarded official statistics on Namibia, authors were reliant on ill-informed estimations (e.g. Rijneveld, 1977; Green, 1979; Mbuende, 1986). Green (1979), for example, extrapolated MVA/GDP estimations from the more easily available data on the fish processing industry. Secondly, and more commonly during the 1980s when South Africa became willing to share data, authors often used official statistics from SWA's Department of Finance, figures which *excluded* Walvis Bay, one of two of Namibia's major industrial hubs (e.g. Zinn, 1985; Sparks & Murray, 1985; UNIN, 1986; UNIDO, 1990; Kaakunga, 1990; Curry & Stoneman, 1993). A third, more speculative, reason for the consistent underestimation of GDP is that authors were happy to accept statistics that painted Namibia's economy as 'backward', conforming, as this did, to narratives of South African exploitation, even when other statistics – though admittedly harder to obtain – suggested a stronger manufacturing sector.

That MVA in Namibia was underestimated is not to suggest that a secret, thriving, manufacturing sector was present in Namibia. But it is important to acknowledge that Namibian MVA/GDP was consistently between 9% and 12% from 1960 to 1989, as official data (including from the current Namibia Statistics Agency), which *includes* Walvis Bay, demonstrates. Figure 3.4 shows how MVA/GDP remained around 9% from 1960 to 1970, before rising in the first half of the 1970s to close to 11%, decreasing during the economic crisis of the late 1970s, and stabilising in the 1980s around the 10.5% to 11.5% mark.

The manufacturing sector continued to grow in the latter half of the 1960s and the early 1970s, averaging 6.6% per annum from 1964 to 1974 (SWA Department of Finance, 1988). Wallace (2011: 257) refers to the "rapid expansion" in manufacturing during the 1960s, and towards the end of the decade Gervasi (1967: 131) stated that "manufacturing industry has been expanding in recent years". Herrigel (1971) too observes the strong growth of manufacturing in the 1960s, led by increased meat and fish processing, the establishment of a copper and led smelter at the Tsumeb mine, and a further boom in construction activities due to the infrastructure projects undertaken in the wake of the *Odendaal Report*.

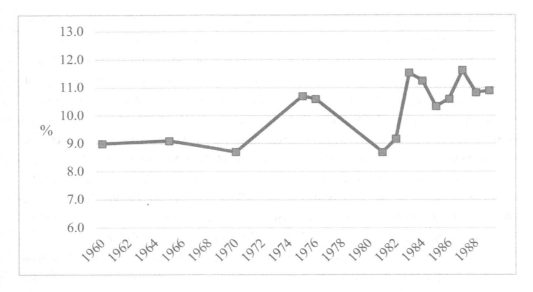

Figure 3.4: Manufacturing value added (% of GDP), 1960–1989. Sources: For 1960 and 1965, Thomas (1978); for 1970, 1975, and 1976, Leistner (1980); for 1980-1989, Republic of Namibia (1996; 1998).

But enormous declines in the fish processing industry, coupled with the economic recession that the country entered in the late 1970s, meant that Namibia's manufacturing sector was to experience its first ever major crisis, with average growth falling dramatically to -2.7% per annum from 1975 to 1980 (SWA Department of Finance, 1988). The recovery of the sector was far quicker than that of the overall economy, however, with growth rates improving to a steady 3.4% per annum from 1981 to 1989 (Namibia Statistics Agency, 2018).

Reflecting the lumbering progress of industrial development from 1964 to 1989, the total number of manufacturing firms and manufacturing employees grew slowly from 1964 to independence. The 212 firms in 1964 had increased to 250 by 1976 and reached around 277 at independence (Republic of South Africa, 1967; Republic of South Africa, 1980; Namibia Department of Economic Affairs, 1989).[11] Total manufacturing employees concurrently increased from 8,400 in 1964 to 12,000 in 1976 and roughly 13,500 in 1989 (*ibid.*). This meant that a higher proportion of the total population had been employed in manufacturing in 1964 than was employed in the sector at independence.

---

[11] The 277 firms for 1989 is based on the Namibia Department of Economic Affairs (1989) manufacturing industry survey, which found there to be 271 firms in Namibia. Their figure, however, excludes Walvis Bay. In later surveys (e.g. as reported in UNIDO, 1994), Walvis Bay was reported to have six manufacturing firms (though this seems like an underestimation to me).

Not only was manufacturing expansion to slow over the final twenty-five years, but the sector also failed to diversify to any significant extent, as is shown in Table 3.4, with manufacturing continuing to be dominated by fish and meat processing, with no other sectors even came close in terms of economic importance.

	% of firms		% of employees		% of output	
	1962/63	1994/95	1962/63	1994/95	1962/63	1994/95
Food and beverages	30.4	41.8	75.4	65.0	83.4	74.9
Metal products	17.7	14.7	13.0	13.6	11.6	11.3
Paper products, printing and pub-lishing	5.7	7.2	2.5	4.2	1.5	2.4
Wood, wood prod-ucts, and furniture	17.7	8.3	3.3	4.2	1.4	1.6
Non-metallic miner-als products	5.7	10.1	4.3	5.2	1.2	2.6
Textile, clothing and leather	12.0	6.5	1.1	3.3	0.3	1.0
Chemical products	1.4	8.6	0.0	4.0	0.0	6.1
Other	3.3	2.9	0.5	0.5	0.6	0.1
Total	100.0	100.0	100.0	100.0	100.0	100.0

Table 3.4: Manufacturing sector breakdown (%), 1962/63 and 1994/95. Sources: Republic of South Africa (1963); Ministry of Trade and Industry (1994). The two surveys are largely comparable, though an important difference, particularly concerning '% of firms', is that in the 1994/95 survey firms with less than ten employees were excluded.

Nevertheless, the final twenty-five years did see the emergence of some new manufacturing activities in the country and the expansion of some pre-existing ones. Food products other than processed meat and fish were to grow quite strongly. Most notably, *Namib Mills* established a maize mill in 1982 which proved extremely successful – by the early 1990s its production covered 75% of national demand for maize meal and 55% for wheat flower, employing 250 people (UNIDO, 1994). Several other maize mills were established over this period, as well as the largest animal feed producer yet seen in the country in 1983, a chocolate factory, and smaller firms producing cooking oil and peanut butter (Namibia Department of Economic Affairs, 1989).

In construction-related manufacturing, several large firms emerged during a construction boom in the late 1960s, including firms manufacturing calcium silicate bricks, fabricated steel, tanks, corrugated steel, and basic mining products. *Wispeco*, which quickly became the largest producer of steel and aluminium windows and door frames, and three large-scale wood products and furniture firms were also founded at this time (UNIDO, 1994). Very few firms were involved in the production of machinery, with two exceptions being *Swachrome*, who manufactured hydraulic cylinders for the mining industry, and *Gearing Ltd*, a ship-repairing firm which ran a small foundry to produce bearings and propellers for the fishing industry (*ibid.*).

The production of chemical products was the sub-sector of manufacturing which grew most markedly in this period. Prior to 1964 this sector only included firms producing paint or soap, but during the 1960s and 1970s firms emerged in the production of detergents and cleaners,[12] shampoo, plastic bags and other plastic materials,[13] charcoal, and salt (Department of Economic Affairs, 1989; UNIDO, 1990). In 1964 production started at the Tsumeb copper and lead smelter, which was to become a statistically important contributor to the manufacturing sector. No large firms emerged in apparel production, and, similarly, there continued to be only a handful of tanneries or companies processing karakul wool into higher-value products (UNIDO, 1994).

Manufacturing exports failed to grow over this period, with manufacturing exports as a percentage of total exports averaging 16.5% from 1981 to 1989, as compared to 20.2% in 1954 (the last year prior to 1981 for which trade data is available), though manufacturing exports were more diversified (i.e. less dominated by fish processing) in the 1980s than in the early 1950s (Republic of Namibia, 1996; 1998).[14] In the 1980s processed meat, smelted copper, and beer were exported in large quantities, as well as smaller amounts of charcoal, steel wire, and leather products (Ollikainen, 1991; UNIDO, 1994). Manufacturing continued to be concentrated in Windhoek and Walvis Bay, and ownership remained the almost exclusive reserve of Namibia's white (male) population.[15] Manufacturing in Namibia in the final years of colonial rule continued to be dominated by food processing, and the troubled-fortunes of this crucial sub-sector will be discussed below.

---

[12] Including *Cernol Chemicals* in 1978 and *Taurus Maintenance Products* in 1981.

[13] *Plastic Packaging*, founded in Windhoek in 1982, and another firm, *Namibia Plastic Converters*, also operated at this time.

[14] In 1954 processed fish accounted for 78% of total manufacturing exports, whereas from 1981 to 1989 its average annual contribution was 48.1%. Given that the high point in fish processing was to come in the 1970s (Moorsom, 1984), it is likely that manufacturing's contribution to total exports reached its zenith at some point during this decade.

[15] In 1993, 106 of the 274 firms reported were in Windhoek, with the next highest number being Swakopmund with just 25. Walvis Bay had high employment and output, but a small number of firms, given that the industry was dominated by the handful of fish processing firms (Ministry of Trade and Industry, 1994).

Deindustrialisation in Namibia? The collapse of fish processing and dairy production

The most significant development in Namibian manufacturing in the final years of colonial rule was the enormous decline in fish processing and the near-total collapse of the dairy industry.

In fish processing, overfishing – caused by a lack of regulation in Namibia and by highly dubious actions from the South African state – led to enormous stock depletion. Issues had begun in the early 1960s, when, following the death of the Administration's renowned director of fishing policy, the Administration's resistance to fishing companies' attempts to expand their quotas was broken, and a tripling of quotas between 1960 and 1964 saw "rational control of the fishing industry began to crumble before company pressure" (Moorsom, 1984: 22). The situation worsened in 1965, when the South African Government began to license factory ships (large vessels which did the processing onboard) operating out of Cape Town to fish outside of the legal Namibian waters, which at the time only stretched out 22 km from Namibia's coast *(ibid.)*. This led to confrontation between the Administration and the South African Government – the factory ships were banned from being serviced in Namibian ports (fuel, supplies, etc.) and Namibia deployed ships to patrol the 22km border. The Administration also responded, recklessly, by increasing the quotas for the three factories in Walvis Bay that were not affiliated with the factory ships, as well as permitting the establishment of new processing facilities and the allotment of quotas for new firms *(ibid.)*.

The growth in fishing caused Namibia's fish processing facilities to temporarily thrive, with output increasing from 3.6 million cartons per annum in 1964 to nearly 11 million in 1975 and the number of fish processing facilities at Walvis Bay increasing from six to nine (Smit & Rushburne, 1971; Thomas, 1978). By the early 1970s Namibia was "the world's largest producer of canned pilchards" (Smit & Rushburne, 1971: 15). The *Metal Box* tin-can plant was consequently expanded in 1974 and was now equipped to produce 16 million cartons per annum (Moorsom, 1984).

In the late 1970s, however, the pilchard population of Namibia fell off a cliff. Whereas the total pilchard catch in 1975 had been 550,000 tonnes, by 1980 it had fallen to just 11,000.[16] This meant a massive decline for the Walvis Bay canning industry, and by 1982 only four of the nine fish processing facilities remained, and canning output fell to around a tenth of what it had been in the mid-1970s *(ibid.)*. With demand slashed, *Metal Box*, the ·

---

[16] Pilchard fishing has never again brought in an annual catch even remotely close to the 1950 to 1975 era (Paterson et al. 2013).

largest industrial investment in Namibia's history, was forced to close in 1980. From then on, cans were produced in *Metal Box*'s factory in South Africa (*ibid.*).[17]

Even with reduced canning activities, the continued production of fishmeal and oil (which had been less effected by the declining pilchard population[18]) meant that Namibia's fish processing industry, whilst a lot smaller than it had been in the 1960s and 1970s, was still an important part of the manufacturing sector at the end of the 1980s, with five processing facilities at Walvis Bay and two at Lüderitz (UNIDO, 1994). Indeed, at independence Kaakunga (1990: 116) could still rightly cite fish processing "the core of the Namibian manufacturing industry". In 1989 fish processing was still, at 18% of total manufacturing, the largest sub-sector of Namibian manufacturing, though this was a massive decline compared to the 59% contributed in 1964 (Republic of South Africa, 1967; Republic of Namibia, 1998).

But the decline of the dairy industry was even more colossal than that of fish processing. From being one of the largest export-industries of the Namibian economy in the 1930s and 1940s, the industry "disintegrated entirely in the 1960s and had all but vanished by 1974" (Lau & Reiner, 1993: 13). Dairy production in the mid-1970s was just 6% of what it had been in the 1950s and most of the creameries and cheese factories had closed, along with the casein factory in Walvis Bay (Moorsom, 1982). By independence only two large-scale dairy companies survived, both just producing milk.

The declining fortunes of the sector were largely a consequence of the advancement of the South African dairy industry coupled with the withdrawal of active state support for the sector, as the SWA Administration sought to encourage farmers to concentrate on the raising of cattle for meat production.

On the former, the South African dairy industry expanded greatly during the 1950s such that it soon dwarfed that of Namibia (Henderson, 1960). For example, three cheese factories established in the Northern Cape in the early 1950s could alone produce around seven times the total cheese output of Namibia at the time (Henderson, 1960; Lau & Reiner, 1993). In butter production, South Africa overtook Namibia in output around 1955 and continued to advance throughout the decade whilst Namibia's butter industry faltered (Henderson, 1960). The increased production of South Africa's dairy industry meant that in the late 1950s and early 1960s South African dairy exports into Namibia began to increase markedly, offering stern competition to Namibian producers.

---

[17] Following the slight recovery of the fish canning industry in the mid-1980s, *Metal Box* was briefly recommissioned in 1989, and at independence it was producing about half of the cans required for fish processing (Moorsom, 1990; Curry & Stoneman, 1993). It closed soon after.

[18] The processing of fishmeal and oil was more resilient because pilchards could be substituted for the relatively abundant anchovies and horse mackerel of Namibian waters (these fish were at the time considered unsuitable for canning) (Moorsom, 1984).

The rising competition from South African producers was made even more challenging for Namibian producers because of the lack of state support to the industry. Chapter 2 discussed the initial reticence from the Administration to dairy production in Namibia in the 1920s, and these concerns persisted in the post-war era. For example, the 1949 'Report of the Long Term Agricultural Policy Commission' presented a somewhat negative perception of dairying in the country, noting that it was "wasteful of labour" and again highlighting its negative impact on the livestock industry (Agricultural Policy Commission, 1949: 26). This attitude led to the withdrawal of the 'winter premium' on butter in 1950, which had existed to protect dairy farmers from the dearth of milk production during the rainless winter months, on the grounds that this subsidy incentivised farmers to continue to practice dairying even when it was not based on "concept of good farming" (Agricultural Policy Commission, 1949: 69). The removal of the winter premium (whilst it continued to be in place for South African firms) simply made dairy production uneconomical for many farmers of Namibia. Though the Dairy Industry Control Board was opposed to the withdrawal of the subsidy, it was unable to sway the Administration (DICB, 1956).

The 1950s and 1960s were characterised by a stark lack of support from the Administration to the dairy industry (Herrigel, 1971), in contrast to the supportive measures deployed by the Administration during the interwar years discussed in chapter 2. But whilst the state was willing to see the industry largely wane, it did not want its total demise, because although a large dairy industry would be to the detriment of the meat industry, an outlet for farm milk was still considered of use, and as such the Namibian state took measures to ensure the milk industry's survival in the 1980s, stepping in to temporarily nationalise the industry when the remaining firms were close to collapse (FNDC, 1985; Lau & Reiner, 1993). In 1982 the milk industry was "on the brink of collapse" and as such the state-owned First National Development Corporation was requested by the Administration to take over the five remaining milk plants in the country under an SOE to be known as *Milcor* (FNDC, 1985: 13). Soon after, the Administration organised for the sale of these plants to two companies – *Bonmilk* and *Rietfontein Dairy* – and to facilitate these purchases the Government provided generous loans to the companies (Lau & Reiner, 1993).

The general absence of government support for dairy was not an example of outright neglect from the state. Rather, it was a consequence of the Administration's conviction that the industry damaged meat production and should therefore be curtailed. Indeed, the state was highly supportive of the meat industry and, despite challenges, the industry was able to successfully progress over the final years of colonial rule.

Meat processing, unlike dairy production, was regarded by the Administration as vital for the livestock farmers of the country, as during periods of drought, or when illnesses such as foot-and-mouth disease infected the cows, the facilities became the only economically viable outlet for farmers (Rawlinson, 1994). Thus, even from the perspective of the South African Meat Board, it was stated in 1968 that "in view of the exceptional conditions pertaining to the Territory, the local meat processing factories should be seen as an integral part of the stabilising mechanism of the cattle slaughtering industry in the Territory" (quoted in Rawlinson, 1994: 159). As such, both the South African and Namibian Meat Boards supported the industry's progression, with, for example the South African Board financing the revamping of slaughtering facilities in Okahandja, the Namibian Board granting a loan at generous rates to expand the Okahandja's meat processing plant's cooling and deboning facilities, and the two Boards jointly contributing an export levy on canned beef (Rawlinson, 1994).

Despite support, the three meat canning facilities in Namibia were suffering substantial losses during the 1970s, principally because of a lack of cattle-throughput.[19] The situation was exacerbated by the drought of the early 1980s and matters were made worse still when the Administration announced that export subsidies – without which it was "common knowledge that the two canning factories at Windhoek and Otavi could not survive" – were to be stopped, because of South Africa's curtailment of financial support to Namibia in the face of its own economic difficulties and Namibia's impending independence (*ibid.*: 193). The three meat processing plants, along with a fourth which had been established in Gobabis by the state-owned First National Development Corporation (FNDC) in the early 1980s, agreed to a merger in 1983 to rationalise the industry, but it was evident that the state would still have to intervene to ensure the industry's survival.

Accordingly, in 1986 the Administration nationalised the country's meat canning industry, establishing the *Swameat Corporation*, and the firm proceeded to buy all of the assets of the recently-merged private firms and was further awarded with R15 million in working capital from the FNDC (FNDC, 1986; Rawlinson, 1994). The state swiftly consolidated the industry, closing the Gobabis and Otavi plants, and sought to expand its revenue stream, taking over a bonemeal plant in Ossa, commissioning a venison plant, and creating a pet food plant within its Windhoek facilities (Rawlinson, 1994). Very quickly *Swameat* proved a success and became financially self-sufficient (*ibid.*).[20]

---

[19] To support the industry, the early 1980s saw additional measures introduced, including the importing of beef from overseas to be processed in the facilities and the introduction of a subsidy for abattoirs per cattle slaughtered (Rawlinson, 1994).

[20] Though these factories represented the centre-point of meat processing in Namibia, they were not the only facilities in existence. Many towns had their own abattoirs, and lots of butchers in the country of course undertook their own processing. A number of these butchers grew substantially. For example, *Hartlief Continental Meat Products*, founded in Windhoek in 1946, established a small factory in 1966, which, producing meat products such as salamis, went on "to become one of the best-equipped factories of its kind" (Rawlinson, 1994: 171).

All-in-all, despite the evident difficulties experienced by the meat processing industry throughout the post-war era, the industry was able to grow into a significant part of the Namibian economy, largely due to the extensive support measures provided by the state. Whereas from 1946 to 1956 only 8% of Namibia's livestock was processed locally, by 1981 to 1990 it had increased to 49%, and at independence the industry was on a sound footing (*ibid.*).

An assessment

Compared to the strong performance of Namibia's manufacturing sector in the 1940s, 1950s and 1960s, the final two decades of colonial rule were extremely disappointing, with output failing to increase notably, the sector's contribution to the overall economy growing minimally, exports slightly decreasing in relative terms, manufacturing employment as a percentage of total employment decreasing, and manufacturing failing to diversify into more technologically-sophisticated activities. Despite a handful industries emerging from 1964 onwards and some industries declining, the manufacturing sector looked very similar in 1989 to how it had done in 1964.[21]

It appears that Namibia's record from the 1960s through to the end of the 1980s was just slightly below-average by African standards. In terms of MVA/GDP, Namibia's growth was similar to other African nations: of the 18 countries included in table 3.4 above, MVA/GDP increased from an average of 7.7% in 1960 to 12.0% in 1990 for all countries (excluding Namibia), whilst Namibia's increased from 9.0% to 12.5% over the same period (World Bank, 2018). Namibia maintained its position of having a high manufacturing output per capita, reaching US$205 in 1990, the 6th largest in sub-Saharan Africa, nearly double the regional mean and over four times the median (*ibid.*).[22]

Like in Namibian manufacturing, the typical African manufacturing sector continued to be dominated by food processing. In a breakdown of manufacturing for 22 sub-Saharan African countries provided by Tribe (2000), 19 countries had, like Namibia, 'food products, beverages, and tobacco products' as their largest sub-sector. What is evident from Tribe's dataset, however, is that the manufacturing sector of Namibia was far less diversified than most countries. In Namibia, 74.9% of total manufacturing output was in food processing and beverages in the early 1990s, a proportion higher than every single country in Tribe's dataset, bar Burundi, with the average for the 22 countries being 44.0% in 1990.

---

[21] For an example of an industry declining, lime works disappeared in this period, beginning to close in the 1950s when large cement factories were constructed in South Africa (Swilling, 2017). The *Nieswandt Boatyard* in Lüderitz was bought by *Ohlthaver & List* in 1969, and shortly afterwards a second branch of the firm was established at Walvis Bay (Kraatz Engineering, n.d.). The firm struggled however, and both yards were closed during the 1980s (UNIDO, 1990).

[22] Based on the 41 countries with data available.

Constraints and drivers of industrial development

The absence of industrial policy

The above overview paints a picture of an industrial sector that, despite progress in the years up to the mid-1960s, failed to advance notably. The question is, why?

In explaining the industrial and economic structure of a given country there are a host of factors at play. There are what could be called 'structural factors', such as in Namibia's case its small domestic market and distance from major global manufacturing markets. For example, Chenery & Taylor (1968), in their analysis of global industrial patterns, note that what they call 'late' industries (e.g. clothing, printing, durables, and capital goods) are more likely to emerge earlier in more greatly populated countries than in smaller ones because of economies of scale. From the dataset in Tribe (2000), the evidence does suggest that the large countries are more likely to have diversified industrial sectors. Smaller countries are more likely to have specialised manufacturing structures because they do not have the domestic market size necessary to support a multitude of industries with significant scale economies (Streeten, 1993). Because of this, "[a] small country, therefore, will either avoid industries with marked economies of scale or will specialize in a few such sectors where is has special advantages" (Perkins & Syrquin, 1989: 1712).

There are also other factors which, whilst less structural than features such as small population size, represent significant hurdles for prospective industrialists. For example, throughout this period observers noted that, as well as Namibia's small population, Namibia also suffered from "high and variable costs of transportation, power, water and personnel, which render most local manufacturers uneconomic on international markets" (Republic of South Africa, 1967: 71), with another commonly cited factor being the "shortage of exper-tise" to be found in the country (Administration of SWA, 1980: 5).

But the important point regarding these latter factors – which were frequently touted by the South African state and the SWA Administration as justifications for the lack of Na-mibian industrial development – is that they are, essentially, alterable, via programmes to improve transport infrastructure, power and water supply, to train skilled labour, to better coordinate industry, to protect firms from foreign competition and to offer them subsidies to encourage expansion, etc. In other words, they are alterable if the state pursues active in-dustrial policy. This is a point that the South African state rather candidly acknowledged in 1964, when in the *Odendaal Report* it argued that industrial development in Namibia would see "no big new developments unless the Republic of South Africa makes a further real ef-fort to make *capital* and technical assistance available on a broad base for a well-organized programme" (*ibid.:* 431, emphasis in original). Ultimately, this prediction appears to have been correct, with Namibia experiencing extremely limited industrial policy and concurrently extremely limited industrial development from 1946 to 1989.

The immediate post-war period had seen the continuation of the SWA Administration's apathetic attitude towards industrial policy of the interwar years, with the exceptions being the above-discussed interest in meat processing and the fleeting contemplation of establishing a diamond cutting and polishing industry in the mid-1950s. Beyond these two instances, there was no concerted effort to encourage the development of industry, in contrast to the state's continued commitment to supporting agricultural development.

For example, in 1950 "a fund for the promotion of the development of farming activities was established... which by the mid-1960s paid out almost R500,000 of public money to white farmers in support of cattle farming" (Lau & Reiner, 1993: 20). An Agricultural Credit Board was established in 1966 to organise financial support to farmers, and through this the Administration provided loans for the settlement of farmers, the combating of bush encroachment, the construction of property, and the purchase of equipment. The state directly subsidised activities deemed in the "national interest", such as soil conservation and water conservation works (Administration of SWA, 1981: 4). The state also undertook agricultural research, including vineyard cultivation, experiments in fruit and vegetable cultivation, the cultivation of cotton, maize, and other crops. Research continued in karakul and cattle development at the state's experimental farms and the state's agricultural college at Neudamm continued to train farmers (Administration of SWA, 1981; 1982; 1983).

The absence of industrial policy in Namibia appeared to be coming to an end in 1964, with the publication of the *Odendaal Report*, which represented the first time in the eighty years of colonial rule of Namibia that plans for industrial development were advocated by the country's colonial authorities. The South African state wrote that in Namibia "[i]t is clear... that future economic development must be more in the direction of further local refinement of the available raw materials and of manufacturing industries" (Republic of South Africa, 1964: 429). To advance manufacturing it was argued that, for example, "young industries with possibilities should be protected", stating that whilst the costs of living may increase with protectionism, it is "of no interest to a person who had no job, and therefore no money, to learn that products can be manufactured more cheaply elsewhere than in his own country" (*ibid.:* 431).

But any hopes of a targeted industrial policy materialising were misplaced, and the final twenty-five years of colonial rule can most aptly be characterised by the "complete lack of systematic local industrial development strategy" (Zinn, 1985: 59). Various commentators lamented that the SWA Administration failed to provide: exporting marketing channels for industrialists; rail tariffs to favour manufacturing exports (by providing lower costs for goods destined for export); tax incentives to encourage local processing of resources; any form of

protectionism; a training-programme for industrial skills; fiscal instruments to support manufacturing; a Board of Trade & Industry; or preferential procurement policies for local manufacturers (UNIDO, 1984; Thomas, 1985).

Thomas (1985: 2) concluded that "[t]here can be little doubt that, compared to the other
major sectors of the economy... the industrial sector has in the past been Namibia's stepchild"
and that the "[t]otal lack of a research and planning base ... is both deplorable and shocking
(*ibid.*: 9). The only incentives present in the late 1980s were tax concessions wherein machinery was 100% tax deductible for the first year of new industries, and buildings were deductible at 20% in the first year and 4% thereafter (FNDC & Department of Economic Affairs,
1989). FNDC (1986: 25) refers to a cabinet decision in 1985 "to provide interim assistance
to local industry in the form of subsidies and rebates", but it is unclear if this ever took place.

The assessment of a lack of industrial policy was not just the opinion of commentators,
with the Administration itself acknowledging that "there has never been a clear policy of
industrial development, and attempts have not been made to diversify the economy" (Department of Governmental Affairs, 1987: 24) and that "Namibia has no formal incentives for
long-term industrial and regional development" (FNDC & Department of Economic Affairs,
1989: 39).

Clearly, industrial policy in the 1946 to 1989 period of colonial rule was mostly notable
only in its absence. There were, however, exceptions to this general rule. We have already
discussed the support measures taken to support the advancement of meat processing, but
there remains an important further way that the Administration pursued industrial policy:
the work of the state-owned First National Development Corporation (FNDC), to be discussed
below.

The exception to the rule: the First National Development Corporation
Following the publication of Odendaal, the Bantu Investment Corporation (BIC), which had
been established in South Africa in 1959 to encourage development in the South African
'bantustans' through investment and technical assistance, saw its scope of operation expanded to include the 'ethnic homelands' of Namibia (Republic of South Africa, 1964). The aim in
increasing economic prosperity in the 'ethnic homelands' of Namibia and South Africa was to
try sustain the apartheid social system. As Dobler (2014: 93) writes, "[e]conomic development
was seen as a means to sustainably achieve apartheid. It should provide the 'welfare of the
indigenous population' that even the proponents of apartheid saw as a necessary precondi-
tion for a stable white rule".[23]

---

[23] Bob Meiring, Chairman of the FNDC from 1990 to 1993, explained in interview, the *raison d'être*
of the FNDC as follows: "It was all in the fundamentals of grand apartheid. In that, every tribal or

The BIC established several industrial firms in the 1960s and 1970s in Ovamboland, including a furniture factory in Oshakati in 1965, and in the 1970s a soft drinks factory, a large-scale bakery, and a meat factory (South West Africa Annual, 1976; Dobler, 2014). The company further founded or took over a host of non-industrial activities (e.g. restaurants, a construction company, a petrol station, wholesale stores), provided loans to local businesspersons, and built property to be rented by enterprises (South West Africa Annual, 1976).

In 1978 BIC was replaced by the FNDC, which proved more ambitious in its scope.[24] The FNDC's mandate was to "develop South West Africa and its peoples by encouraging new undertakings in agriculture, manufacturing, mining and commerce", and, whilst development ambitions were still to generally target the 'homelands' and 'underdeveloped' communities, the corporation was now interested in *national* development more broadly, and its responsibilities included "strategic undertakings" not restricted to the 'homelands' (FNDC, 1985: 5). Although the stated remit suggests that manufacturing was not necessarily the preeminent sector from the FNDC's perspective, there was a "preference given by the FNDC to industrial development" (*ibid.:* 13).

The FNDC became an important part of the economy and the manufacturing sector, particularly in the north of Namibia. In its first seven year the company dispersed R43.4 million in loans to over 500 businesses, with 80% of funds destined for manufacturing activities (*ibid.*). In comparison the total loans from the FNDC's predecessors in 1978 was just R2 million. A 'small industrialist scheme' was also launched in the early 1980s, giving industrialists workspace that was subsidised with low interest rates and rental costs; assistance with purchases and marketing of products; administrative training; management consultation; and financing for the purchase of production inputs (*ibid.*). By 1985 there were 68 small industrialists (carpenters, dressmakers, metal workers, leather workers, woodcarvers, etc.) in workspaces in Windhoek, 48 in the north, and 23 in other parts of the country, including Swakopmund, Gibeon, Rehoboth, and Okahandja (FNDC, 1983; 1985). The FNDC also continued to undertake research into industries, conducting investigations into the viability of various manufacturing and other economic activities (FNDC, 1988).

---

national, sub-national unit, must have its own environment, where it could settle itself, grow, and progress. And it cannot be done if it doesn't have an economic basis. So, in all [the homelands] development corporations were established" (interview with Bob Meiring, Chairman of FNDC 1990–1993, 14.1.2016).

[24] This is a simplification of what happened. From 1976 to 1977 the BIC was replaced by a variety of ethnic homeland-specific development corporations, with the Ovamboland Development Corporation, Rehoboth Investment and Development Corporation, Caprivi Development Corporation, and Ekuliko Kavango established and operating under the same remit as the BIC (Thomas, 1978; FNDC, 1983; Dobler, 2014). These corporations were amalgamated into the FNDC in 1978.

The FNDC also operated thirteen manufacturing firms in the 1980s: the Gobabis meat factory, the *Milcor* dairy company, a venison plant, a firm producing wood-chips, as well as two smaller meat processing facilities, a maize mill, a soft drink plant, a firm producing gemstones, and some bakeries (FNDC, 1983; 1989). Many of these enterprises benefitted from their close connection with government, often receiving procurement contracts. For example, the furniture factory in Oshakati provided school benches and office desks for the state within Ovamboland, and the meat processing factories sold its meat to the school kitchens of the region (Dobler, 2014). By 1985 the company stated that it had created 4,000 jobs, 2,000 of which were in manufacturing, which was perhaps one-sixth of *total* manufacturing employment at the time, a serious contribution (FNDC, 1985).

Despite the relatively large levels of employment created, the FNDC's impact on industrial development was quite small. As Dobler (2014: 98) argues, whilst the FNDC and its predecessors "founded most of the few industrial companies operating in [Ovamboland] today", its endeavours "did not really lead to sustainable development, least of all to the industrial development the companies had envisaged". Indeed, aside from FNDC's own enterprises, little in the way of manufacturing developed in the north of the country and those entrepreneurs who it supported failed to emerge as major economic players.

The major reason for the FNDC's shortcomings were that its genuine efforts towards industrial development were not shared by the SWA Administration, with the corporation itself complaining that it was "handicapped" by "the lack of [a] national development strategy" (FNDC, 1988: 4). There were consistent tensions between the FNDC and the Administration, with the company having unsuccessfully "campaigned for many years for the introduction of incentive measures and concessions to help promote industrial development" and for policies similar to those in South Africa (FNDC, 1986: 22). The FNDC also complained that it was finding itself under "[i]ncreasing pressure" from the state to privatise its own firms (FNDC, 1988: 5). FNDC's aiding of small-scale enterprises (e.g. through training programmes, supporting firms in their marketing efforts) was also debilitatingly undercapitalised (Thomas, 1985).

Ultimately, the FNDC's role in industrial development was limited. It was allowed to intervene directly in the economy at points of desperation in the meat and milk industries – serving the interests of the nation's farmers and maintaining stability – and to establish industries in the north to try to preserve the apartheid system. But elsewhere its role was only in the small-scale provision of loans, property, and advice. No trade protection and only scant fiscal incentives were available, leaving industrialists with little hope of substantial growth.

What we can see, therefore, is a state that was willing to intervene in the economy (which sometimes included support to manufacturing firms) to preserve the status quo but which was unwilling to embark on a programme of structural transformation. And as will be shown in the following sections, the motivations of the South African state and the SWA Administration largely explain the failure to adequately support manufacturing.

The interests and actions of South Africa

The most common explanation of the limited development of Namibian manufacturing during the colonial era has been the actions of the South African state (Green, 1979; Green & Kiljunen, 1981; Zinn, 1985; Witulski, 1985; Thomas, 1985; UNIN, 1986; UNIDO, 1990). The broad consensus amongst commentators was that Namibia's "industrial sector is not only small but has also been deliberately designed to serve the interests of South Africa and its allies... The main reason for lack of significant industrial development is the design of the colonial power to turn Namibia into a source of raw materials and a market for South African manufacturers" (UNIN, 1986: 337).

The clearest way in which the South African state was undermining industrial development in Namibia was through its failure to pursue active industrial policy in the country. This, despite the fact that South Africa was domestically doing all that it could to foster industrial development (Feinstein, 2005). A telling example is how South Africa's industrial decentralisation programme of the 1970s and 1980s – which provided tax concessions, cash grants, and other supportive measures to firm in regions of South Africa which had yet to see significant industrialisation – excluded Namibia (Wellings & Black, 1986).

Namibian industry also continued to struggle because of trade relations with South Africa due to Namibia's *de facto* membership of the Southern African Customs Union (SACU), with UNIN (1986: 339) observing that the "[l]ack of adequate protection has discouraged the establishment of new industries and led to the closing down of some of the existing ones". Not only were South African firms operating at much larger economies of scale, but, just as in the interwar years, they were also benefiting from state support, including that the South African railway company offered subsidised transport of goods from South Africa to Namibia, such that South African firms were, in most manufacturing sub-sectors, able to outcompete Namibian firms (Zinn, 1985; UNIDO, 1990).

The Namibian market and those of the other SACU countries, were, despite their small size, extremely important to South Africa, because South Africa's products were mostly uncompetitive on the global market (Innes, 1981; Mbuende, 1987). The importance of the Namibian economy to South African producers was well-illustrated in a report commissioned by the Association of Chambers of Commerce and Industry of South Africa, which stressed that Namibia provided "a natural export market for all types of South African merchandise which needs to be fostered and cultivated" and stating that "[w]e must do our utmost do [sic.] preserve those profitable relations and ventures" (van Rensburg, 1989: iv; 48).

Accordingly, South African firms were often ruthless within SACU. Following the independence of Botswana, Lesotho and Swaziland (BLS), the SACU agreement was reworked in 1969. The free trade area and common external tariff of the 1910 agreement remained intact, but the BLS states, who felt that SACU was enabling South African industrial growth at the expense of the others, sought compensation (Maasdorp, 1982). Consequently, a 'revenue-sharing formula' was established which meant the BLS states received more revenue from SACU customs and excise receipts than was due to them. In effect, the BLS countries were being paid to accept that South African firms would dominate the SACU market, at the expense of BLS firms. The new 1969 agreement did, however, include a provision to allow the non-South Africa members to impose protective tariffs to develop new industries for up to a period of eight years, thereby raising the prospect of industrial development.

However, "South Africa found itself unwilling to allow [the BLS states] to protect infant industries that could undermine the competitiveness of South African industry" (Gibb, 2006: 594), fearful "of the damage which this would do to South African industry" (Selwyn, 1975: 114). It later transpired that the 1969 SACU agreement included a 'secret memorandum' which stated that an infant industry seeking protection had to be able to supply 60% of the demand requirements of the customs union, a stipulation which "represented an almost insurmountable obstacle to industrial development" in the BLS countries (Gibb, 2006: 594). Moreover, "there were numerous instances where Pretoria withheld permission or, worse, actively pursued policies to undermine industrialisation" in the economies of the other SACU countries (ibid.: 594). Examples include pressure from South Africa to close a textile mill established in Swaziland by Hong Kong investors in the 1970s (Maasdorp, 1982), a fertiliser plant in Swaziland, and a television firm and car assembly plant in Lesotho (Gibb, 2006). Such an approach was certainly evident in Namibia, with UNIDO (1990: 13) writing that South African firms "often undercut prices when Namibian firms tried to produce a specific product".

And, in many ways, the situation was worse for Namibia than it was for Botswana, Swaziland, and Lesotho, due to its status as a South African colony. For one, the colonial links between the two countries meant that the Namibian retail sector was dominated by South African firms, which tended to source goods from South Africa, given their preestablished national procurement systems (Green & Kiljunen, 1981; Witulski, 1985). As Zinn (1985: 58) observed, "[a]s suppliers of products for the local market, i.e. as 'agents' and service outposts of RSA firms, local subsidiaries are usually unwilling to implement local assembly or processing". Moreover, the South African state was purposefully organising for specific firms to be granted effective monopolies in the Namibian market. For example, when the company *Namib Mills* first sought to establish its maize mill in Namibia in 1982, the firm was called for a meeting with the country's Administrator-General, who told them in no uncertain terms that they could not sell their products in the Namibia because the market had already been allocated to a firm in South Africa.[25]

The assessments of this section demonstrate how industrial development in Namibia was curtailed by its relationship with its coloniser, South Africa. However, as the following section will argue, at various points the governing elites of Namibia did have reasonable scope to support industries but failed to do so, as it was not their ambition to foster industrial expansion.

The attitude of the Namibian elite

Prior to when South Africa withdrew some of the powers of the SWA Legislative Assembly in the late 1960s, Namibia did have scope to pursue industrial policy, but chose not to. We know this because in the 1950s South Africa, remarkably, criticised Namibia for failing to pursue industrial policy. In a report on South Africa's financial relations with Namibia, the South African treasury was highly critical of the SWA Legislative Assembly's decision to set income and corporate tax significantly lower than rates in South Africa, arguing that greater taxation was necessary to finance development: "the choice for both the Union and the Territory lies between lower financial demands and a more rapid development of the Territory" (Union of South Africa, 1952: 7).

The report argued that the common-held view in Namibia at the time "that a low rate of taxation would attract secondary industries" was "based on a misconception", stating that in reality industrial progress in Namibia has been "limited to those industries which are able to supply the local market more profitably by establishing a branch business in the Territory than by importing their goods" (*ibid.:* 8). If industrial development was to occur to a significant extent, the report argued, Namibia's high transport costs, energy and water scarcity, and relatively high labour costs would have to be addressed: manufacturing growth was not simply achieved by the setting of low taxes to encourage firms to locate to Namibia.

---

[25] The Administrator-General's verdict would have stood, but because the firm had already invested large sums of capital in the project prior to being summoned by the Administration, it was finally allowed to sell in the Namibian market, but only south of Otjiwarongo, with the northern part of the country still the domain of the South African firm. *Namib Mills* was run by South Africans, which perhaps explains why the Administration was lenient. It also interesting to note that, in an example of the conflicting views held by the Administration and the FNDC, the FNDC actually financed loans for the *Namib Mills* project to start (interview with Frans Meyer, Operations Manager and Pieter van Niekerk, Commercial Manager, *Namib Mills*. 13.6.2017).

Evidently, the highly-developmental South African state viewed the policy choices of its colony as short-sighted, failing to invest in the economy in a manner that could make industrial development conceivable. The lack of interest in industrial policy from the SWA Administration in the 1950s appears to have been a consequence of its complacent attitude towards Namibia's economic development, with the economy at the time in an unprecedented boom. As the South African report scathingly noted, "one will have to turn the blind eye to reality in order to maintain the illusion of never-ending prosperity", with the governing and economic elites of Namibia having had their views on economic development "completely distorted" by the country's strong growth (*ibid.:* 8).

During the 1960s the policy freedom of the Administration and Legislative Assembly was curtailed. But irrespective and unsurprisingly, the disinterest from Namibia's elites in pursuing industrial development persisted. For example, one of the country's most high-profile bankers wrote in his assessment of the economy that because "[t]he odds against industrial development in South West Africa are heavy" (due to the lack of water and power supply, small population, and distance to major markets) it would make more sense for Namibia to develop non-manufacturing activities, "of which tourism is the most promising" (Collins, 1971: 71–72).[26] Collins was not alone in this contemptuous assessment of manufacturing. The following quote from Thomas (1985: 6) presents the attitude of Namibia's major economic actors at the time:

> Neither the Government sector nor the largest mining concerns really support local industry... The mines, a large segment of the large scale farmers and probably a substantial segment of the local bureaucracy and trading class only have a short to medium run time horizon with respect to their involvement in the local economy. This almost inevitably dampens efforts towards the steady, yet determined exploration and utilisation of industrial opportunities."

SWA's political landscape was dominated by farmers, with many politicians having become so via the SWA Agricultural Union. The Union, along with other agricultural bodies, were, throughout the 1950s, 1960s, and 1970s, closely connected to the Administration and able to push for the aforementioned measures supporting the agricultural sector. In a rural country like Namibia, politics was really about farming, and there were very few voicing support for manufacturing.

The negative or apathetic attitude of most of the private-sector actors towards structural transformation was well-reflected in the Administration in the 1970s and 1980s, which was "heavily indoctrinated with 'free market' ideology" and firmly against the state intervening

---

[26] At the time tourism was growing rapidly, with the number of visitors to Namibia increasing from 12,350 in 1960 to 185,238 in 1970 (South West Africa Annual, 1973: 129).

in the economy to support the advancement of industry (Thomas, 1983: 145). In the 'National Development Strategy of South West Africa', the Administration pointedly identified the country as being based on a "free market economy" (Department of Governmental Affairs, 1987: 22), whilst an earlier report argued that "at this stage efforts should not be made to convert the SWA/Namibian economy by means of policy measures, in an 'artificial' way, to greater industrial intensity", given that "greater industrial self-sufficiency would place too heavy a burden on the consumer and taxpayer of SWA/Namibia" (Economic Advisory Committee, 1978: 34).

Clearly, then, the SWA Administration had no intention of intervening in the economy to stimulate industry and there was no support for such intervention from the country's elites. One could rightly ask whether the views of the SWA Administration and the key economic actors of Namibia would have any influence on industrial development. After all, was the SWA Administration not merely obligated to follow the directives of South Africa, and therefore the views of Namibia's elites can have had little impact on the direction of industrial development? Indeed, Zinn (1985: 59) argued that South Africa "dominated local economic and development policies", whilst Thomas (1985: 6) described the Administration as "(semi-)autonomous", with the "de facto autonomy" to implement industrial policy "still very much restricted". The point of interest, however, is that it appears highly unlikely that an independent Namibia politically dominated by the country's white population would have pursued industrial development with any more fervour than the Administration did under the colonial rule of South Africa, due to the nature of the most powerful economic interests within society. The case of *Namib Mills*, which was eventually permitted to establish itself in Namibia when the Administration acquiesced, demonstrates that there was some room to manoeuvre, were the Administration to have been willing to support the manufacturing sector. This was not to be, and Namibian industry was forced to cope with South African competition and various structural issues single-handedly.

Thomas (1985: 11) well summarises the Namibian experience of industrial development in this era, concluding that "[w]ith respect to Namibia's industrial sector we have seen that fundamental limitations (population size and dispersal, low income, etc.) and the unequal relationship with the RSA leave a very limited – though not insignificant – scope for industrial activities, the activation of which are seriously hampered by structural and political constraints, and the absence of a systematic and determinate sectoral strategy." Industrial development would always be challenging, but its main obstacle was the disinterest from the South African and SWA states.

Conclusion

This chapter has chronicled the progression of Namibian industrial development from the end of the Second World War up to 1989, the year before Namibia was to achieve independence. Using archival sources and secondary literature, it has been possible to provide rich detail as to how the sector evolved over time and the factors behind said evolution.

Manufacturing in Namibia was to boom during the late 1940s, 1950s, and most of the 1960s, driven principally by the establishment of large-scale fish processing and to a lesser extent by construction-related activities, and the era also saw the establishment of relatively large firms manufacturing high-volume, low-value products, such as soap and paint. The experience of Namibia's manufacturing growth over these decades reflected a near-continent-wide trend of strong industrial growth centred on food processing (Ewing, 1968), though the extent was even greater in Namibia, which by 1960 had emerged as one of the most industrialised countries on the continent.

But Namibia's manufacturing fortunes were to falter from the late 1960s to independence, at a time when momentum towards Namibian independence was gathering and the status of the country became shrouded in controversy and uncertainty. Overfishing caused a major collapse in the fish processing industry in the late 1970s, which also led to the closure of the significant can-manufacturing firm at Walvis Bay, and dairy – which had been the largest manufacturing sector in Namibia prior to 1945, was to fall away entirely in the face of strong South African competition and the withdrawal of state support for the sector. Whilst some further new industries emerged over these final decades of colonial rule (again in high-volume, low-cost industries), the sector was to experience only piecemeal expansion, and manufacturing employment as a percentage of the total population was to decline from the mid-1960s onwards. By 1989 Namibia had lost its place as one of the more-industrialised countries in Africa and exhibited one of the least-diversified industrial sectors on the continent.

The 1946 to 1989 period can ultimately be characterised by the failure for structural transformation of the economy to occur, with the manufacturing sector remaining small, and the economy remaining dominated by mining, agriculture, and services (particularly retail, real estate, and financial/business services), as is demonstrated in figure 3.5.

There are inevitably a host of factors that at various stages affected the course of Namibian industrial development. For example, firms appeared to be wary of investing in Namibia in the late 1940s and early 1950s due to the uncertainty over the country's constitutional future (Union of South Africa, 1952). Conversely, Namibia's industrial boom of the 1950s was in large part a consequence of increased global demand for canned fish (as a cheap source of protein), and rapid Namibian growth in the 1950s following a surge in diamond

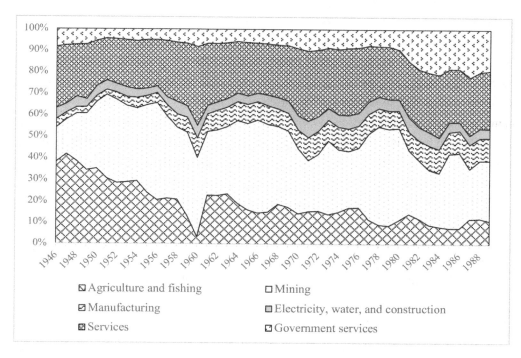

Figure 3.5: Change of Namibian GDP by sector (%), 1946–1989. Sources: Figures for all sectors
excluding manufacturing are from SWA Department of Finance (1988; 1990), with figures for manufacturing based on author's calculations.[27]

production also helped to stimulate the manufacturing sector, with money in particular
flowing into constructing activities which needed manufactured inputs. In turn, Namibia's
industrial stagnation of the late 1970s and early 1980s was closely associated with the general economic crisis of the time, itself a consequence of the global oil crises of the 1970s,
drought, and political uncertainty due to the war of independence.

---

[27] The situation for manufacturing is more complex because the SWA Department of Finance figures exclude Walvis Bay. As such, manufacturing figures from 1946-1956 are from Krogh (1960).
For 1960, 1965, 1970, 1975, 1976, and 1981-1989 I've calculated the sum based on the MVA/
GDP data-obtained from other sources (Thomas, 1978; Leistner, 1980; Republic of Namibia,
1996; 1998). For missing years (1957-1959; 1961-1964; 1966-1959; 1971-1974; 1966-1980),
I've calculated the difference between the data points that I have e.g. (made up example) for
500,000 in 1956, 1,200,000 in 1960, the answer is 700,000. I have then divided the answer by
the number of years between the two data points (in this case, 4) and then assumed man facturing output to have increased at the same rate over these four years. This means that in this example I estimate manufacturing output to have increased by 175,000 per annum, so I have inputted
manufacturing output to be 675,000 for 1957, 850,000 for 1958, etc. This is a more accurate way
of representing the Namibian economy for these years than just using the SWA Department of
Finance figures, which typically underestimate the size of the manufacturing sector by half.

But the argument put forth here has been that large-scale industrial development failed to occur primarily because of the near-total absence of industrial policy throughout this period, given the nature of the system of accumulation in the country. Both South Africa and the Namibian elites presented a consistent disinterest in industrial development, leaving the manufacturing sector to mostly fend for itself, with structural issues left unaddressed and South African industry permitted to have free reign over the Namibian market, meaning that Namibian firms had the odds of success stacked against them. The prevailing economic interest groups of Namibia and South Africa were opposed to industrial development, which meant that there was no ambition from the state to seriously pursue industrial policy.

In 1990, after over a century of colonial rule, Namibia was to finally become independent, with the authority to set its own economic policy. As chapters 2 and 3 have shown, industrial development had up to this point been curtailed by the actions of the South African colonisers and by the lack of commitment to industrial development from Namibia's white elite. Would an independent Namibia, governed democratically, be able to successfully drive forward industrial development for the wellbeing of the population? This question is addressed in the following chapter.

4 Economic change in independent Namibia: dashed hopes

Introduction

In May 1988, negotiations to end the military conflict and to facilitate UN-supervised elections in Namibia finally began. Independence was in sight, and Namibian exiles – who had been spread across 42 countries – began to return en masse, with nearly 43,000 having returned to the country by the end of 1989 (Wallace, 2011). Amongst the returnees were the leading figures within the independence movement SWAPO, including its leader, Sam Nujoma. On the momentous occasion of the first elections held for independent Namibia in 1989, SWAPO won power, and accordingly Nujoma was sworn in as President of Namibia on the 21st of March 1990, the day which marked the official independence of the country. SWAPO has remained in power to this day, winning all five of the subsequent general elections handsomely.

Unlike at any point in the previous century, Namibia's governing elite now appeared committed to achieving industrial development and the structural transformation of the economy. Indeed, manufacturing has "held a special place in the Namibian Government's affections since independence", with Government ministers having "regularly declared that stimulating the manufacturing sector held the key to development for Namibia" (Sherbourne, 2016: 271). Namibia's 'Vision 2030', a document published in 2004, encapsulated the industrious ambitions of the state, with President Nujoma's foreword reading "[b]y the year 2030, with all of us working together, we should be an industrial nation enjoying prosperity, interpersonal harmony, peace and political stability" (Republic of Namibia, 2004: 11). For the independent Namibian state industrial development was, evidently, a central ambition.

What success was Namibia to have in realising its ambitions of industrial development? As the title of this chapter has communicated, progress in manufacturing since independence has been disappointing, with the sector exhibiting no signs of substantive growth or technological advancement. The objective of this chapter is to provide a thorough overview of manufacturing's stuttering progress, highlighting first the Government's economic and industrial policies and secondly the empirical performance of the economy, particularly the manufacturing sector.

SWAPO's Namibia: free markets, foreign investment, and limited government intervention

During most of the pre-independence era SWAPO had adopted strongly socialistic rhetoric, aligning itself with the Soviet bloc. SWAPO's 1976 constitution stated that the organisation's aim was "to unite all Namibian people, particularly the working class, the peasantry and progressive intellectuals into a vanguard party capable of safe-guarding national independence and of building a classless, non-exploitative society based on the ideas and principles of scientific socialism" (quoted in Melber, 2014: 143), and a later party document stated SWAPO's commitment to "the social ownership of Namibia's natural resources" (SWAPO, 1981: 294). Many of SWAPO's early publications, and those of writers affiliated with the party, deployed traditional Marxist analyses of the Namibian economy (see, for example, Mbuende (1986) and Kaakunga (1990)). This stated commitment to socialism was supported by many academics in Europe and the United States, who often vehemently denied that such rhetoric was mere posturing to secure financial and military support. For example, Beilstein (1982: 10–11) stated that "[w]hen SWAPO accedes to power it can be expected to act upon its political economic strategy of socialist transformation with conviction. To expect SWAPO to be co-opted... like Botswana, Tanzania, Zambia or Kenya is to truly misunderstand the historical realities of underdevelopment and exploitation in Namibia".

But SWAPO's commitment to socialism notably wanted towards the end of the 1980s, and by independence there was a consensus within SWAPO over maintaining Namibia's free-market, private-sector led economy (Melber, 2011). For example, SWAPO's 1989 election manifesto pledged that "[n]o wholesale nationalization of the mines, land and other productive sectors is... envisaged in the foreseeable future" (SWAPO, 1989: 10). There were several reasons behind SWAPO's volte-face. For one, its rhetorical commitment to socialism was "a consequence of pragmatism, not conviction", appealing to the Soviet Union to secure financial and political support, and as such it was "easily revived or abandoned when circumstances demanded" (Dobell, 1998: 59). Brian Urquhart, the former undersecretary-general of the United Nations, who was involved in negotiations for Namibian independence, quipped of President Nujoma: "I doubted if Nujoma would know a Marxist-Leninist idea if he met one in the street, but like most liberation leaders, he would take help from wherever he could get it" (quoted in Melber, 2011: 104).

Ultimately, "SWAPO regarded national independence (and not the proletarian revolution) as the primary goal of its struggle" (Jauch & Tjirera, 2017: 145). SWAPO's shift also had much to do with the party's acceptance that for the economy to maintain its stability SWAPO would "need to reassure the (white) business community" that it was not going to impose too radical a change in the ownership of production to ensure that there was no sudden outflow of capital (Rosendahl, 2010: 13). Large companies in Namibia, particularly the mining firms, had spent much of the final fifteen years of colonial rule preparing themselves for independence by reaching out to SWAPO, and were able to forge "a rather relaxed relationship between government and the business community" (*ibid.*: 13).

SWAPO's economic policies in the post-independence years proved conservative. The choice made seems to have been to assure economic stability and continuity as a basis on which to launch a programme to improve the provision of social services to the population and for the gradual rectification of massive social injustices. As Jauch & Tjirera (2017: 145) observe, "[e]conomic structures were left intact" as the Government directed itself towards the achievement of "a non-racial capitalist order".

SWAPO appointed Otto Herrigel, a conservative white Namibian, as independent Namibia's first Minister of Finance, "[i]n what was widely regarded as a signal that the new Government intended to follow orthodox economic and fiscal policies" (Sherbourne, 2016: 37). The decision was made to remain part of SACU, maintaining free trade relations with South Africa, and Namibia continued to use the South African Rand as its official currency up until 1993, when it introduced the Namibia Dollar, which continued to be pegged to the Rand. The major industries, in mining and fishing, remained in the hands of private foreign firms and in land reform the issue of racial imbalances was to be addressed with a state policy of 'willing seller-willing buyer', making the process extremely slow (Jauch & Tjirera, 2017). In the subsequent years, the Namibian Government has been characterised as subscribing to "neoliberal fundamentals", focusing on ensuring macroeconomic stability and encouraging foreign direct investment via incentives and liberalisation (Winterfeldt, 2007: 66). The state has been committed to securing "low inflation rates and low budget deficits" (Jauch & Tjirera, 2017: 171) and "has maintained a cautious approach to monetary policy" (Sherbourne, 2016: 35).

In the 1990s and 2000s the principal view of the Namibian Government with regards to economic development was that foreign direct investment would drive growth, and that therefore the state must "attract investment by offering increasing concessions to foreign investors" (Jauch, 2001: 6). Consequently, "all [Namibian] governments since independence have endeavoured to create a national image that advertises a friendly attitude towards free markets and investment" (Bertelsmann Stiftung, 2014: 40). Government documents consistently projected a pro-foreign investment and non-interventionist approach to the economy. For example, the MTI's 'Business Guide to Namibia' pronounces that "[t]he attitude of the Government of Namibia to foreign investment is positive and hospitable, as the Government firmly believes that the private sector has a major role to play in the economic development of the country" (Ministry of Trade and Industry, 1996: 202).

Beyond a rhetorical commitment to foreign investment, Namibian policymakers were also said to be "hard at work" making the country an attractive investment destination (Kahuika et al., 2003: 65). The most important policy document was the Foreign Investment Act of 1990, which has been described as "a free-market investment code with considerable protection against state expropriation, extensive incentives for foreign firms, and no requirements for participation or share holding by local firms" (Klerck, 2008: 359). The Act stated that "a foreign national may invest and engage in any business activity in Namibia which any Namibian may undertake" (Republic of Namibia, 1990a: 4), with a national law firm noting that this clause "ensures that investors to Namibia can be assured of a measure of security which is not normally present with investment in developing countries" (Cronjé & Co, n.d.1).

Namibia's investor-friendly economic policy approach was in line with the free-market principles that pervaded development thinking in the 1990s and early 2000s. The earnestness of Namibia's efforts to model itself as an ideal investment destination is emblematised by the fact that in 1999 UNCTAD rated Namibia amongst the top ten countries globally with the most attractive environment for FDI (Jauch, 2001). Ultimately, as Klerck (1997, quoted in Jauch, 2007: 60) concluded, independent Namibia had failed "to conceive of an economic policy that departs in substance from that of the colonial powers".

'Neoliberal' industrial policy in the 1990s and 2000s: ineffective and misguided

Whilst the Namibian Government in the 1990s and 2000s put forward conservative economic policies rather in-keeping with those of the late-colonial era, an important difference in rhetoric was the independent Namibian Government's stated view that industrial development was necessary for the country. Despite such assertions, the free-market ideology of the Namibian state in the 1990s and 2000s meant that industrial policy effectively adhered to a principle of 'industrial development via foreign investment via generous tax cuts and an enabling environment'. This perspective, coupled with a lack of funding and mismanagement of the Ministry of Trade and Industry (MTI) and other relevant government agencies, meant that progress was extremely lacklustre.

Namibia's MTI was established at independence and Ben Amathila, who had joined the forerunner to SWAPO[1] as a teenager in the 1950s and who became SWAPO's Secretary for Economics in 1976, was appointed as its first minister (Hopwood, 2007). The Ministry, how-

---

[1] The Ovamboland People's Organisation.

ever, was not awarded high status amongst government ministries. As well as having one of the smallest staffs in the early 1990s,[2] it also consistently had one of the lowest allotted budgets of any of Namibia's eighteen ministries (Republic of Namibia, 1993a).

The MTI, was not, however, to be solely responsible for Namibia's industrial development. The FNDC of the colonial era continued its operations and was renamed the Namibia Development Corporation in 1993, with the intention being that it would play a key role in industrial policy (Smith, 1993). Also related to industrial policy was the National Planning Commission, established at independence "to plan the priorities and direction of development" and to be the "principal adviser to the President in regard to all matters pertaining to economic planning" (Republic of Namibia, 1990b: 71).

Namibia's early approach to industrial development was highly free-market. The first industrial policy document, the 'White Paper on Industrial Development' of 1992, stated that the Government's "primary commitment" was "to create an enabling environment within which the private sector can prosper" and that the "Government's overall policy is one of non-interference with market mechanisms" (Republic of Namibia, 1992: i, 15).[3] Whilst lengthier than the colonial Government's writing on industrial development, there are unambiguous similarities between the advice and tone of the 1992 white paper and those of the policy documents of the 1980s (see, for example, Department of Governmental Affairs, 1987).

Early assessments of Namibia industrial policy suggested that a great deal of confusion presided over government thinking. A report for the Namibian Government in 1994 concluded that "as yet, industrial strategy for the country is not fully developed" (Commonwealth Secretariat, 1994: 28). Whilst there was consensus around the aim of creating an 'enabling environment', there was no such consensus about what that would look like: "[t] here is belief that Government's role should be enabling and not interventionist but Government's role in bringing about an enabling environment is not clearly defined nor is it clear how MTI will create such an environment" (*ibid.*: 31). And whilst flaws in the MTI were identified in the report (e.g. MTI is "generally inexperienced at policy formation"), it was most critical of central government, which was seen to have failed to coordinate its ministries and to clearly direct the MTI (*ibid.*: 31).

---

[2] 82 at the start of 1992, compared to say 264 in the Ministry of Foreign Affairs and 166 in the Ministry of Information and Broadcasting.

[3] The Government was supported in the production of the document by UK academics, UNIDO, and the Namibia Economic Policy Research Unit (NEPRU) (Curry & Stoneman, 1993). At just twenty-five pages long, the White Paper was light on detail, with its policy proposals including the provision of tax incentives, the expansion of serviced industrial sites, and the promotion of Namibian industry at international trade fairs. It was critical of the idea of government providing infant industry protection.

The first major industrial policy announced in independent Namibia was a generous package of incentives for manufacturing firms in 1993. In its first guise, the 'Special Incentives for Manufacturing Enterprises' offered all manufacturing firms excellent benefits, including: a 50% reduction on the corporate tax rate for five years, phased out over a subsequent ten years; buildings erected could be written off at 20% for the first year and 8% over the following ten years; and cash grants for exporting firms to support marketing efforts (Republic of Namibia, 1993b). Whilst these benefits sound generous and of value to firms, the reality is that the incentives have, for the most part, proved "virtually impossible to obtain" (Sherbourne, 2016: 274).[4] In 2016 there were only 114 firms registered for the incentives, likely only around one-fifth of all manufacturing firms in the country. The main reason that it has proven so difficult to secure the incentives is because the Ministry of Finance does not want to lose revenue through these tax exemptions.[5]

Exporting Processing Zones and the drive for foreign direct investment

The flagship industrial policy of the early independence years was undoubtedly the Export Processing Zone (EPZ) Act of 1995, with a stated objective "to attract, promote or increase the manufacture of export goods" (Republic of Namibia, 1995: 6). The idea of EPZs was in currency globally at the time, and the Namibia Investment Centre (NIC), part of the Ministry of Trade and Industry, had sent several its staff, as well as Government Ministers, to Hong Kong, Thailand, and Malaysia to see how their EPZs functioned. The Ministers were enamoured by what they saw and decided to emulate the model in Namibia.[6] The subsequent EPZ Act emblematised Namibia's commitment to industrial development via generous incentives, with the Government proclaiming that the Act "laid down an even more favourable regime for foreign investors than that created by the Foreign Investment Act" (Namibia Investment Centre, 1996: 205).

EPZs, as outlined in the Act, were not strictly physical 'zones', but rather 'EPZ status' was something that all manufacturing firms could apply for, so long as they exported at

---

4   The difficulties in achieving registered manufacturing status were explained to me by the Director of a manufacturing firm in Windhoek: "being able to get manufacturing status in Namibia is key because of the tax benefits associated with it... [but] the process is almost – I don't want to say impossible – but it is almost impossible. It took us more than a year to get our manufacturing status, with a lot of drama and a lot of visits to their offices. It hasn't been an easy process by any means. So, I can only imagine that, for a new firm, that is a big hiccup" (interview with Antonie Vermaak, Director of *WV Construction*, 22.3.2016).

5   Added to this is that the general process of applying, even to MTI, is itself cumbersome, reflecting bureaucratic issues. It does not seem, for example, that MTI even hold a list of registered manufacturing firms, and there appears to be only one member of staff responsible for conducting assessments of firms, contributing to the slowness of the process.

6   Interview with Steve Galloway, Managing Director at *Rand Merchant Bank*. 15.12.2015.

least 70% of their produce outside of SACU. Benefits of having EPZ were wide-ranging, including: exemption from sales tax, stamp and transfer duties on goods and services; guarantee of free repatriation of capital and profits; exemption from VAT, and exemption from corporate tax (Republic of Namibia, 1995; Jauch, 2006; Sherbourne, 2016). Extraordinarily, the EPZ Act further stated that Namibia's Labour Act of 1992 would not apply *at all* to companies with EPZ status, with President Nujoma explaining that this was "a delicate compromise, which is necessary to achieve the larger goal of job creation" and to allay investors' "fear of possible industrial unrest" (quoted in Jauch, 2006: 214).[7] Clearly, there was very little that the Namibian Government was not willing to offer to attract foreign manufacturing firms.

The Government enthusiastically predicted that the EPZ scheme in Namibia would create 25,000 jobs. But the initial results were highly disappointing and by the end of 1999 only 400 jobs had been created by 18 companies (Winterfeldt, 2007), whilst "millions of dollars had been spent on promoting the policy and on developing infrastructure" (Jauch, 2006: 215).

The case of Ramatex: the epitome of misguided industrial policy
The EPZ scheme's first major coup was to come, however, in 2002, with the arrival of Ramatex, a textile firm from Malaysia (Jauch, 2006). Ramatex, like many Asian textile and apparel firms, was at the time seeking to relocate some operations to sub-Saharan Africa in the early 2000s following the passing of the African Growth and Opportunity Act (AGOA) in the United States in 2000, which gave firms based in Africa preferential access to the US market (Lee, 2014).

The Namibian Government was desperate to secure a significant EPZ investment and as such, when *Ramatex* proposed an investment of N$1.2 billion in the country – equivalent to one third of manufacturing's total contribution to GDP in 2001 and ten times the total investment from EPZ companies so far – the Namibian Government offered enormous incentives even *beyond* the EPZ provisions to entice the company (Winterfeldt, 2007). These included: leasing the land for the factory (valued at N$16.9 million) for a nominal fee of N$1 a month; the building of an access road; the provision of free electricity, water and sewage infrastructure up to the factory site, as well as preferential rates for water and electricity; and exemption from wharfage and the promise from the Government to build a new container terminal at the Walvis Bay port (*ibid.*).

Ramatex accepted the proposal, rejecting a less lucrative offer from the Eastern Cape regional Government in South Africa, and arrived in Namibia in 2002, eventually setting

---

7   Following pressure from the major trade union this decision was overturned almost immediately, but from 1995 until 2001 workers of EPZ companies were still banned from striking (Jauch, 2006).

up four subsidiaries in Windhoek producing garments, principally for export to the United States, but also to the EU and the Middle East. At their peak the four subsidiaries employed around 8,000 people, a massive amount in the Namibian context, where total employment in manufacturing in 2000 was only 22,000 (Jauch, 2006). Labour-intensive manufacturing had finally arrived in Namibia, much to the delight of Government, vindicated for its implementation of a pro-foreign investment structure. In a surreal development, former Minister of Trade and Industry, Hidipo Hamutenya was awarded 'FDI Magazine's African FDI Personality of the Year' for 2003, "in recognition for having snatched the Ramatex investment from under the noses of the South Africans" (Sherbourne, 2016: 281).

But *Ramatex*'s investment was immediately fraught with difficulties. The firm appeared reluctant to conduct business with government amicably, ignoring numerous national laws and policies. Its discrepancies included: not publishing an environmental impact assessment report; issuing a written demand to female workers to undergo pregnancy tests; not registering the factory at the Ministry of Labour; and denying unions access to the premises for the purpose of unionising (Winterfeldt, 2007). Workers were subjected to terrible conditions, particularly those brought in from Bangladesh, leading to strikes and social unrest (Jauch, 2006). In an incident emblematising *Ramatex*'s footloose business model, when the firm sought a spatial extension of their lease in September 2002 and the City of Windhoek showed hesitance, the *Ramatex* Executive Director angrily told the Prime Minister that "we are now faced with the dilemma of whether to move to Malawi or Botswana for expansion" (quoted in Winterfeldt, 2007: 73).

Tensions persisted, and the writing appeared to be on the wall when in 2005 one of *Ramatex*'s four Namibian subsidiaries closed and rumours of full closure began to circulate (Sherbourne, 2016). Facilities continued to gradually close, when finally, in March 2008, the company's remaining 3,000 employees arrived at work "only to be left standing in front of a closed gate" (Isaacs, 2008). *Ramatex* had permanently closed its final subsidiary. Namibia's big manufacturing FDI had remained in the country just six years, leaving nothing but environmental pollution and misspent government infrastructure funds in its wake. In the national press the incident was lamented as an embarrassment.

The reason that *Ramatex*'s operations in Namibian failed was because *Ramatex* always regarded Namibia as a temporary location for its activities (Jauch, 2008). As noted, the firm's operations in Namibia represented a small shift in global textile and apparel production to sub-Saharan Africa following the passing of AGOA. Concurrently, their departure mirrored trends across the region, which saw an exodus of firms back to East Asia from 2005 onwards (Lee, 2014). By 2010, sub-Saharan African exports of textiles and apparels were almost exactly what they had been in 2000. This rise and fall can largely be explained by the expiration of the Multi Fibre Arrangement (MFA) at the end of 2004. MFA came into force in 1974 under the General Agreement on Tariffs and Trade and allowed high-income countries to impose quotas on imports of textile and apparel goods to protect their industries from principally Asian competition. With the establishment of the WTO in 1995, it was agreed that these quotas would be phased out over ten years. The onset of AGOA in 2000 had given Asian firms the opportunity to circumvent the MFA restrictions, knowing full-well that they could return to Asia once MFA expired in 2005 (*ibid.*). This is likely what occurred in the case of *Ramatex*.

The *Ramatex* debacle clearly showed the problem with Namibia's industrial development strategy. As commentators noted, "[f]or the Government maybe the most important lesson is that attracting investment involves far more than dolling out incentives" (Flatters & Elago, 2008: iv). Indeed, the view that industrial development does not occur solely by providing rich incentives for foreign firms is well established. For example, Kozul-Wright & Rayment (2007: 149) posit that "carefully weighing the costs and benefits of hosting FDI and designing policies tailored to local conditions and preferences are among the common traits in countries that have successfully used FDI in their development process", traits that were evidently lacking in Namibia's approach to *Ramatex*.

The EPZ programme continues to limp on in Namibia, poorly managed, and with outcomes having remained disappointing. The Offshore Development Company (ODC), responsible for running the EPZ programme, has proved to be largely idle, with the programme representing a "striking" example of poor policy implementation (Rosendahl, 2010: 1). The high-point in enrolment in the programme was 2004, when 33 firms had EPZ status. By 2007 the number had reduced to 20, and by the end of 2015 it had reduced to 16 (Ministry of Trade & Industry, 2009; Sherbourne, 2016). Of the remaining 16 firms in 2015, nine were diamond cutting and polishing firms, one was the copper smelter in Tsumeb, and one was a zinc refinery established in Rosh Pinah in 2004, leaving just five firms that were not involved in mining.[8] The EPZ scheme was supposed to serve as the driving force behind industrial development, but has instead offered little more than tax breaks for mineral processing companies, most of which would likely have been operating in the country regardless. Employment provided by EPZ companies stands at just 2,000 people, a far cry from the hopes of the Government.

It was not just with regards to the EPZ programme that Namibia encountered issues with foreign investors, with the plight of the Namibia Development Corporation (NDC)

---

[8] A cigarette manufacturing firm, a plastic manufacturer, a firm making specialised nuts and bolts for machines used to stamp emblems onto machinery, a firm involved in vehicle refurbishment, and a manufacturer of vehicle components.

illustrative of general mismanagement and the perils of an indiscriminate approach to for-eign investment. NDC became involved in a handful of foreign investments into the country through joint-ventures during the 1990s and early 2000s, but its record on this front was disastrous, with the Government's desperation to secure foreign investment leading to some highly dubious companies being welcomed into Namibia.

The five largest foreign investments that NDC was involved with up to the early 2000s all ended unsuccessfully: a tomato paste factory; a cotton gin; a cement factory; a pipe manufacturing enterprise; and a tractor manufacturing assembly plant. The cotton gin saw NDC construct the premises for the operation, but the entrepreneur eventually vanished before the machinery was installed. With the pipe manufacturing initiative, NDC placed money into an international account for the procurement of equipment, and the money vanished along with the prospective investors, costing the corporation some N$5 million. The tomato paste factory never got off the ground, whilst the cement plant closed in 2000 (Schade, 2016). In the early 2000s the Chinese tractor production enterprise quickly came and went, when it became clear that the tractors were not suitable to Namibian conditions.[9]

Despondency and absence of industrial policy in the wake of EPZ's failures

By the late 1990s the Namibian Government, faced by limited foreign investment in manu-facturing, found itself having to reassess its industrial development strategy. In 1999 the MTI commissioned a review of its 1992 white paper, which, written by the think tank the Namibia Economic Policy Research Unit (NEPRU), was frank in its criticisms (Hansohm, 2000). The review criticised the failure for the white paper's ideas to be properly dissemi-nated through the Ministry and wider government; the lack of monitoring instruments; that many of the statements in the document were general platitudes; the failure to target specific industries; and that the MTI did not have the capacity to implement the policy.

Following NEPRU's assessment, the MTI decided to develop a new industrial policy framework, but efforts proved problematic. NEPRU was commissioned to lead the writ-ing of the new industrial policy document, and though a first draft (titled 'Industrial Policy Beyond 2000') was already written by the end of 1999, a change of leadership in MTI led to it being shelved (Hansohm, 2007). A new draft was finally accepted by the MTI in 2003, but "[f]or reasons one can only speculate on" the new industrial policy "was never presented to Parliament or even formally adopted" (Rosendahl, 2010: 21). The policy

---

[9]   Interview with Pieter de Wet, Acting Managing Director of the Namibia Development Corpo-ration, 20.1.2016. A similar example to those described above is *Pidico*. *Pidico* was set up in Namibia in 1992 by an Egyptian businessman, supported by the MTI, pledging to establish an export processing zone. A shell structure for such a zone was built close to Walvis Bay, but was never completed, and soon the company left Namibia (Amupadhi, 2004).

document was never to see the light of day, indicative both of the "institutional weakness" of the MTI and that "industrial policy is not prominent... in the eyes of government" (Hansohm, 2007: 233).

The failure to develop a new industrial policy is all the more remarkable given that this mishap was occurring just as the Government, via its much-touted 'Vision 2030' in 2004 was pledging that the industrialisation of Namibia would occur by 2030 (Republic of Namibia, 2004). More incredulous *still* was that 'Industrial Policy Beyond 2000' was not even particularly different to the 1992 white paper and was rather a "fine-tuned" version of it (Ministry of Trade and Industry, 2001: 54), or in the words of a critic, still well "in line with a neoliberal approach – that free trade and trade liberalisation were important for industrial development" (Knutsen, 2003: 564).

The result of this impasse was that industrial policy in the 2000s was mostly aimless, lacked drive, and was poorly administered. The main industrial policy of this era was the construction of industrial parks, with industrial sites then leased out to SMEs under what was known as the 'Sites and Development Programme'. By 2001 14 industrial parks had been established throughout the country and the number increased gradually throughout the 2000s to 32 by 2008 (Ministry of Trade and Industry, 2001; Rosendahl, 2010). Industry specific facilities were also established, such as the Automotive Common Facility Centre in Ondangwa, the India-Namibia Plastic Technology Centre in Ondangwa, the Wood Common Facility Centre in Rundu, and the Garment Centres in Ovitoto and Windhoek.

The Sites and Development Programme, aside from its small-scale, suffered from "significant shortcomings": sites often lacked water, electricity, and other basic infrastructure, with firms on the sites experiencing a "total lack of support services" (Rosendahl, 2010: 31). Moreover, the programme soon gave up on its concern for supporting *small* and *medium* enterprises. Because rent for SMEs on the sites was highly subsidised the programme, struggling to recover costs, was forced to begin renting out sites to larger enterprises – typically retail firms (*ibid.*). Further, the programme seemed to do little to target *industrial* firms, with the sites also aimed at service industries, with trading units or small shops become more common than industrial units. It is little exaggeration to say that this underfunded programme, which failed to support either SMEs or manufacturing firms, was the centrepiece of industrial policy in the mid-2000s.

Most other programmes to aid industrial firms emanating from the MTI at this time proved unsuccessful. A 'Group Purchasing Scheme' (to helps SMEs to reduce costs by buying in bulk) failed to get off the ground, despite being planned for at least four years; a 'Vendor Development Programme' (to establish links between SMEs and larger firms) ceased operations after only a few years; and the 'Small Business Credit Guarantee Trust' (to secure loans for SMEs and provide them with advice) proved largely defunct, eventually becoming a much-criticised 'white elephant' (Ministry of Trade and Industry, 2000; 2001; 2009a).[10]

Beyond the Ministry, inactivity and unclear policy was maintained. For example, in 2002 the Development Bank of Namibia (DBN) was founded, responsible for mobilising capital for firms and planning and monitoring development schemes. This brief was seen as stepping on the toes of the Namibia Development Corporation (NDC), and as such the Act of Parliament that established the DBN also stated that the NDC was to be wound-up. But the closure of the NDC never occurred, and to this day the corporation continues to operate, clearly confused as to what its role should be.[11] The ambiguity over the roles of the NDC, the DBN, and the Offshore Development Company[12] (ODC), meant there was a confusing amount of overlap between their activities. From the mid-2000s there were two SOEs constructing industrial sites (NDC and ODC) and two offering finance and partial ownership of developmental projects (NDC and DBN). None of the organisations, moreover, were operating particularly effectively, contributing to the general impasse and confusion of industrial policy in this era.

There are some exceptions to this general narrative of laissez-faire industrial policy, particularly with regards to trade policy. In trade negotiations Namibia was willing to fight against the imposition of prohibitive rules that would curtail policy space. For example, in negotiations with the EU over the Economic Partnership Agreement (EPA) Namibia consistently proved stubborn in the face of EU attempts to curtail the country's right to provide infant industry protection (IIP) (Melber, 2013). And, indeed, in the 2000s Namibia did choose to use tariff IIP on two occasions: for long-life milk from 2000 to 2012 and pasta from 2002 to 2014.

Evidently, Namibia's industrial policy up to 2010, as was the case during the South African era of colonial rule, was notable mostly only in its absence. As Rosendahl (2010: 21) observed, "there is currently a 'policy void' in Namibia when it comes to policies and strategies for private sector development and industrial transformation", and as a local economist remarked to me in interview, "in general we had a lull in [industrial] policy making from the

---

[10] See, Namibia Economist (2012).

[11] The NDC's activities in the 2000s seem to have been limited to the management of its three major remaining projects: a small date farm in the east of the country founded in the late 1970s; the Naute irrigation project in the south founded in 1991, which produces dates and table grapes for export; and the Kavango cattle ranch in the north of the country, founded at some point in the pre-independence era (interview with Pieter de Wet, Acting Managing Director of the Namibia Development Corporation, 20.1.2016).

[12] The ODC was established under the 1995 EPZ Act and was to promote, market and co-ordinate the Act.

end of the 1990s until 2010 or so. For ten years or so there weren't many new policies, if at all".[13] Despite over a decade's worth of attempts to try to establish a new industrial policy framework, industrial policy in Namibia in 2010 was still guided by the openly-criticised and clearly limited 1992 white paper. As one anonymous member of staff at the MTI told me, in the 2000s there was "really no policy framework or legislation that we would follow". Even generally approving accounts, such as the following from the Bank of Namibia, acknowledged that the Government has "not developed and executed a clear-cut manufacturing strategy for the country" (Kadhikwa & Ndalikokule, 2007: 26).

After the failure of the EPZ programme it was as if the Government ran out of ideas on how to foster industrial development, restricting itself to smaller measures, such as the building of industrial parks. As Calle Schlettwein, former Minister of Trade and Industry and current Minister of Finance, aptly summed up to me in interview, for the first twenty years of independence:

> The Ministry of Trade and Industry forgot the 'industry' part – they were just the Ministry of Trade. They were involved in trade negotiations, in market access negotiations, which are very tough things and it was quite successfully done. But what lagged behind was the need to also industrialise in parallel in order to have commodities to trade with.[14]

The 2010s: the emergence of active industrial policy?

Things, however, were seemingly about to change. As Minister of Trade and Industry from 2008 to 2012, Hage Geingob did a commendable job of raising the profile of the Ministry. Historically an important member of SWAPO, his appointment as Minister of Trade and Industry was of benefit to the Ministry, which was to see its budget more than quadruple between 2007/8 and 2011/12 (Republic of Namibia, 2008; 2012a). Geingob, by all accounts, was a far more energetic and competent Minister than his predecessor, Immanuel Ngatjizeko.[15]

And, under Geingob's leadership, a decided change occurred within the MTI. The Ministry commenced work on a new industrial policy document in 2011 and, as the document neared completion, it became clear that it would present a noticeable shift in SWAPO's thinking on industrial and economic policy.[16] Rather than be based on free-market prin-

---

[13]   Interview with Klaus Schade, Head of Economic Association of Namibia. 1.4.2016.
[14]   Interview with Calle Schlettwein, Minister of Finance. 23.3.2016
[15]   Interview with Tangeni Amupadhi, Editor-in-Chief, *The Namibian.* 25.1.2016
[16]   Namibian economists such as John Steytler, Rowland Brown, and Klaus Schade, as well as a team from MTI and support from the German development agency GIZ were charged with creating the

ciples, the new document was to emphasise the essential role that the state must play in assuring industrial development. In November 2011 an article in *The Namibian* announcing the completion of the first draft of the new industrial policy document claimed that "[a]fter 21 years Government has finally woken up to the need for an industrial policy in Namibia" (Duddy, 2011a). Just three days later heterodox economist Ha-Joon Chang, a leading proponent of state-led economic development, ran a whole-day seminar for the Cabinet, deputy ministers, permanent secretaries, and the heads of SOEs on Namibia's developmental approach, as the Government sought inputs to finalise the industrial policy paper (Duddy, 2011b).

When the new industrial policy white paper was released in 2012 it did indeed present far more activist industrial policy principles and pointedly distanced itself from previous government rhetoric emphasising the primacy of macroeconomic stability, trade liberalisation, and foreign investment. For example, it was written that: "there may be times where it will be necessary to temporarily relax the macroeconomic stability condition in order to accelerate economic growth and job creation"; that "Government is aware that opening the economy too much or too quickly... [may] result in undesirable investment and unintended consequences that may thwart and negate local industrialisation efforts and initiatives" (Ministry of Trade and Industry, 2012a: 5), and that "[f]irms that are not locally owned might focus too much on a short-term profit objective, compared with domestically owned firms" (*ibid.*: 7).

The document was, moreover, far more positive about the role that the state can play in industrial development that its predecessor, noting the "pivotal role" that the state played in the industrialisation of the East Asian states, as well as the likes of Germany, the UK, and the US, thus arguing that "[i]n some instances, it might be necessary for Government to play a much more proactive role in economic development that what is currently the case" (Ministry of Trade and Industry, 2012a: 7).

The shift in rhetoric was also perceptible amongst government officials. In 2013, recently-appointed Minister of Trade and Industry Calle Schlettwein said that "Government has decided to focus on industrialisation... We are convinced that government must accept a new role to unlock the industrial potential of different sectors and projects" (quoted in Insight Namibia, 2013). When parliament discussed the industrial policy paper it was reported in the press that "parliamentarians on both sides of the National Assembly... agreed in principle that Government has to become an active development agent to propel the country into an industrial nation" (Sasman, 2012). The concept of 'developmental states'

---

document (interview with Rowland Brown, *IJG Securities* and Economic Association of Namibia. 13.1.2016).

began to be discussed openly by SWAPO, and an article posted on the party's website said of the concept that "[i]n Namibia, many, including myself, see this as a possible panacea to the country's social and economic challenges" (Shipale, 2012).[17] As one current affairs magazine commented at the time, the Government seemed to have now "sincerely embarked on a state-led development approach" (Insight Namibia, 2014a). In 2015 the decision was even taken to change the name of the Ministry of Trade and Industry, becoming the Ministry of Industrialization, Trade, and SME Development (MITSMED). The change, reflecting that the Ministry was to now focus on industrialisation, was explained by the Minister as being "the clearest statement we as a government... can make when it comes to our intentions" (MITSMED, 2016: 42).

In 2015 MITSMED finally released its promised 'implementation strategy' for the new industrial policy. Titled 'Growth at Home: Namibia's Execution Strategy for Industrialisation', it is the most detailed, coherent and well-structured document ever produced by the Ministry. The report endorsed the view that the state would need to intervene heavily in the economy to effect industrial development. As Calle Schlettwein stated in his speech to the National Assembly introducing the strategy:

> [T]he debate on the industrial policy has shifted in recent years from the question of whether developing countries should or should not seek to industrialise, to the question of how to best design strategies and subsequent intervention tools which can promote a process of inclusive and sustainable industrial development. Namibia should therefore internalize the positive experience of the best performing countries in the world and become one of them (Schlettwein, 2015: 2).

To achieve industrial development, Growth at Home outlined a host of policy tools, including the following:

- Providing "tariff protection, quantitative restrictions, incentives and other appropriate supportive measures" to support infant industries (Ministry of Trade and Industry, 2015: 9)
- Enhancing the various incentive schemes for manufacturing firms
- Widening the scope of the Industrial Upgrading and Modernisation Programme, such that 80 enterprises are supported by the scheme by 2020
- Passing a Public Procurement Bill with price preferences for locally manufactured products

---

[17] In 2018 it was reported that SWAPO, concerned about the lack of a clear ideology within the party, was seeking to return to its more socialist leanings of the 1980s, with a 'developmental state' approach seen as being a part of this: "Swapo party adopts the ideology of socialism with Namibian characteristics where the role of the state is, amongst others, that of a developmental state within a market system" (quoted in Shikongo, 2018).

- The creation of a Retail Charter to encourage retail firms in Namibia to stock more locally produced goods

- Easing the import and export of goods through a new National Export Strategy

- Making it easier to start a business by establishing the Business and Intellectual Property Authority and creating an online registry for new companies

- Establishing the Namibia Trade Forum, a public-private dialogue platform

- Establishing the Namibia Industrial Development Agency, "which will drive the economic transformation process in close collaboration with MTI", by merging the pre-existing NDC and ODC (ibid.: 49).

- The writing of 'Sector Growth Strategy Documents' for ten sectors identified for targeted support for whom specific measures would be implemented.[18]

The Government's approach to foreign investment also appeared to be changing. In 2016, MITSMED put forward the Namibia Investment Promotion Act (NIPA) to replace the Foreign Investment Act of 1990. Rather than the indiscriminately pro-foreign investment perspective of the 1990 Act, NIPA took as its premise that 'foreign investment at any cost' was not a viable developmental strategy. Unlike in the 1990 Act, the 2016 version required all foreign investors to attain the approval of the Minister, and the Act listed out nine criteria (e.g. employment creation, technology and skills transfer), stating that, for MITSMED to approve a foreign investment, "a substantial number of [these] requirements [should be]... fulfilled" (Republic of Namibia, 2016: 8). Aside from this change, the policy differences between the 1990 and 2016 Acts are minor, though the language deployed by the 2016 Act revealed that much more was expected from foreign investors to support economic development. To date, the 2016 Act has yet to be officially adopted and is under review. For UNCTAD (2016: 34), the Growth at Home strategy and NIPA showed that "Namibia's current domestic policy envisions a more interventionist state approach" than has been seen at any point in independent Namibia's history.

Indeed, were the policy measures outlined above to be implemented it would represent a great increase in the level of state intervention in the economy and support for manufacturing firms. The question remained, however, as to whether the Namibian Government would 'walk the walk' as well as 'talk the talk' of industrial policy. In many ways the stage was well set, Hage Geingob, Minister of Trade and Industry at the time that the new white paper was released in 2012, became President of Namibia in March 2015, whilst Calle Schlettwein, Minister of Trade and Industry at the time that Growth at Home was formulated, was appointed

---

[18] The ten sectors to receive sector growth strategies were: cosmetics, game meat, handicrafts, jewellery and gemstones, leather, metal fabrication, seafood, swakara wool, taxidermy, and wood charcoal.

Minister of Finance by Geingob at the same time. The two most powerful positions in the Namibian Government were now held by apparent proponents of active industrial policy.

Dashed hopes

It is now seven years since the Namibian Government first announced its commitment to a more interventionist-approach to industrial policy. But the track record to date has been disappointing, with the current era exhibiting far more similarities with industrial policy in the 1990s and 2000s than many would have hoped for. Despite some policy advancements, industrial policy continues to be marred by poor planning, a lack of funding, mismanagement, and a failure to turn plans into action. As a Professor of Economics at the University of Namibia concluded in an editorial in 2017, it had become evident that "Namibia's industrialisation policy is not succeeding" (Grynberg, 2017).

From the very beginning the signs were not encouraging. For one, Growth at Home was not released until early 2015, even though in 2012 the MTI stated that writing of the document was at an "advanced stage" and was to be completed "before the end of the 2011/2012 financial year" (Ministry of Trade and Industry, 2012b: 26).[19] And just two months after Growth at Home was finally released the document lost its chief orchestrator, with Schlettwein appointed Minister of Finance. In a disappointing move, Schlettwein was replaced as Minister by Immanuel Ngatjizeko, who had already served in the role previously from 2005 to 2008, during what was probably the low point of industrial policy since the country's independence. The choice was not a dynamic one, particularly given continued concerns over Ngatjizeko's health, and early assessments of his performance were damning.[20] Appointing Ngatjizeko meant that, as one leading Namibian economist told me, efforts towards industrialisation clearly "lost momentum".[21]

Little progress has been made in terms of new policies. Most debilitatingly, the Namibia Industrial Development Agency (NIDA) has failed to be established. To be formed through the merger of the much-maligned NDC and ODC, NIDA is supposed to be a "core element" of Namibia's industrial development strategy, positioned to "drive the economic transformation process" (Ministry of Trade and Industry, 2015: 49). MTI's intention to establish

---

[19] Part of the reason for the delay appears to be that under Hage Geingob the Ministry had (via external consultants) been writing the implementation strategy and had neared completion, but this document was shelved when Calle Schlettwein became Minister in December 2012 (interview with Klaus Schade, Head of Economic Association of Namibia. 1.4.2016.).

[20] Insight Namibia, which publishes an annual 'Cabinet Scorecard' grading the performances of all the Ministers, gave Ngatjizeko a 'U' (Ungradable) in 2016, with the reasoning being that "[t]he man has just been MIA and has been sickly. Everyone knew he was not going to perform when handed the portfolio and that has turned out to be true" (Insight Namibia, 2016a).

[21] Interview with Klaus Schade, Head of Economic Association of Namibia, 1.4.2016.

NIDA has been consistently voiced since 2012 (Duddy, 2012), and whilst a parliamentary bill establishing NIDA was finally gazetted in December 2016, at the time of writing (August 2018) no move has been made by the MITSMED to formally create the agency. This, even though in 2015 Ngatjizeko said that the supposedly imminent establishment of NIDA "means that we can and will very soon be able to implement practically what we are talking about" (quoted in The Namibian, 2015).

Elsewhere, the establishment of a Namibia Board of Trade, which was "to oversee the implementation of infant industry protection and anti-dumping measures" has not yet occurred (Ministry of Trade and Industry, 2013: 56), despite intentions to have it finalised by the end of 2015 (WTO, 2015). Thus, whilst infant industry protection was provided for two industries (cement in 2012 and poultry in 2013), no further developments have occurred and at present there is no intention from Government for further protectionist measures to be deployed.

The Ministry has also experienced great difficulties in developing its 'Sector Growth Strategy Documents'. Through these documents, as the MITSMED Deputy Permanent Secretary of Industrial Development told me, "the role of the state is going to become much, much more proactive".[22] The documents, however, took an enormously long time to write. As an anonymous member of staff working on them told me, whereas the initial plan had been to have the strategies ready within six months (by mid-2015), and then have a period of two and a half years of implementation, the documents were only launched in November 2016, and as of January 2017 "we are now two years into the programme, and we haven't started implementing anything". Implementation finally started in 2018, "without much commitment of the Ministry, though".

Other initiatives have been hampered by recent major cuts in government spending, a consequence of the alarming growth in Namibia's public debt-to-GDP ratio. MITSMED's budget fell from N$998 million in 2014/15 to N$527 million in 2016/17, severely curtailing the Ministry's activities (Republic of Namibia, 2016b; 2018). Rather than being expanded, Namibia's Industrial Upgrading and Modernisation Programme (IUMP), a machinery purchase scheme for firms launched in 2012, saw its budget slashed from N$10 million to just N$1.6 million in 2017, only enough to cover the costs of staff, meaning the programme was effectively at a standstill. Other programmes and bodies, such as the Equipment Aid Scheme the Namibia Trade Forum, are also presently in a state of greatly curtailed functioning due to funding cuts.[23]

---

[22] Interview with Michael Humavindu, Deputy Permanent Secretary, MITSMED. 14.12.2015.
[23] The Equipment Aid Scheme, which provides equipment to SMEs, has seen enormous budget cuts: in 2016 the scheme helped just 6 SMEs, compared to assisting 433 SMEs in 2013 and 743

By far the most significant example of the failure to improve industrial policy is the planned withdrawal of special incentives for manufacturing firms. Growth at Home had committed the Government to "enhancing" the generous incentives offered to firms (Ministry of Trade and Industry, 2015: 18). Despite these claims, in March 2018 Schlettwein surprisingly announced plans to scrap the preferential tax to manufacturers which had been in place since 1993. Rather than enhancing incentives, the Government of Namibia intends to remove the most tangible means of support offered to firms. As representatives of *Namib Mills*, a company that has received the incentives previously, told me in interview (prior to the announcement of their planned withdrawal), "if you don't have these types of incentives, you don't see manufacturing growth".[24]

Budget cuts alone do not explain the plight of MITSMED. As an employer of the German development agency GIZ who had been seconded to MITSMED told me, "I would say, even if we wouldn't have any budget at all to start implementing the industry growth strategies we would have at least in each industry four or five interventions which could be started without having budget".[25] But the Ministry has maintained its pre-existing ineffective patterns of work and organisation. An anonymous member of staff said that the Ministry is "not properly managed", with another calling the Ministry "a big mess", even in comparison to other government ministries, suffering from a lack of motivation, and a distinct lack of direction from senior members of staff. For example, the excessive delays in the publishing of the sector growth strategies were said to be the consequence of infighting within the Ministry, with two rival factions to-ing and fro-ing once the external consultants had completed the reports, both keen to receive final credit for the strategies, even at the expensive of majorly delaying their completion.

This latter anonymous interviewee argued that, because of this disorganisation, concerted industrial policy was very difficult: "in the past years of course you have nice documents – Industrial Policy, Growth at Home, and now you have the Growth Strategies – but in terms of implementation there hasn't been much going on". The general atmosphere of lethargy permeates such that even the motivated members of staff find it challenging. As the interviewee continued: "The good guys, they come in, start their jobs, and then they realise that they can't move anything here, it is way to slow, people are stubborn, it is like they are working for their own ego and not seeing the greater good. And then they have two options – they either adapt, or they get another job". For example, another anonymous member of staff in the Ministry told me the following: "I came from the private sector, so I

---

firms in 2014 (Ministry of Trade and Industry, 2013; 2014; MITSMED, 2017a).

[24] Interview with Frans Meyer, Operations Manager, and Pieter van Niekerk, Commercial Manager, *Namib Mills*. 13.6.2017.

[25] Interview with Wolfgang Demenus, Advisor at Deutsche Gesellschaft für Internationale Zusammenarbeit (GIZ) and MITSMED, 28.4.2016

realised eventually to relax. I now don't feel bad about days going by where I have not done much work". This same interviewee said that early in their tenure at the Ministry a more senior official, responding to their energetic first few weeks in office, said "you need to learn to relax, this is government".

Many of the other government ministries and SOEs involved in Namibia's industrial policy have been equally disappointing. The National Planning Commission (NPC), charged at independence with planning and coordinating government's economic policy, has proved toothless, devoid of the de facto authority to dictate the actions of ministries. The Director-General of NPC described to me the difficulties in getting other ministries to be cooperative: "[i]t is not always easy. What normally will happen is people [in ministries] might think, 'oh they are just trying to prescribe to us what we should do, why should we do that?'... Then you find that at times, because maybe we didn't do a good job in convincing them, or maybe they changed their minds, that implementation of what had been agreed has not always been smooth" (interview with Tom Alweendo, Director-General of the National Planning Commission. 27.1.2016).

Development funding has proven to be a major issue, most notoriously in the case of the SME Bank. Replacing the defunct Small Business Credit Guarantee Trust, the SME Bank was launched in 2012, with the Ministry of Trade and Industry (2013: 7) emphasising that "[t]he significant role to be played by the recently established SME Bank should never be underestimated". Yet, its contribution remained limited, before a scandal broke in early 2017 and the Bank of Namibia was forced to seize control of the Bank "over alleged unsound and questionable financial and asset management practices" (Nakashole, 2017). The Bank was subsequently wound up in November 2017, with N$175 million of its assets appearing to have disappeared (Menges, 2018).[26]

As proposed in Growth at Home, the Government successfully passed the Public Procurement Act in 2015 and a Retail Charter (to encourage retails firms to stock more locally produced goods) in 2016. Nevertheless, both have been blighted by issues. The Public Procurement Act has so far failed to reform the procurement system, with local commentators noting that whilst the Act "was supposed to be a turning point in public procurement governance, by mid 2018 all the evidence pointed to a system still in deep crisis" (Links, 2018: 1). The Retail Charter, meanwhile, as a purely voluntary commitment for retail firms, has not led to significant changes in the practices of retail firms.

---

[26] The other state institution funding investments, the Development Bank of Namibia (DBN), which commenced operations in 2004, has a much better reputation, but its impact appears to be limited, itself estimating to have created some 22,000 jobs from 2004/5 to 2016/17 through funding to firms (Development Bank of Namibia, 2017).

All in all, the quality of Namibia's industrial policy has failed to improve in the 2010s. In a recent MITMSED document, the Ministry concluded that its progress from 2013 to 2017 had been unsatisfactory and "severely hampered" (MITSMED, 2017b: 17). The candid report argues that "[t]he quality of the masterplan was low hence rendered management with little confidence to fully implement it as per the blueprint" (*ibid.*: 17), adding that the Directorates of the Ministry suffer from "decision paralysis", making the achievement of stated objectives extremely difficult (*ibid.*: 20). Further factors explaining the lack of progress that were identified included budgetary constraints, poor human resource and institutional capacity, and the slow implementation of policies, programmes and projects, and a lack of continuity in planning due to high staff turnover (*ibid.*).

Despite the fanfare which surrounded the reformulation of Namibia's industrial policy, the subsequent years have failed to see significant progress made in industrial policy. MITSMED has continued to be poorly managed, NPC has next-to-no authority, the now defunct SME Bank was mired in controversy, and the central Government has financially abandoned industrial policy as it seeks to reduce public debt. Rather than the 2010s representing a decisive break with the past, industrial policy has continued much as it had done throughout the independence era.

From the perspective of industry, this is to be seen as a missed opportunity. As the CEO of the Namibian Manufacturers Association told me, if the ideas included in Growth at Home were to be implemented it would be of enormous benefit to manufacturing companies in Namibia:

> [I]f you take the procurement bill, tenders from government, retail charter, the new investment bill, incentives to the manufacturing sector, we can have a huge success. What is in this book [Growth at Home] must be implemented, executed, and controlled ... The execution is what is lacking.[27]

Ultimately, the Namibian era of independence has seen very little intervention from the state in the economy and a near-total lack of industrial policy measures. Accordingly, the extent of structural transformation has been extremely limited. The following sections will detail the course of economic and industrial development over the independence years, thereby completing this exhaustive account of economic and industrial progress in Namibia since 1900.

---

[27] Interview with Ronnie Varkevisser, CEO, Namibian Manufacturers Association, 28.1.2016. Similarly, a GIZ member of staff seconded to MITSMED stated to me, "[w]hat I found as a good sign, when we did the growth strategies, was that industry was happy to see government approaching them to talk openly about issues" (interview with Wolfgang Demenus, Advisor at Deutsche Gesellschaft für Internationale Zusammenarbeit (GIZ) and MITSMED, 28.4.2016).

Economic progress since independence: steady but unspectacular

At independence Namibia's economy was dominated by the primary industries, particularly the mining of diamonds, uranium and copper, which together contributed 18% of GDP and 59% of exports of goods (Republic of Namibia, 1998). Fishing and fish processing, which had recovered from its enormous collapse of the 1970s, was the largest contributor to exports after mineral products (14%), and cattle and (to a lesser extent) karakul rearing continued to be the chief activities of Namibia's agricultural sector. The manufacturing sector contributed 12.5% to GDP in 1990 and little by way of exports aside from processed fish. The country had a large services sector, contributing 46% to GDP, almost half of which was accounted for by Government. Other important services sectors were real estate and business services; transport and storage; and wholesale and retail trade (Moorsom, 1990).

All sectors of the economy were still dominated by Namibia's white population, which now made up some 6% of the population. The country was highly unequal and had one of the highest Gini-coefficients in the world (Kaakunga, 1990). Poverty was pervasive, particularly in rural areas, with around two-thirds of the population living in absolute poverty at independence and unemployment was rife (Christiansen, 2011; Jauch & Tjirera, 2017). Hage Geingob, then Prime Minister, argued that "independent Namibia had inherited enormous problems", including a bloated civil service, mismanaged public sector, inequality, and a skewed economic structure (i.e. an over-reliance on the primary sector) (Geingob, 1992: 9).[28]

Whilst steady growth has occurred throughout the independence era, the economy has failed to structurally transform, remaining much as it had done in 1990. Namibia's economy grew at an average of 4.2% per annum from 1990 to 2016 in constant prices, with only one year of negative growth (in 1993) (Namibia Statistics Agency, 2018).[29] For the whole of sub-Saharan Africa GDP growth from 1990 to 2016 averaged 4.3%, suggesting that Namibia's performance has been steady but unexceptional (World Bank, 2018). Accordingly, Namibia has maintained its position as one of the wealthiest countries in the region, with its GDP per capita of US$4,415 in 2016 only bettered only by neighbouring Botswana and South Africa, oil-rich Gabon and Equatorial Guinea, and the islands of Mauritius and Sey-

---

[28] Other commentators have been more positive about Namibia's economic situation at independence. Christiansen (2011: 42) argues that, given its large endowments of natural resources, its stable political situation, and its comparatively good GDP per capita performance, Namibia at the time of independence "definitely had substantial advantages" over most other sub-Saharan African countries. In its report on Namibia's politics and economy the German foundation Bertelsmann Stiftung (2016: 29) concur, stating that the "relatively high levels of economic and social development" at independence were "good fortune" for the Namibian state.

[29] The preliminary national accounts for 2017 show Namibia's GDP to have also experienced negative GDP growth in 2017 (Republic of Namibia, 2017).

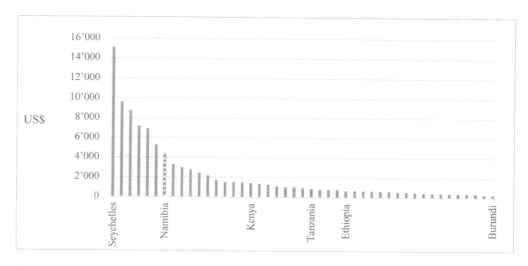

Figure 4.1: GDP per capita for sub-Saharan African Countries (US$), 2016. Source: World Bank (2018). Countries named for comparative purposes.

chelles. Figure 4.1 demonstrates how much higher Namibia's GDP per capita is than most sub-Saharan African countries.

Growth has been accompanied by some evidence of improved quality of life, with access to safe water and electricity increasing, child mortality rates decreasing, and poverty levels decreasing (Sherbourne, 2016; African Development Bank et al., 2017). These improvements have, again, closely mirrored trends across the African continent, though there have been some questions raised over the quality of data collected on Namibian poverty rates (see Sherbourne, 2016),[30] as well as for Africa in general (see Hickel, 2016).[31]

But despite these markers of improvement, "poverty and inequality have remained widespread" in Namibia (Jauch & Tjirera, 2017: 165). For example, the percentage of the population said to be undernourished increased from 30.4% in 2001 to 42.3% in 2016, making Namibia one of only four countries across Africa to have seen this figure increase over the time period (African Development Bank et al., 2017). The proportion of the population living in slums remained at 33–34% between 2000 and 2014, life expectancy has only increased minimally, and Namibia's performance in the UN Human Development Indicators shows a lack of progress, with its index score remaining largely unchanged from 1990 through to present day (UNDP, n.d.). Melber (2007b: 115) has called Namibia's performance

---

[30] Sherbourne (2016) speculates that data may have been massaged by the Government, or poverty may have been simply overestimated at independence.

[31] Hickel (2016: 749) argues that evidence from the likes of the UN and the World Bank of global poverty reduction is "misleading at best and intentionally inaccurate at worst".

in the Human Development Indicators (it is currently ranked 135th out of 188 countries) "nothing less than a scandal... given the country's relative resource wealth". Namibia also remains one of the most unequal countries in the world by Gini-coefficient, and unemployment persists. The unemployment rate was 34.0% in 2016, compared to 34.5% in 1997 (Ministry of Labour/Central Bureau of Statistics, 1998; Sherbourne, 2016).

Most commentators today argue that Namibia has been relatively successful in diversifying its economy since independence. For example, Sherbourne (2016: 22) writes that "[t]he structure of Namibia's economy has changed and become more diversified. In 1990 more than half of the country's GDP was generated by just three sectors: agriculture, mining and government. By 2014 these three sectors accounted for under 40 percent of GDP". Kambonde & Rena (2014: 27) similarly state that since independence the "economy has become less dependent on mining and agriculture and has diversified its exports to include a variety of goods and services".

Despite such assertions, there has in fact been little diversification of the Namibian economy. Figure 4.2, below, presents changes in Namibia's GDP structure over time. It shows the remarkable consistency of the economy over the first 26 years of independence, aside from

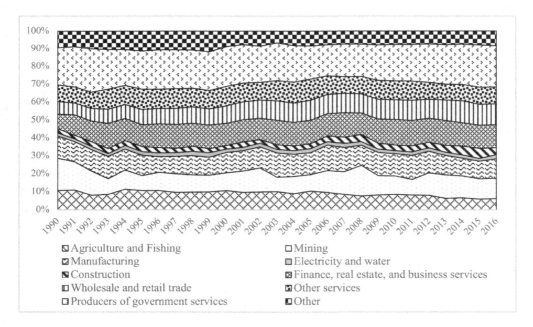

Figure 4.2: Change of Namibian GDP by sector (%), 1990–2016. Sources: Republic of Namibia, 1998; 2000; 2006; 2011; 2012b; 2016d. Figures are based on current prices. 'Other services' = 'hotels and restaurants', 'transport and communication', 'community, social and personal service activities', and 'private household with employed persons'. 'Other' = 'taxes less subsidies on products'.

the drop in the mining sector that occurred in the early 1990s. Sherbourne's claim that the relative contribution of agriculture, mining, and government has reduced since 1990 is correct, but this reduction only occurred up to 1993. Indeed, the combined contribution of the mining, agriculture and government sectors is slightly higher now than it was in 1995.

Exports, whilst not having increased their relative contribution to GDP, present a slightly more dynamic story of diversification, with refined copper and zinc (driven principally by the onset of operations at the Skorpion Zinc mine in Rosh Pinah in 2003) and cut and polished diamonds having been added to Namibia's export basket. Beyond these sectors, however, there has been very little diversification of Namibian exports since independence, with exports having continued to be dominated by minerals, with small quantities of food products and beverages also exported, as is shown in figure 4.3.

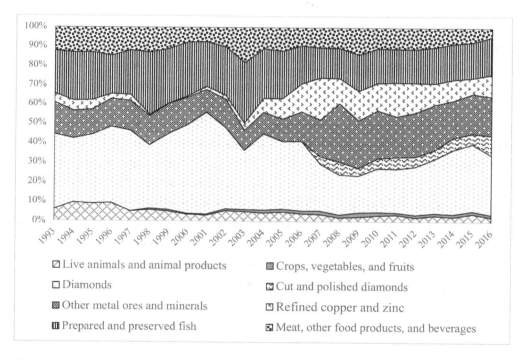

Figure 4.3: Namibia's exports of goods by product type (%), 1993–2016. Sources: Republic of Namibia, 1998; 2000; 2006; 2011; 2012b; 2016d. Figures are based on current prices. 1993 was chosen as the starting date because only from this year is a more detailed export breakdown available. Note that the large section, 'other manufacturing products n.e.c. incl. reexports' has been excluded from the above graph. This is because it appears that almost all this category refers to reexports, which is of little relevance to the illustrative exercise here. Other sectors excluded are 'electricity' and 'fish prod-ucts', both of which are very small. The figure also excludes 'exports of services'. This category showed a gradually declining contribution to exports from 1993 to 2016.

It has been argued, however, that the "aggregate [GDP and export] figures ... hide changes at a more disaggregated level and therefore the diversification that has taken place in the economy" (Schade, 2017: 1). Schade points to several economic activities to have emerged or grown strongly beyond diamond cutting and polishing and copper and zinc refining: fruit and vegetables (particularly grapes[32]), tourism, pasta production and cement production.

These industries have indeed advanced, though to date they are still reasonably small parts of the economy.[33] And importantly, these sectors represent *exceptions* to the Namibian Government's free-market approach. Growth in fruit and vegetable production followed the onset of the Government's Horticulture Market Share Promotion scheme in 2004. The scheme requires all importers of fruit and vegetables to source a certain percentage of their produce from within the country. Set at just 3% in 2004, this percentage has since increased steadily, reaching 44% in 2016 (Namibian Agronomic Board, 2016; Sherbourne, 2016). The scheme was had an extremely positive effective on local production, with Namibia now supplying around 40% of the domestic demand for fruit and vegetables, up from just 5% fifteen years ago (Schade, 2017). The state's involvement in the onset of pasta and cement production will be discussed in the following section on industrial development.

To conclude, Namibia's economic track record since independence exhibits reasonable growth but the absence of structural change coupled with the persistence of poverty and unemployment, much as in the late-colonial era. Sherbourne (2016: 19) writes that "Namibia has benefitted from the global boom in resources but has not succeeded in engineering more fundamental economic transformation. Growth has fallen far short of what is required to substantially reduce poverty and unemployment and is nowhere near what is needed to attain... high-income status". As Melber (2014: 111) further argues, Namibia is "a case study for a resource-rich but structurally underdeveloped economy with a so far absent or failed strategy to turn the relative natural wealth into substantial benefits for the majority of the people. Instead, the society remains characterised by massive socio-economic disparities".

---

[32] The industry, first started in the late 1980s, grew notably during the 1990s, exporting mainly to Europe and the United States. Operating in the south of the country, it is essentially an extension of the pre-existing grape industry in the region of South Africa immediately below the Namibia-South Africa border. Exports have increased from N$22.4 million in 1998 to N$407.2 million in 2015 (data provided by the Namibia Statistics Agency, via email), and the industry employs over 11,000 people (in largely atrocious conditions) (Hamutenya, 2017).

[33] The exception being tourism, which consists principally of large safari lodges and the selling of Namibian crafts and has become a more important feature of the economy. It is difficult to know exactly how large a contribution tourism presently makes to the Namibian economy, though it has been estimated that its contribution to GDP is over 12% (World Travel & Tourism Council, 2017).

Meanwhile, the Government itself has acknowledged that whilst the economy has "expanded at a healthy pace" since independence, "its structure [has] remained virtually unchanged" (Ministry of Trade and Industry, 2012a: 3). This lack of development has proved perplexing for proponents of 'economic development via sound investment climate' approaches, with Godana & Odada (2008: 243) concluding that "the post-independence investment activity and economic growth have not been good as [sic.] one might expect given the favorable economic and political environment".

The disappointing record of industrial development, 1990 to 2018

The manufacturing sector has failed to advance to any meaningful extent over the independence years. Few new industries have emerged and in terms of employment, value added, and exports, its relative size has not increased. Sherbourne (2016: 269) notes manufacturing's "disappointing" performance, with Christiansen (2012: 45) referring to the secondary industry as "the problem child" of the Namibian economy, noting that "[d]evelopment in the manufacturing sector has been particularly slow with hardly any progress towards a more diversified product palette" (*ibid.*: 52). A recent article also concluded that "industrial development has not advanced notably over the past 26 years" (Insight Namibia, 2016b).

MVA/GDP, peaking in 2006, has consistently hovered between 10% and 14%, showing no upwards trajectory, with MVA/GDP in 2017 at 10.8% as compared to 12.5% in 1990. MVA (constant prices) grew at 3.4% from 1990 to 2017, very similar to the 3.3% per annum growth of the 1964 to 1989 period, and far less than the 12.6% from 1946 to 1963 (SWA Department of Finance, 1988; Namibia Statistics Agency, 2018).

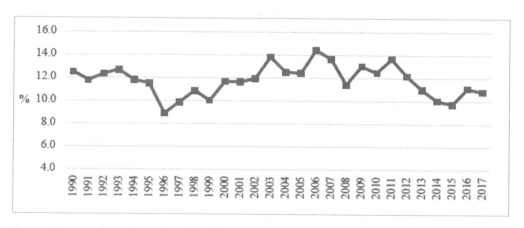

Figure 4.4: Manufacturing value added (% of GDP), 1990–2017. Source: Republic of Namibia (various years).

The record in job creation has been especially disappointing. As table 4.1 presents, Namibia's manufacturing employment increased by only 25% between 1997 and 2014, despite the total number of employed persons increasing by 100% over the same period. Even with the large spike[34] in manufacturing employment that was recorded between 2014 and 2016, manufacturing's contribution to total employment is still unchanged from its level in the 1990s.[35]

Year	Total manufacturing employment	Total employment	Manufacturing employment as percentage of total employment
1991	22,837		
1994	21,000		
1997	22,840	356,849	6.4%
2000	22,445		
2003	31,851		
2008	20,961		
2009	26,129		
2010	29,119		
2012	28,409	630,094	4.5%
2013	32,769	685,651	4.8%
2014	28,706	712,710	4.0%
2016	44,419	676,885	6.6%

Table 4.1: Manufacturing employment, 1990–2018. Sources: For 1991, 2000, 2008, and 2010, information is from Sherbourne (2016). For 1994 information is from Ministry of Trade and Industry (1994). For 1997, information is from Ministry of Labour/Central Bureau of Statistics (1998). For 2003 information is from Kadhikwa & Ndalikokule (2007). For 2009 information is from Ministry of Trade and Industry (2009b). For 2012, 2013, 2014, 2016, information is from Namibia Statistics Agency (2013; 2014; 2015; 2017).

Information on the number of manufacturing firms operating in Namibia has become difficult to obtain because the Government has been poor at conducting industrial censuses. In 1993 the Government estimated that there were roughly 400 manufacturing enterprises, whilst a 1998 publication from the MTI listed 481 firms (Ministry of Trade and Industry, 1993; 1998). Since then the Government has released no official figures, though the Na-

---

[34]   A spike which reportedly baffled staff at the Ministry of Industrialization, Trade, and SME Development.

[35]   And little more than it was in the pre-independence era. In 1978 manufacturing employment as a percentage of the total labour force was 4.6% in 1978 (Kaakunga, 1990).

mibian Manufacturers Association (NMA) published a supposedly exhaustive directory of manufacturing firms which included 517 firms.[36] Evidently, the number of firms operating in the country has not increased substantially. Manufacturing has continued to be concentrated in the centre of the country – in Windhoek and at the coast. According to the NMA's manufacturing directory, 305 of the country's 517 manufacturing firms were based in Windhoek, whilst a further 65 were based in the Erongo region. And although there are now more black people owning and managing manufacturing firms in the country, the sector continues to be dominated by white men.[37]

Despite the seeming lack of progress, there has been a change in the structure of Namibia's manufacturing sector. The dominance of food and beverages within the sector has relatively waned, falling from 73% of total value added in 1993 to 44% in 2017, even reaching as low as 32% in 2007 (Republic of Namibia, various years). This diversification is not, however, as impressive as first appears, as its major catalyst was the establishment of the zinc mine and refinery in Rosh Pinah in 2003. This meant that the contribution of 'basic non-ferrous metals' to manufacturing value added increased from just 1.8% in 2003 to 24.2% in 2006. Similarly, in the late 2000s output began to increase at the Tsumeb copper smelter. Beyond the copper smelter and zinc refinery, the other sector to contribute to manufacturing's changing structure has been the onset of diamond cutting and polishing, which began in earnest during the 2000s. As figure 4.5 shows, excluding these two large mining operations and the dozen or so diamond cutting and polishing firms, the relative contribution of other manufacturing activities has actually decreased since the year 2000.

Manufacturing exports have failed to increase their relative share of total exports over the independence years, staying around the 35–45% mark, as is shown in figure 4.6.[38] The contribution of processed fish to manufacturing exports has declined due to tightened fishing quotas, but this shortfall has been made up by the increasing export of refined zinc, smelted copper, and cut and polish diamonds, whilst food and beverage products (mainly beer, meat and, since 2002, pasta) have maintained their minor share of exports. Exports of cut and polished diamonds, zinc and copper are said to be exported to Europe (though

---

[36] My experience was that several the firms in the directory were either not *manufacturing* firms or were yet to start operations.

[37] Women are poorly represented in the industry, with Ally Angula, founder and Managing Director of *Leap Holdings*, a firm involved in garment manufacturing and horticulture, a notable exception.

[38] This figure excludes the subsection 'other manufactured goods', because this section is dominated by re-exports, which have grown enormously over the independence era (or, at least, have begun to be included in export data more consistently). Having to exclude this subsector is inconvenient, but no major exports have emerged in this subsector. The exception is textiles, which we know increased massively during the era of *Ramatex* in the mid-2000s but fell away entirely by 2008.

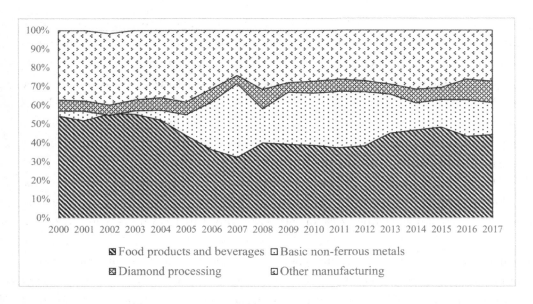

Figure 4.5: Manufacturing sector breakdown (%), 2000–2017. Source: Republic of Namibia (various years).

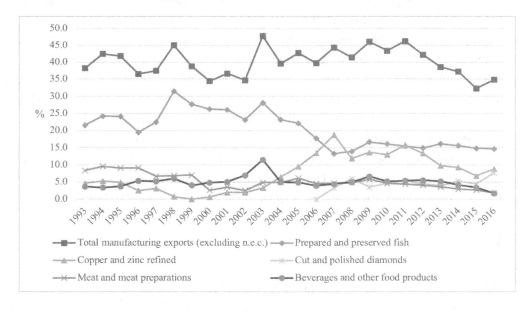

Figure 4.6: Manufacturing exports (% of total exports), 1993–2016. Sources: Republic of Namibia (various years). Excludes subsector 'manufactured products n.e.c., including reexports'.

this is likely only stated for tax purposes, with zinc and copper likely ending up in China), as is processed hake, and processed pilchards, meat, pasta, and beer have South Africa and other neighbouring countries as their major export destinations. Beyond this, the extent of manufacturing exports is very limited. Much smaller quantities of goods such as charcoal, paint, agricultural equipment, cement, printed works, carpets, pharmaceutical products, and clothing are exported to other Southern African countries, but exports are generally sporadic rather than consistent elements of firms' revenue streams.

Namibia's manufacturing sector today, as it did throughout the 20th century, remains dominated by food processing, beverages, and construction-related products, though mineral beneficiation has taken on a much larger role. There are only be limited upstream linkages between Namibia's manufacturing and mining sectors. Some small firms have provided mining equipment, whilst a lot of the construction-related firms see an uptick in their business when large mining projects are being built. A small number of clothes manufacturers have also supplied uniforms for mining firms. By value of sales, the largest manufacturing companies in 2013 were *Namib Mills*, *Namibia Breweries*, and the *Coca-Cola Namibia Bottling Company*, with the companies employing roughly 1,900, 800, and 1,000 people respectively in their operations.[39]

Foreign investments dominate Namibia's mineral processing activities, with the copper smelter, zinc refinery, two cement plants, and all of the diamond cutting and polishing facilities majority-owned by foreign interests. Fish processing, too, continues to have several South African firms involved in the industry. Meat processing has remained principally the reserve of local capital, and *Namibia Dairies* and *Namibia Breweries* are both owned by the local company *Ohlthaver & List*. The smaller firms in Namibia tend to be owned by Namibian nationals, though there are exceptions to this rule. For example, of the two firms in Walvis Bay producing packaging materials for the fish industry, one is a Chinese firm, and the other is South African. There is another Chinese firm which makes bedding in Oshikango on the northern border of the country. The firm, *Oryx Textile Manufacturing and Trading*, is owned by infamous local Chinese businessman Jack Huang. Huang was arrested in 2017 over an alleged customs duties and foreign currency scam (Menges, 2017). In early 2018 the French car manufacturer *PSA Group*, announced that it was going to set up an assembly plant in Walvis Bay in the latter half of 2018, producing *Peugeot* and *Opel* vehicles.

---

[39] Employment figures provided by interviews with Frans Meyer, Operations Manager, and Pieter van Niekerk, Commercial Manager, Namib Mills 13.6.2017; Graeme Mouton, Finance Director, Namibia Breweries, 15.2.2016; and Frik Oosthuizen, Managing Director, Coca-Cola Namibia Bottling Company, 15.2.2016. Other large employers include the half-a-dozen fish processing companies (typically employing around 800 people); *Namibia Dairies* (750 employees); a firm making cardboard boxes (700 employees); a plastic bag manufacturer (500 employees); the meat processing firms (around 350 employees); and a cement company (300 employees).

Category	Contribution (%)	Principle industries/products
Basic non-ferrous metals	19.3%	Skorpion zinc refinery, Tsumeb copper smelter
Other food products	17.7%	Processed fish, animal feed, baked goods
Beverages	14.3%	Beer, soft drinks, water
Diamond processing	10.8%	Diamond cutting and polishing
Chemical and related products	7.5%	Pharmaceuticals, paint, soap, domestic cleaning products, charcoal, cosmetics
Grain mill products	7.2%	Pasta, wheat, maize, mahangu
Non-metallic mineral products	3.9%	Cement, bricks, tiles
Fabricated metals	3.9%	Windows, doors, pipes, pumps, gutters, trailers, fences, road signs, water troughs
Meat processing	3.6%	Processed meat
Other	11.7%	Plastic bags, packaging materials, clothing, carpets, wooden windows and doors, furniture, leather products, publishing and printing

Table 4.2: Manufacturing value added breakdown (%), 2016. Source: Namibia Statistics Agency (2016d).

New industries to have emerged

There are only four major manufacturing industries (excluding zinc refining) that have emerged over the independence period: pasta, pharmaceuticals, cement, and diamond cutting and polishing. The establishment of all four of these was a direct consequence of actions of the state, whilst the survival and expansion of a fifth industry – beer production – was also in part due to support afforded to the industry by Government.

Pasta production in Namibia has been a resounding success. The industry was started in the early 2000s by *Namib Mills*, after it approached the Government to ask for infant industry protection in the form of an import tariff. From 2002 a tariff was imposed, originally until 2010. Without this tariff the launching of the pasta industry would have been next-to-impossible. As a senior member of staff at Namib Mills told me, "[t]he only reason that we could really get involved, and that the investors even decided to put in money, was because the Government said that they will help protect the market".[40] A second firm, *Bokomo Foods*, also began producing pasta in 2008, and at its request IIP for pasta was extended until the end of 2014. The sector's growth has been impressive. Whereas in 2001 all of Namibia's pasta was imported from South Africa, today *Namib Mills* alone hold about 90% of the country's pasta market. Moreover, the company has successfully began exporting, holding an estimated 60% of the Zambian market, and an 8% share of the lucrative South African market, producing and selling its pasta more cheaply than the major South African firms. *Namib Mills* and *Bokomo Foods* now compete with imports without tariff protection.[41]

The pharmaceuticals industry has gone on to achieve considerable growth. The sole major player in pharmaceuticals is *Fabupharm*, founded in 1990 by a trained industrial pharmacist. The company makes products such as paracetamol, antibiotics, vitamin supplements, body lotions, and sunscreens in their factory of some 70 employees in Otjiwarongo. The Managing Director of the company told me that at independence the Government "supported us fully", with, for example, the Minister of Health and Social Services officially opening the factory.[42] The Government agreed to award the company all of the tenders that it needed to reach sufficient economies of scale. Although relations between the company and the state have been fraught in recent years (discussed in chapter 5), that the firm would not have been able to establish itself without state support is evident.

Domestic cement production has recently been established in the country, again due to infant industry protection offered by the state.[43] In 2010 *Ohorongo Cement* was established in Otavi by a German company. The cement industry was granted tariff protection in 2012, and although the protection has been taken to court by a Chinese cement importing company and is therefore not being enforced, South African firms have agreed, in a "gentleman's agreement", to not compete in the Namibian market at present.[44]

Diamond cutting and polishing in Namibia, as first been envisaged by entrepreneurs in Namibia the 1950s, was finally to emerge in the independence era. In 1999 Government passed the Diamond Act, which gave the Minister of Mines and Energy the power to oblige

---

[40] Interview with Frans Meyer, Operations Manager, and Pieter van Niekerk, Commercial Manager, *Namib Mills* 13.6.2017. The interviewee further added "would we have gone in without infant industry protection? Ufffff it would have been very difficult".

[41] As the Namib Mills senior member of staff told me, "we are not infants anymore, we can handle the competition".

[42] Interview with Fanie Badenhorst, Managing Director, *Fabupharm*. 21.1.2016.

[43] A cement firm was also established in the early 1990s by *African Portland Cement* in Otjiwarongo, though this endeavour proved unsuccessful and was shut down in 2000 (Schade, 2016).

[44] Interview with Rudolf Coetzee, General Administration Manager, *Ohorongo Cement*. 18.2.2016. On an aside, I am curious as to how long the South African firms will be willing to leave the Namibian market to *Ohorongo*. A second cement company, *Cheetah Cement*, began production at a newly established plant in 2018 (Cemnet, 2018).

diamond miners to sell a proportion of their production to domestic cutting and polishing factories (Sherbourne, 2016). The possibility of local cutting and polishing companies getting access to Namibia's high-quality diamonds was an instant draw to international firms, and several companies set up in the country (*ibid.*). In 2007 the Government pushed *De Beers* to establish the *Namibia Diamond Trading Company* (a joint venture between *De Beers* and the state), which formally states that a specific proportion of diamonds mined in Namibia must be processed locally (at the time, 16%). Consequently, Namibia's cutting and polishing industry could at last be launched, and though the industry has been blighted by issues and appeared close to collapse in 2015 in the face of low international prices, the situation for the industry is starting to improve.[45]

Finally, beer production has been well-supported in the independence era and has been able to expand. By 1990 the sole major player in Namibian beer production was *South West Breweries*, and soon after independence the company changed its name to *Namibia Breweries*. The company "put much effort in establishing a good and mutually beneficial relationship with the newly formed government" and the Government, accordingly, was willing to protect the company (van der Hoog, 2016: 101). For example, in 1994 *South African Breweries* (SAB) officially proposed the establishment of a large-scale brewery in the north of the country and applied for a liquor license, but the Government rejected the license request. As the Minister of Trade and Industry said at the time, "[w]e have a company that is Namibian, that pays tax, and is the largest manufacturing plant employing 8,700 [sic.] Namibians. We cannot let it be overrun by SAB" (quoted in van der Hoog, 2016: 104). This protection meant that Namibia Breweries "could grow and look for export markets" and this the company proved able to do with aplomb (van der Hoog, 2016: 109). By 2011 Namibia was the world's largest exporter of beer, excluding countries in Europe and North America, and the 14th largest overall, with most exports destined for South Africa and other neighbouring countries (UN Comtrade, 2018).

Beyond these exceptions, it appears that those companies that have been able to survive in Namibia without direct government support are those which have taken advantage of their proximity to the consumer and to find niches in high-volume goods markets. Senior staff of a successful plastic packaging firm, for example, told me that its competitive advantage was in doing branded packaging for firms that could not make the kind of large-scale bulk orders that South African firms were interested in.[46] A furniture manufacturing firm

---

[45] For example, value of cut and polished diamond exports more than doubled from 2015 to 2016, and their contribution to total exports of goods (current prices) increased from 4% to 8% (Republic of Namibia, 2016d). See also Brandt (2017).

[46] Interview with Bennie Venter, Financial Director, and Jan Hendrik Duvenhage, *Plastic Packaging*. 16.1.2016.

only makes bespoke products (typically conference room tables made to a certain size or shape, etc.) which the South African firms would be less likely to do or that would take them much longer.[47] Paint manufacturing firms can organise the production of personalised colours or grades at a faster turnover time than firms based in South Africa,[48] whilst a company making light steel framing for buildings said that its competitive advantage came in fast mobilisation and flexibility – if the client wanted a building design adjusted the company would be able to have the new materials ready far quicker than South African firms would be able to.[49] This flexibility appears key in explaining why construction-related industries have been able to survive and prosper in Namibia.[50]

Conclusion

This chapter has provided the most detailed account of industrial policy and development in independent Namibia yet written, benefitting from a thorough review of primary documents, interviews with government officials and manufacturing firms, the compilation and analysis of GDP and export data, and the contextualisation of developments through a broader assessment of economic policy and development.

Namibian economic and industrial policy in the 1990s and 2000s was characterised by an adherence to free-market principles and a dogmatic commitment to the attraction of foreign investment. And whilst a shift in Namibia's industrial policy approach occurred in the early 2010s, to date it has continued to suffer due to a lack of funding, an ineffective MTI unwilling to transition from planning policies to implementing them, and a lack of coordination between ministries on matters related to industrial development. In this context, Namibia's economy has remained structurally very similar to its state in 1990, and industrial development has failed to advance.

The culmination of this chapter concludes an account of Namibian industrial development and policy from 1900 to present day, the first such attempt ever made. I have tried to make the account as accurate and unbiased as possible, providing detailed descriptions of the changing structure of the Namibian economy and the role that the state was playing in these changes.

---

[47]   Interview with Bertie Kotze, Managing Director, *Cecil Nurse Business Furniture.* 14.4.2016.
[48]   Interview with Erich Muinjo, Manager: Material Requirement Planning & Projects, *Neo Paints Factory (Pty).* 8.2.2016
[49]   Interview with Antonie Vermaak, Director, *WV Construction.* 22.3.2016.
[50]   It is also of benefit to firms if transport costs prove detrimental for South African operations. This is true of paint, which, as a relatively heavy product, has high transport costs. Transport costs serve as a sufficient buffer of non-governmental protection for a number of high-volume goods.

The conclusion is that Namibia, like most countries on the African continent, has not seen marked industrial development. Namibia has seen fundamental change over this period – scarred by colonialism and its integration into the global economic system – but since the onset of colonialism the economy has remained remarkably similar. How different is the economy today to 1990, 1960 or even 1930?

Is the absence of industrial development in a small, sparse country an inevitability, or have there been other 'constraints' on the process of industrial advancement? I subscribe to the latter view, pointing to two essential factors in explaining industrial development: how committed the state is to achieving industrial development and how permissive the international political economy is to such ambitions. In chapters 2 and 3 I gave assessments of how these two factors were at play in colonial Namibia (the ambition of the SWA Administration of creating an agricultural economy, the interests of Namibia's economic elites in continuing to concentrate on agriculture, mining and trading, the interests of South Africa in maintaining Namibia as a market for its own manufactured goods). Now, in chapter 5, I wish to provide a political economy assessment of the constraints of industrial policy and industrial development in Namibia today.

5 The political economy of industrial policy and economic change in Namibia

Introduction

Chapter 4 identified what can be thought of as cosmetic causes of Namibia's failing industrial policy in the independence era. A lack of coordination of strategy across ministries, serious inefficiencies within the MITSMED, cut development budgets, and an inability for the state to transition from planning to executing industrial policies have all undermined progress.

But such assessments do not take us very far. One could look at the above cited factors and conclude that Namibian politicians and civil servants are inherently lazy, corrupt, or incompetent, thereby making industrial policy implementation next-to-impossible, and leading one to concur with the 'government failure' standpoint that "[i]mperfect markets [are] superior to imperfect planning" (Lal, 1983: 106). Rather than adopt such a view, my position is that the major cause of Namibia's shortcomings in industrial policy is that the Namibian state is not sufficiently committed to the achievement of structural transformation – that it does not have the 'developmental mindset' that is necessary to drive industrial development (Thurbon, 2016). Accordingly, in understanding issues in industrial policy it is necessary to consider the factors that are affecting the state's mindset.

As Whitfield & Buur (2014: 126) state, "we cannot understand why some governments pursue and implement industrial policy better than others without understanding its politics". Consequently, following Fine (2013: 26), what we need to analyse are "the systems of accumulation associated with particular economies... the underlying interests and the structure and dynamic of the economy through which these interests are formed and expressed". This is what is meant by 'system of accumulation' – the recurring structure through which economic society is organised in a politically sustainable manner.

What I want to achieve in this chapter is the articulation of how the system of accumulation in Namibia works to recreate itself and how its maintenance often stands as a direct obstacle to effective industrial policy. The chapter seeks to demonstrate how this system does not exist exclusively at the domestic level, but is linked inseparably to the international sphere, keeping in mind the observation from Wade (2018: 537) that "[t]he world economy seems to contain something analogous to a 'glass ceiling'".

My argument is that the presence of a functioning system of accumulation that is in some ways opposed to industrial policy and development has made their successful establishment a lot more challenging in Namibia. There are four features of Namibia's system of accumulation to be discussed: the functioning of SWAPO's political system; the interests of Namibia's economic elites; the actions of South Africa; and the role played by international bodies and globally predominant ideologies. Though discussed in the following discretely, it should be remembered that they are closely linked. What I want to build up is an understanding of the logics at play that contribute to the retainment of the status quo, and with it a limited industrial policy.

The functioning of SWAPO's political system

In interview, Robin Sherbourne, the leading independence-era economist of Namibia, described the political and economic system in Namibia as working in the following way:

> [SWAPO] ensure that foreign investors stay in the country and are satisfied. The foreign investors (mainly in mining and fishing) do the clever stuff, are taxed, and this money, as well as the money received from SACU revenues, is distributed enough to keep relevant parties satisfied. The system is based on SWAPO's unchallenged authority.[1]

This conceptualisation is quite straightforward: the state receives revenue from the large foreign enterprises and the SACU tariffs, and the money is then distributed nationally by SWAPO to a sufficient extent to stop unrest, either from prospective additional political factions or from the general public. As the Editor-in-Chief of the leading national newspaper told me, the President of Namibia can, through the country's political networks, "dispense patronage with ease", whilst leading political analyst Herbert Jauch described one of the main characteristics of the Namibian state as being "a huge network of state institutions that can be used to accommodate allies, sometimes even foes" that "serve for political patronage services".[2]

As Sherbourne says, the system works because of SWAPO's unchallenged dominance of Namibian politics. Indeed, SWAPO has near-absolute control over the Namibian political system. 'It's cold outside of SWAPO' is a common refrain, and to date all attempts to form meaningful opposition parties have been unsuccessful. In an extraordinary showing of political strength, Hage Geingob won the 2014 presidential election with 87% of the popular vote and SWAPO won 80% of votes in the concurrent National Assembly elections.[3] SWAPO

---

[1] Interview with Robin Sherbourne, former researcher at the Namibian Economic Policy Research Unit, founder of the Institute for Public Policy Research Namibia, and author of the *Guide to the Namibian Economy*, 16.11.2015.

[2] Interview with Tangeni Amupadhi, Editor-in-Chief, *The Namibian*. 18.12.2015; interview with Herbert Jauch, Head of Research, Metal and Allied Namibian Workers Union. 14.12.2015.

[3] Turnout was a high 72%, in what was by all accounts a fair election.

thus currently holds 77 of the 96 seats in the Assembly, with the largest opposition party holding just 5.

Within and around the powerful SWAPO has emerged a "post-colonial elite", centred on the President and some thirty leading figures in SWAPO and further made up of a "middle stratum of SWAPO politicians, senior civil servants, security chiefs and black empowerment entrepreneurs, [whose] personal affluence is derived from privileged access to power" (Cooper, 2012: 193). Melber (2011, 2014) has been particularly vocal in his criticism of the "new elites" who recreated colonial-era inequalities, and who appear "to be about self-enrichment within a given and unchallenged system of crude capitalism and class. In other words, it's business as usual" (Melber, 2014: 143, 149). Jauch & Tjirera (2017: 182) have similarly argued that the ideological orientation of the independent Namibian state has been "towards a system of patronage that is geared towards personal gratification rather than any higher ideal".

Clearly, a powerful, centralised political elite has emerged in Namibia which, over the past 28 years, has proved successful in achieving political, economic and social stability – particularly through its effective distribution of patronage – but has failed to notably advance economic development. The point of relevance here is how the system described by the likes of Sherbourne affects industrial policy and development. As the following will show, the nature of SWAPO's political system has, at times, directly undermined industrial policy and development.

A first example is the phenomenon of 'tenderpreneurship', which became widespread in Namibia in the years following the global financial crisis.[4] The term 'tenderpreneur', a portmanteau of 'tendering' and 'entrepreneur' originating in South Africa, refers to individuals who make their money through the obtaining of government tenders (e.g. contracts to supply school textbooks). The archetypal tenderpreneur operates without any productive business in place (i.e. they do not produce the goods or provide a service) and sources the item which they have been contracted to supply from a third party. Tenderpreneurs are typically businesspersons intimately associated with SWAPO, and their existence is linked to ambitions of the state to address racial inequalities and to create "a non-racial capitalist order" by supporting the emergence of a black capitalist class (Jauch & Tjirera, 2017: 145). For example, a member of SWAPO remarked in interview that "[a]ny tender, any contract of government that is going out must meaningfully and practically be seen to empower ... the poor" (quoted in Cooper, 2012: 202). The corruption and inefficiencies associated with the tenderpreneurs has led to the practice being chastised in the media, as well as by politicians,

---

4   It appears that tenderpreneurs have been suffering greatly in the wake of the large cuts in government spending in recent years. See The Patriot (2017).

with one member of parliament recently stating that the country must "move away from the dependence on tenderpreneurs" (quoted in Kahiurika, 2017).[5]

Concerning industrial development, the primary issue with the tenderpreneur system is that it makes it harder for manufacturing firms to secure government contracts. For example, the Managing Director of a printing and publishing firm told me in 2016 that until 2011 his firm would often win government tenders (or lose out to other printing press firms in Namibia). From then on, however, tenderpreneurs began winning *all* government contracts, with the middlemen then approaching the firm to actually conduct the work.[6] In the case of printing and publishing the practice tends not to negatively affect firms (because most often they still, eventually, get the business), but in most other manufacturing industries it is cheaper for tenderpreneurs to source the goods that they are supplying to Government from abroad, meaning that local firms lose contracts to foreign firms. This, for example, is the case for *Fabupharm* – the successful pharmaceutical firm mentioned in chapter 4 – which relies on the Government for contracts. In 2015, when a new Minister of Health and Social Services was appointed, the firm suddenly lost some 70% of its government contracts.[7] An anonymous government source told me that the contracts were instead awarded to tenderpreneurs who were importing the products from other African countries. The case of *Fabupharm* is particularly emblematic of industrial policy issues – *Fabupharm* had in fact received financial support from the Government as part of the Industrial Upgrading and Modernisation Programme in 2014, yet just one year later the Government cancelled the majority of the firm's contracts.

The tenderpreneur system is also part of the story of the failure of the SME Bank to support industrial development, as discussed in chapter 4. The SME Bank, it transpired, rather than financing the growth of productive enterprises, was effectively a conduit for the tenderpreneur system. Staff of the now defunct bank told me that the majority of the loans that they gave out were to individuals seeking government tenders and that in most cases these individuals were importing the goods that were to be supplied to Government.[8] The Government was, essentially, via loans from the SME Bank, giving funds to well-connected individuals, then awarding these individuals tenders so that they could accrue massive profits. This was both a drain on state resources and a distortion of the developmental role that the SME Bank should have been playing.

---

[5]   See, for example, Hamata (2013), Kamati (2018).

[6]   Interview with Henry Fernandes, Managing Director, *Solitaire Press*. 19.4.2016.

[7]   Interview with Fanie Badenhorst, Managing Director, *Fabupharm*. 21.1.2016.

[8]   Interview with Fillemon Nditya, Head: Business Lending, and Mr. Onesmus Kandenge: Senior Account Relationship Manager, SME Bank. 29.4.2016

Moreover, the system of elite individuals profiting from government projects can serve to dictate government investment policy, with recent proposed projects (such as an expansion of the Windhoek airport or the construction of a lavish new parliament building) seemingly prestige projects linked to the kickbacks that certain parties would receive from their construction.[9] Consequently, government investments can often be driven principally by the aim of satisfying narrow interests. As Jauch & Tjirera (2017: 182) state, "[t]he awarding of tenders and scholarships to family members of the political elite... the continuous increase of politicians' earnings and benefits, the enormous amounts spent on civil servants' and politicians' travel and subsistence allowances... plans to build an even more luxurious new parliament, houses for regional governors and a N$450 million state of the art military hospital... are all elite projects that will have very little developmental impacts".

Beyond the diversion of government contracts for manufacturing firms and funds from developmental activities, there are other ways in which SWAPO's political system inhibits industrial policy and development. In the face of persisting high levels of unemployment, public sector jobs and enterprises have served SWAPO as an essential way to generate employment and distribute wealth. Mkandawire (2015: 580) offers a critique of the "standard view of the African state" as being bloated or unusually large, arguing that public sector employment as a percentage of total population is actually much smaller in sub-Saharan Africa than it is in Latin America and the Caribbean, Middle East and North Africa, and Asia and the Pacific. He concludes that "African states are not singularly more likely to spend large shares of gross national product, to employ high ratios of the population in bureaucratic jobs, or to own extensive state-owned enterprises" (*ibid.*: 581). My contention, however, is that Namibia's government spending and level of government employment are particularly high by global standards.

The number of people working in the sector has grown gradually since independence, such that today nearly one in four employees in the country work for the Government or one of its SOEs, a ratio that puts Namibia amongst the most public-sector dominated economies in the world (Namibia Statistics Agency, 2017). Throughout the independence era government expenditure as a percentage of GDP has been amongst the highest in sub-Saharan Africa (generally between 22% and 26%).[10] The number of SOEs has also grown dramatically: whereas in 1990 there were some ten SOEs, by 2015 there were over seventy.[11] It is hard to overstate how large an overt role the state plays in Namibian society.

---

9 Interview with Herbert Jauch, Head of Research, Metal and Allied Namibian Workers Union. 14.12.2015. For a discussion of the wasteful tendencies of the governing elite, see Lister (2016).

10 In fact, in 2015, excluding countries with populations under 60,000, Namibia's government expenditure as a percentage of GDP was the 10th highest globally.

11 This was partly because of pressures during the 1990s to commercialise activities typically un-

For industrial policy implementation the concern is not the presence of a large number of bureaucrats and SOEs, which *could* serve to make industrial policy more effective. Rather, the issue is that the presence of a large government sector in Namibia is mainly about employment creation. This has led to oversaturated ministries, including MITSMED, with many staff more-or-less idle.[12] Overstaffed ministries serve to undermine effectiveness, with the assurance of the near-impossibility of one losing their job leading to gross inefficiency. For example, a high-ranking member of staff at MITSMED is widely regarded as being corrupt and disruptive, but despite their reputation (one extremely senior member of staff in another ministry was said to have remarked of them in a meeting "why [are they] not behind bars yet?") remain in their post, according to an anonymous source within MITSMED.

Meanwhile, SOEs, embedded in the "neopatrimonial" system of the state (Insight, 2014b), are an "ever growing fiscal burden", plagued by "numerous high-profile instances of mismanagement and poor performance" (Sherbourne, 2016: 420). The likes of *Air Namibia* and *TransNamib* have been particularly criticised, with *TransNamib* having "become a black hole into which taxpayer funds are continuously poured" (Brown, 2017: 10). Over the past ten years "mismanagement and outright fraud [within SOEs] have continued unabated and possibly even increased" (Sherbourne, 2016: 417), such that recently even the Minister of Finance acknowledged that SOEs in Namibia need serious reform (Nakashole, 2016). Rather than serving as productive enterprises, SOEs have diverted government revenues, limiting the availability of funds for the pursuit of industrial policy and undermining the provision of productive services, such as water and electricity.

A final example of the interaction between SWAPO's political system and constraints on industrial policy was the decision to re-appoint Immanuel Ngatjizeko as Minister of Trade and Industry in 2015, despite his poor performance in the role during the 2000s and the negative effects that his appointment had on the implementation of the Growth at Home strategy. The decision seemed to totally jar with the espoused ambition to achieve industrial development, but experts consider the move to have been one of political expediency, with the need for the Herero ethnic group – the third largest ethnic group in the country,

---

dertaken by the central government, with SOEs seen as a step towards privatisation, but SOEs also served "as an important training ground for new black Namibian professionals" (Sherbourne, 2016: 419). SOEs in Namibia include firms in public utilities, transport, a national broadcasting company, financial institutions, regulatory bodies, welfare organisations, and universities. There are also a handful of SOEs in other commercial activities, such as the *Meat Corporation of Namibia*, and *Windhoek Maschinenfabrik* (which produces armoured personnel carriers on a small scale for the Ministry of Defence).

[12] Despite this, the Government has reiterated its commitment to not laying off public sector employees (Brown, 2017).

of which Ngatjizeko is a part – to hold some senior positions within Government so as to continue to present SWAPO as the party of Namibia, as opposed to of the Ovambo ethnic group.[13] In this instance the re-entrenchment of SWAPO's political power, as opposed to the pursuit of industrial development, took precedence.

This section has served to outline the link between SWAPO's political system and hurdles to effective industrial policy and development. The system described is not an inherent feature of Namibian or 'African' politics. The point is that, as the examples above indicate, the Government acts in certain ways (e.g. handing out lucrative contracts to well-connected individuals, appointing unsuitable candidates for key positions) in order to maintain the stability of the system of accumulation, and these choices are frequently unconducive to industrial policy. The Government, pivotal to how money moves around Namibia, has been argued by commentators to have created "the environment for initiating and allowing private sector corruption to take place" as part of this important feature of how profit is generated in the country (Coetzee, 2018: 31). In a system where the amassing of individual wealth is, more often than not, related to government actions, it is little exaggeration to say that the state *is* the economy (at least its centre), and the way that this state-economic system works has had negative effects on industrial policy and development.

Mkandawire (2015) offers a rich critique of the idea that negative economic performance in Africa can be explained by 'neopatrimonialism' – the prevalence of patronage, corruption, factionalism, despotism, and clannish behaviour in the politics of a country – arguing that the approach appears guided by "strong preconceptions and prejudices about African politics" (*ibid.*: 601). I have wondered if Mkandawire would consider my above depiction and argument to be neopatrimonial. Essentially, I am of the view that he would not, based on his stated view concerning industrial development that "leadership's commitment to development... trump[s] neopatrimonialism" (*ibid.*: 587). In other words, Mkandawire views neopatrimonialism as not being able to explain differences in industrial development between nations, because what is more important is the commitment of the state to achieving said development. I concur with this view. But my position is that the functioning of SWAPO's political system helps to stifle said commitment to industrial development. The system and the commitment to industrial policy are, for me, part of the same story. But as the following sections demonstrate, there are many other factors at play.

---

[13] Email exchange with Graham Hopwood, Executive Director, IPPR. 27.7.2018.

The interests and views of Namibia's economic elites

In chapters 2 and 3 I charted the disinterest of Namibia's leading economic actors in industrial development during the colonial era. This attitude was well appraised by Thomas (1985: 6), who wrote that "the mines, a large segment of the large-scale farmers and probably a substantial segment of the... trading class only have a short to medium run time horizon with respect to their involvement in the local economy. This almost inevitably dampens efforts towards the steady, yet determined exploration and utilisation of industrial opportunities." As was noted in chapter 1, the presence of such a 'traditional class' of economic actors has long been identified as an impediment to structural transformation (see, for example, Hirschman, 1968; Cardoso & Faletto, 1979). It appears that such is the case in Namibia today, where actors from the trading, mining and finance sectors, which dominate the economy, have continued to show aversion to industrial development and policy in influential ways.[14]

This, at least, is the view of Namibia's Minister of Finance, who described the challenges of industrial development to me in the following terms:

> The reason is also to be found in a certain extent in the fact that our business community is a bunch of agents. They are actually only trading. They are buying finished goods from South Africa and trading in the market. And they are doing fine with that ... So the big players are trying very hard to maintain the status quo and not transform the economy.[15]

This is, I think, an enormous statement, with the Minister arguing that the major economic actors are fighting against state-led industrial development. And indeed, trading and retail firms have shown resistance towards industrial development. Due to Namibia's colonial history retail firms in Namibia are mostly South African, and have shown a profound reluctance to integrate Namibian firms into their supply chains.[16] For example, the retail firms in Namibia were vocal in their disapproval of the onset of infant industry protection for dairy (2000), pasta (2002), and poultry (2013), lobbying strongly within the Namibia Chamber of Commerce and Industry for the organisation to oppose the protectionism so as to assure the retailers of continued access to South African dairy, pasta and poultry.[17]

---

[14] The largest companies in Namibia by revenue are: the banks (*First National Bank of Namibia, Standard Bank of South Africa, Bank Windhoek*); the mining companies (*Rössing Uranium, Langer Heinrich Uranium, Namdeb Holdings*); the energy companies (*Namibia Power Corporation, Vivo Energy Namibia, Engen Namibia*); the retail firms (*Shoprite, Woermann Brock, Edgars Stores*); and the large trading firms (*Pupkewitz & Sons, Ohlthaver & List*).

[15] Interview with Calle Schlettwein, Minister of Finance of Namibia. 23.3.2016.

[16] Prominent South African retails firms include *Clicks, Shoprite, Pick n Pay, Edgars Stores*, and *Woolworths*. Namibian firms include *Cymot, Pupkewitz Holdings,* and *Woermann & Brock*.

[17] Interview with Tarah N. Shaanika, CEO, Namibia Chamber of Commerce and Industry. 31.3.2016

Namibia's liberal attitude to foreign investment meant that there was no effort to induce the retailers to source more locally manufactured goods, until finally Namibia introduced its 'Retail Charter' in March 2016.[18] The charter is a voluntary agreement that retail firms can sign, pledging to sourcing more locally, with the Namibia Trade Form (NTF) then giving each firm a score on compliance. It seems that the soft formulation of the charter (there is no consequence if your firm receives a poor score) was the result of pressure from the retailers. And even in its tame format, firms have proved slow to change their supply-chain practices and, moreover, the charter has effectively been at a standstill since March 2017, when the Namibian Competition Commission received a complaint (most likely from the South African retail firms) that the charter violates the Namibia's Competition Act of 2003 and consequently instructed the NTF to cease implementation. One of Namibia's flagship industrial policies of Growth at Home was now dead in the water.

The mining companies, meanwhile, have resisted increased value-addition to Namibia's minerals. In 2011 the Government announced the establishment of an export levy tax of up to 5% on unprocessed mineral exports to increase its tax revenues and to encourage local processing (Sherbourne, 2016). The industry, represented by the Chamber of Mines, was in uproar, arguing that the tax changes would "have led to mine closures and huge disinvestment", and the chamber lobbied strongly and effectively against the imposition of the levy (*ibid.*: 215).[19] The export levy was eventually introduced in 2016 in a greatly watered-down form, with individual levies for specific minerals as opposed to a blanket 5% rate, and no minerals receiving a levy greater than 2% (Republic of Namibia, 2016c). Uranium oxide – one of Namibia's largest mineral exports – became subject to a levy of just 0.25%.

Mines, like retail firms, also tend to source very few locally manufactured inputs for their operations.[20] For example, a firm manufacturing steel drums for the storage and transporta-

---

[18] Interview with Maria Immanuel, Trade & Investment Policy Analyst, Namibia Trade Forum. 9.2.2016; interview with Ronnie Varkevisser, CEO, Namibian Manufacturers Association, 28.1.2016.

[19] The validity of this claim – frequently repeated by those associated with the industry – is unclear, given that mining firms' financial accounts are typically shrouded in secrecy. It is often stated in Namibia that mining firms are involved in transfer pricing. See, for example, New Era (2017a). Irrespective, it should be noted that there is a relatively limited opportunity in Namibia for increased value addition of minerals, as concluded by a recent report on beneficiation (SNL Metals & Mining, 2014).

[20] It appears that the only Namibia-manufactured product that *Rössing Uranium* purchases are uniforms which have been manufactured overseas but had the stitching of the Rössing logo done in Swakopmund (interview with Edmund Roberts, Supply Chain Manager, *Rössing Uranium*. 2.3.2016). Similarly, the only significant locally-sourced input at the Tsumeb Copper Smelter, run by Dundee Precious Metals, is labour (interview with Buks Kruger, Technical Director Tsumeb Smelter, *Dundee Precious Metals*. 15.4.2016). The Skorpion Zinc mine in the south of the country has been provided with uniforms more substantively manufactured in Namibia (interview with David Namalenga, Managing Director, *Dinapama Manufacturing & Supplies*. 26.4.2016).

tion of uranium was established in 2012 adjacent to Namibia's uranium mines in Erongo. The firm, however, was forced to close down in 2015, with one of the largest mines *Rössing Uranium* (owned by *Rio Tinto*) failing to purchase a single drum from the company, leaving it unable to repay its initial capital expenditure.[21] *Rössing* told the company that this was because of the complicated process of changing suppliers within the *Rio Tinto* supply-chain system, but from the perspective of the drum manufacturer, the securing of a local supplier was "just not a priority" for *Rössing*.[22]

Namibia's important and relatively large financial sector – closely linked to the mining sector – shares an attitude that borders on disdain towards Government efforts to advance manufacturing. For example, the Managing Director of one of the largest banks in the country, reflecting on early ambitions towards industrial development in independent Namibia, remarked to me that "President Nujoma used to talk about manufacturing helicopters! [laughs] We laugh about it, but that is the level of political thinking... it's just crazy".[23] The opinions held by these leading economic figures matter for the economy. Indeed, this same individual was head of the MTI's Namibia Investment Centre during the 1990s and was advising the Government against the pursuit of mass manufacturing.

Similarly, most major economists in independent Namibia have been ardent free-market enthusiasts. The think tank NEPRU was the country's leading economic research centre in the 1990s and 2000s, with its staff, including the likes of Robin Sherbourne and Dirk Hansohm, largely adhering to free-market principles and advocating 'neoliberal' policies from the state (Jauch, 2001; Hansohm, 2007). Hansohm (2007: 233) writes that "[w]hile NEPRU presents an economic view emphasizing the role of the private sector, government – and particularly the MTI – tend to have a more public sector view, emphasizing stronger involvement of government itself in the economy". Jauch (2001: 36) states that Sherbourne's view is that "globalisation will only be a threat to Namibia if she continues to protect economically non-viable enterprises... Sherbourne suggests that employment creation and the reduction of poverty are best addressed by opening-up the Namibian economy". In interview Jauch also stated to be that NEPRU subscribed to a neoliberal framework, promoting the type of economics that its staff had been taught (interview with Herbert Jauch, Head of Research, Metal and Allied Namibian Workers Union. 14.12.2015). NEPRU was often closely associated with Government and was one of the key authors of the highly non-interventionist industrial policy white paper of 1992 (Curry & Stoneman, 1993).

---

[21] Interview with Robert de Villiers, Managing Director, *Yellow Drum Manufacturing*. 29.3.2016.
[22] In 2016 it was announced that another firm had bought up the drum manufacturing plant, with this firm seemingly confident that they had the political capital necessary to encourage the mining companies to procure locally (Kaira, 2016).
[23] Interview with Steve Galloway, Managing Director, *Rand Merchant Bank*. 15.12.2015.

The free-market view continues to be prominent amongst Namibia's leading economists today, with Rowland Brown, founder of the Economic Association of Namibia in 2012, particularly vociferous in his disapproval of government intervention and in his belief that Namibia's economy needs further liberalisation.[24] Brown has significant influence within Government, having (according to his own bio) "worked with Namibia's core financial ministries, offices and agencies, providing advice to various ministers and high level advisors" (Cirrus, n.d.). Brown was part of the small team that wrote Namibia's industrial policy white paper in 2012 and the Growth at Home strategy document, and he stated to me in interview that "we tried to push as much as we could to have a more free-market industrial policy".[25] A further example of the predominance of free-market views amongst economists in Namibia is the online magazine the *Namibia Economist*. A recent article written by the editor on the state of the economy argued that: "[f]undamentally, there is only one overarching economic problem and that is, the Government has gradually crowded out the private sector" (Namibia Economist, 2017).

The anti-government intervention stance of most of the private sector and the economic policy-related civil society of Namibia was well-emblematised in the case of the Namibia Investment Promotion Act (NIPA). As discussed in chapter 5, the Government attempted to replace the extremely liberal Foreign Investment Act (FIA) of 1990 with NIPA in 2016 to try to encourage foreign investors to contribute more to the Namibian economy. Despite the minor differences between NIPA and FIA, the negative response to NIPA was enormous. For example, *Cronjé & Co.*, a law firm in Namibia who specialise in assisting private investors, wrote in their brief on NIPA that it "proposes [sic.] a very real threat to the current economic order in Namibia" (Cronjé & Co, n.d.2). Amongst their grievances were that NIPA empowers the Minister to reserve economic sectors either solely for the state or for Namibians and that it grants the state wide powers of expropriation, yet both provisions were actually already part of the FIA. On reserving economic sectors, the 1990 Act states that the Minister may "specify any business or category of business which... no foreign national shall... become engaged in" (Republic of Namibia, 1990a: 6). On expropriation, the Act states that "[w]here an enterprise... is expropriated, the Government shall pay to the holder of the Certificate just compensation" (*ibid.*: 12).

Meanwhile, Rowland Brown (2017: 3) stated that NIPA contains "anti-business clauses" and that it has "led to a loss of investor confidence in the country". The strong campaign against NIPA was successful. Even though the Act was promulgated in August 2016 it has

---

[24] Brown's twitter page is, for the most part, a stream of pro-free market statements and re-tweets.
[25] Interview with Rowland Brown, *IJG Securities* and Economic Association of Namibia. 13.1.2016.

still not been officially implemented, with the Government having been forced to withdraw and fundamentally review it following the public outcry.[26]

To conclude, the private sector in Namibia has been a stalwart of the status-quo, advocating effectively for the continuation of 'business-as-usual' and for limited government intervention in the economy. Leading economists, too, have been highly critical of Government, contributing to a palpable atmosphere of disdain towards the state. There is a racial element to the tension between the private sector and the state, with most of the leading members of the private sector white and most government officials black. The tensions are also a question of class. Colonial SWA was evidently a capitalist state ruled by white capitalists with a black working class. The end of the apartheid system in Namibia and South Africa can be interpreted as one of the only times in the 20th century that the Western powers endorsed the overthrow of the capitalist governing class and its replacement by a previously working class. That the white capitalist class has lost its ability to direct policy appears to fuel resentment, contributing to the unwavering criticism from the private sector of government economic policy. This matters for industrial policy. NIPA, the Retail Charter, and the export levy tax have all been undermined or watered down due to the influence of Namibia's lead economic actors.

So far this chapter's analysis has resembled something like a 'political settlements' analysis of constraints on industrial policy and development, arguing that "the distribution of power in society shapes the specific form of clientelist politics present in a developing country, and in turn, how variations in the organization of patron-client networks affect ruling elites' ability to change institutions governing the distribution of economic benefits in society" (Whitfield et al., 2015: 13). What is necessary is to extend analysis beyond occurrences solely within the Namibian state and society, and to look at the role that other countries and broad international phenomena play in industrial policy and development in the country. This should not be seen as a separate analysis. Rather, the point stressed is the interconnectedness between the domestic and the international.

The role of South Africa

Industrial development is often more difficult in countries with small populations, such as Namibia, with one of the major reasons being that it is harder for small countries to reach

---

[26] In October 2018 an official of MITSMED told the media that a new version of NIPA was ready and would be promulgated either at the end of 2018 or the start of 2019 (Nakale, 2018). Nevertheless, the statement was not widely reported or publicised, and opinion within Namibian civil society maintains that it is improbable that NIPA will be passed at all during 2019, particularly given that the country's general elections will take place in November 2019

high economies of scale in manufacturing production merely through production for the domestic market (Streeten, 1993; Briguglio, 1998). As such, on purely economic terms, it can be challenging for small countries to compete in the same market with larger ones. But the issue of large countries being able to outcompete smaller countries in their respective markets is not merely 'economic'. As this section demonstrates, in the case of the relationship between South Africa and Namibia, the former's political power has enabled it to limit Namibia's industrial development.

South Africa's economy dwarfs that of Namibia. Its GDP is nearly thirty times as large, and although South Africa's manufacturing sector has been declining markedly since the 1990s (Rodrik, 2006), its MVA is close to thirty times that of Namibia. Moreover, South African colonial rule and uninterrupted free trade between the countries since 1915 have left the economies extremely connected, with South Africa the largest export and import destination of Namibia. South African firms are prevalent throughout the Namibian economy, dominating the retail, banking, and fishing sectors. Namibian manufacturing firms have been struggling in the face of South African manufacturing competition since at least the 1930s, and the negative effects of competition from South Africa have continued to be extremely important for manufacturers in the independence era, according to surveys of the sector (Kadhikwa & Ndalikokule, 2007).

South Africa is most effectively able to exercise power in Namibia (and Southern Africa more broadly) through SACU, an organisation which South Africa has politically dominated ever since its creation in 1910. Chapter 3 discussed how apartheid-era South Africa jealously guarded the SACU market for its own manufactured goods and undermined industrial development efforts in Botswana, Lesotho, Swaziland and Namibia. As apartheid ended in Namibia and South Africa, the future of SACU was ambiguous, with Nelson Mandela having referred to the organisation as a "reflection of the colonial oppressor's mentality" (quoted in Gibb, 2006: 595). Nevertheless, efforts towards reform in the 1990s were painfully slow, and the familiar power dynamics of the region's economies continued, with South African firms, for example, obstructing efforts towards the establishment of car assembly plants in Botswana (Good & Hughes, 2002; Simon, 2003).

In Namibia, there are clear examples of the power of South African firms to undermine industrial development. The tendency during the colonial era of South African firms to undercut prices when Namibian firms attempted to produce a new product continued in the 1990s, with numerous instances of local firms being "forced to close following the dumping on the market of cheap South African goods" (Lee, 2003: 76).

Large-scale investments also failed to get off the ground because of South Africa's influence. For example, in the early 1990s *Citroen* were close to setting up a car assembly plant in Gobabis. As soon as plans for the plant emerged in 1990 the National Association of Automobile Manufacturers of South Africa began lobbying against its establishment, fearful of the competition that it would pose (Minney, 1991). SACU (whose external tariff rates are set by South Africa) already had a tariff of 110% on the import of cars not produced within the union, and in response to the prospect of the Gobabis plant being established SACU altered the definition of 'manufactured within SACU' in 1991 such that at least 75% of the car had to be made within the region for it to avoid paying the 110% duty (Minney, 1992). Consequently, it was reported that *Citroen* was left with little choice but to pull out, telling Namibia's MTI that "they could not see any way to come to Namibia under customs union regulations recently imposed by South Africa" (*ibid.*).

In view of the disparities in power within SACU, the union was finally reworked in 2002, with parties seeking to make it more democratic and equitable, such as by establishing a SACU secretariat and a joint tariff board (Gibb, 2006). Nevertheless, there remains a "profoundly unequal" relationship between South Africa and the other members (*ibid.*: 584), and efforts towards reform have continued to be slow (Kropohl & Fink, 2013; Erasmus, 2014). Tellingly, sixteen years later the SACU tariff board has still yet to be established, with a Namibian trade expert arguing that "certain of the structurers being provided for in the [2002] agreement are not yet set up because South Africa do not want them to be set up".[27] Tariffs in SACU continue to be largely dictated by South Africa, meaning that, just as in the 1990s, "Namibian firms in all sectors therefore suffer from a double disadvantage in that they get no protection from South African firms, but have to pay high tariffs on their extra-regional inputs (or above world prices for South African inputs) so as to protect South African firms" (Curry & Stoneman, 1993: 51). SACU is currently in a state of limbo, with South Africa unwilling or unable to radically change its structure.

As well as dominating the Namibian market, South Africa has also proved wary of Namibian firms penetrating its domestic market. For example, the Namibian pharmaceuticals firm *Fabupharm* has been unable to export its products to South Africa because South African regulation – despite purported free trade between Namibia and South Africa – stipulates that medical goods can only be imported through certain airports and harbours. The *Fabupharm* trucks have therefore been turned around at the South African-Namibian border.[28] Other firms, too, have complained of cumbersome regulations serving to effectively cordon off the South Africa market. The Managing Director of the Windhoek-based firm *Machine & Tool*, told me: "South Africa are very smart and crafty in finding loopholes within

---

27 Interview with Wallie Roux, Manager of Research and Development, *Namibia Agricultural Union*. 21.1.2016.
28 Interview with Fanie Badenhorst, Managing Director, *Fabupharm*. 21.1.2016.

the Customs Union", explaining that "it's just not cost-effective to get there [South Africa] because there is a lot of hidden detail... South Africans have designed [their regulations] in a way where it would almost take twenty-four months to get approval [to export] three lousy machines. To get all those approvals would probably cost N$1 million".[29]

The above has shown the negative impact of South African competition on industrial development in Namibia, with South African firms, typically via the regulatory and political support of the South African state, posing a major challenge to the emergence and expansion of Namibian firms. Moreover, established institutions concerning the relationship between Namibia and South Africa are helping to sustain Namibia's system of accumulation. The most fascinating element of the impact of SACU on Namibian industrialisation, for example, is how, via the 'revenue-sharing formula' described in chapter 4, South Africa is effectively paying the other SACU members *not* to develop industry and to accept the disparities between their economic structures and that of South Africa. It would take an incredibly bold leader to decide to walk away from SACU, and thereby forego the valuable additional revenue that it brings the state. The price to pay is unwavering competition from South African firms and the acceptance that trade policy is largely dictated by South Africa.

The actions of South African firms (and firms of other countries) can also have a direct impact on industrial policy implementation in Namibia. For example, Namibia has used infant industry protection (IIP) four times since independence (commencing in 2000 for milk, 2002 for pasta, 2012 for cement, and 2013 for poultry). However, on three of these occasions the Namibian Government has been taken to court – twice by groups of South African firms, once by a Chinese firm. In milk, once tariff protection had expired in 2012 the Namibian Government sought to impose a quota restriction on its import. In response, two South African dairy producers who export to Namibia appealed to the Namibian High Court, and in 2014 the court ruled in the firms' favour, on what appeared to be largely arbitrary grounds.[30] As one anonymous senior ranking member of staff within MITSMED told me, "only in Namibia would the Government lose a court case against a South African

---

29   Interview with Brian Christian, Managing Director, *Machine & Tool*. 16.2.2016.
30   The main reason for deeming the quota restriction invalid was that "[t]he Control of Importation and Exportation of Dairy Products and Dairy Products Substitutes Act of 1986, instead of the Import and Export Control Act of 1994, should have been used by the Minister of Trade and Industry if he wanted to place restrictions on the importation of dairy products into Namibia" (Menges, 2014). Additional reasons put forward by Judge Smuts were that the way the quota was imposed was improper because companies were not given proper opportunity to express their views prior to the quota system being implemented and that the decision had been made by the Namibian Government Cabinet when in terms of the law it should have been made by the MTI (*ibid.*).

company". As such, the dairy industry has seen all protection lifted and is floundering (New Era, 2017b).

In cement, it was a Chinese cement importer that took the Government to court when it introduced a tariff on cement, arguing that the Government had violated the Customs and Excise Act of 1998 (Sherbourne, 2016). This was indeed the case, but again on largely spurious grounds.[31] Judge Smuts – who was also to preside over the dairy case – ruled in favour of the company, and the tariff protection of the industry was revoked, with the Chinese import company able to import duty free (Menges, 2012).[32] Meanwhile, in poultry, the South African Poultry Association took the Namibian Government to court over its decision to impose a quota on the import of poultry, arguing that this "violated the Protocol to the SADC Agreement and also the SACU Agreement" (High Court of Namibia, 2016: 7). In this case, the court ruled in Namibia's favour, and to date Namibia continues to be allowed to enforce the quota.

The consequence of these time-consuming and costly court cases has been that the Government's willingness to use IIP – a device that featured notably in the Growth at Home strategy document – has visibly cooled.[33] As one Namibian trade expert put it, because of the court cases "the Government has lost its appetite for infant industry protection".[34] In interview, the Minister of Finance expressed to me his frustrations with the court proceedings:

> We assisted the poultry industry, we assisted the dairy industry, we assisted the cement industry, all of them ended up in court. So there is strong resistance, and that's the establishment that kicks back, that doesn't like what we aim at with transforming the economy.[35]

In this regard the actions of foreign firms have directly led to less industrial policy in Namibia, and it is unlikely that IIP will be used to any significant degree in Namibia again in the near future. Here again, we see how the likelihood of active industrial policy emerging being thwarted by the actions and interests of foreign actors.

---

[31] The company argued that when a tariff is introduced it must be promulgated in the Government Gazette by Government first, and then be tabled in the National Assembly, whereas in this case the Government first tabled the bill at the National Assembly (Menges, 2012).

[32] The case is ongoing, as it has been referred to the Namibian Supreme Court (The Southern Times, 2018).

[33] For example, it has recently been reported that a MITSMED member of staff "criticised" Namibia's IIP scheme, "saying the scheme never worked and questioned whether the protection granted was aimed at safeguarding specific industries or protecting monopolies" (The Southern Times, 2018).

[34] Interview with Wallie Roux, Manager of Research and Development, *Namibia Agricultural Union.* 21.1.2016.

[35] Interview with Calle Schlettwein, Minister of Finance of Namibia. 23.3.2016.

The international political economy of industrial policy and development in Namibia

What the preceding sections of this chapter have shown is the way that Namibia's system of accumulation contains an assortment of elements – be it the way in which SWAPO seeks to maintain its position of power, the resistance of the influential mining sector to increased value addition, or the power that South African firms (both based in Namibia and in South Africa) exert over Namibian policy – that stand as significant obstacles to the successful implementation of industrial policy and help to quell any motivation to pursue industrial policy to begin with. In this section I will point to the way that international ideologies and bodies have shaped and often further thwarted Namibia's efforts towards industrial development.

Firstly, on ideology. Governments' approaches to economic policy are affected by the prevailing ideological frameworks of the time. The 1990s was a perfect example, a decade which saw "the forging and embedding of an ideological, political and technical consensus both globally and with governing regimes in key developing countries" (Craig & Porter, 2006: 63). This consensus was around what Craig & Porter term 'embedded neoliberalism', wherein to foster development states should create an enabling environment (through e.g. practices of good governance) within which markets can flourish, but do little more. Ikpe (2014) has discussed the importance of the global dominance of neoliberal ideology in energising the change of approach from the Nigerian Government. And in Namibia, as was plainly shown in chapter 4, the Government's approach to industrial policy in the 1990s and 2000s was strongly shaped by this predominant discourse on developmental policy, most notoriously in the case of Namibia's EPZ scheme, with the Government's focus time and time again on the provision of an enabling environment.

It does not even matter whether these policies were 'right' or not. What matters is that the direction of industrial policy in Namibia, and with it the direction of industrial development, was being importantly influenced by global developments. Moreover, the process of Namibian policy mirroring global trends is not just a case of the Namibian Government benignly observing global trends and concluding 'yes, this is what is necessary to achieve economic development'. Rather, the late-20th and early 21st century saw the systemic and well-financed dissemination of an ideology committed to free markets as the panacea for development (Harvey, 2005), even when the rich nations espousing such ideologies had themselves achieved development via a highly interventionist approach to economic policy (Chang, 2003).

In Namibia, this dissemination was evidently taking place, particularly through the interventions from the likes of the World Bank and the IMF. In the 1990s these institutions, despite Namibia having never received a SAP, became "regular visitors to Namibia and 'assisted' with the country's public expenditure review and with 'training' high-ranking staff members of government economic institutions" (Jauch, 2007: 60). The Governor of the Bank of Namibia from 1997 to 2010 recalled in interview with me how high-income nations and international organisations would advise against industrial policy:

> There are people who say governments should not even bother to try and have industrial policy because it does not work, and that is the view you normally hear from the developed countries. When I was at the Bank of Namibia that argument would always be brought up by the IMF. People would boast 'we don't have those industrial policies and things are working for us, so why do you have them?'[36]

The great body of counsel being afforded to the newly independent Namibian state was advocating a free-market, business-enabling approach to economic development. As mentioned above local economists also unwaveringly subscribed to such an approach and advised Government accordingly. Here, the attitude of local economists is also linked to the international transmission of ideology, with many of Namibia's leading economists having been educated in the economics faculties of the universities of Europe and the Unites States, as well as South Africa, most of which had become bastions of neoliberal ideology from the 1970s onwards (Harvey, 2005).[37]

Particularly in the 1990s and 2000s, it is reasonable to conclude that the scope for Namibian industrial policy was constrained by the recommendations emanating from the rich countries of the world. As Jauch (2007: 60) argues, deviation from the neoliberal policy framework was "extremely difficult in the face of an onslaught by the neoliberal ideology that was usually portrayed as the only practical policy option for Namibia". Although Ikpe (2014: 557) is correct to point to examples of countries that have been able to "negotiate the stranglehold of neoliberalism" in forming their developmental policy, that these cases are in the minority is testament to the significant power of ideology and of those who wield it. The point to bear in mind is that it was indeed a *stranglehold*.

In reflecting on the importance of the diffusion of ideologies on industrial policy, it is pertinent to examine the change in Namibia's approach to industrial policy that occurred in the early 2010s. The emergence of purported active industrial policy was not solely occur-

---

[36] Interview with Tom Alweendo, Director-General of the National Planning Commission and former Governor of the Bank of Namibia. 27.1.2016.

[37] For example, Robin Sherbourne received his MSc in economics from LSE, whilst today's most prominent economist Rowland Brown received his MSc in economics from the University of Aberdeen. It is perhaps not coincidence that one of the leading proponents of active industrial policy in Namibia, Calle Schlettwein, was a student of natural history, not of economics (interview with Calle Schlettwein, Minister of Finance of Namibia. 23.3.2016).

ring in Namibia. Rather, as noted in chapter 1, in the late 2000s and early 2010s industrial policy was experiencing a "renaissance" (Wade, 2014: 2). Just as the absence of industrial policy in Namibia in the 1990s and 2000s coincided with an era of the "ideologically-motivated wilful neglect" of industrial policy, so too did the return of the subject in the 2010s reflect international changes (Chang & Andreoni, 2016: 3). Clearly, the Namibian Government's approach to industrial policy was being influenced by external forces.

But, importantly, even if a country changes its attitude to industrial policy institutional legacies can thwart actual change. The case of Namibia shows that once a free-market framework had been established, its institutional structure can become an impediment to industrial policy, even when the policy ambitions of the Government have changed. Constitutional acts designed to foster foreign investment and propagate the primacy of private sector privilege, such as the Foreign Investment Act of 1990 and the Competition Act of 2003, can continue to be used to defend the rights of investors and curtail the actions of the state. The example above, of how implementation of Namibia's 'Retail Charter' has been halted due to suspected violation of the Competition Act, is a case in point.

A further example is the attempt in early 2018 by the Government to repeal the EPZ Act of 1995. Following outcry from the two major mining operations benefiting from the act – the copper smelter in Tsumeb and the zinc refinery in Rosh Pinah – the Government was forced to backtrack just one week after the announcement, stating that EPZ companies would be able to retain their status. As written in a national newspaper, the CEO of the Chamber of Mines stated that, "the EPZ regime is a contractual document between government and the players which cannot be cancelled without the other party's consent" (quoted in Windhoek Observer, 2018). Namibia, it seems, has institutionally painted itself into a free-market corner due to the dictates of neoliberal development theory.

Moreover, during the recent era of marginally increased industrial policy efforts from the Namibian state, international institutions and agencies have proven obstacles to its implementation. An example is the international credit rating agencies, which have been highly influential in shaping countries' economic policies, because a downgrade from one of the three major credit rating agencies can have serious effects on the finances of a government by increasing the interest rate that they pay to borrow money (Hanusch et al., 2016). Whilst organisations such as the World Bank applaud the agencies' "positive role in emerging democracies around the world as private guardians of public fiscal discipline" (Hanusch & Vaaler, 2013: 8), others have raised concerns as to how the "sharp and narrow rationalities" of the agencies serve to constrain governments' policies (Craig & Porter, 2006: 65). For example, Elkhoury (2008: 11), writing for UNCTAD, has argued that agencies lead to countries favouring "orthodox policies focusing on the reduction of inflation and government budget deficits".

The influence of the credit rating agencies over economic policy in Namibia has been clear, with the agencies contributing to heavily reduced government spending in recent years, including on industrial policy. Namibia, as part of a trend in low-income countries globally (Hanusch et al., 2016), saw its public debt-to-GDP ratio grow greatly in the years after the global financial crisis due to countercyclical government spending.[38] In their roles as 'guardians of public fiscal discipline', the ratings agencies loomed ominously over the spending habits of Namibia. In 2015 Moody's warned that a downgrade could occur were Namibia's debt-to-GDP to continue to increase (Moody's, 2015), and in 2016 the firm changed Namibia's rating outlook to 'negative' – a step away from downgrading a rating (Moody's, 2016). Partially in response to these pressures (similar concerns were being voiced by Namibia's economists and financial sector[39]), the Namibian government launched massive budget cuts in 2016, but nevertheless in 2017 both Moody's and Fitch downgraded Namibia from 'investment grade' to 'non-investment grade' status (also known as 'junk' status).[40]

It is not just over the question of managing Namibia's debt-to-GDP ratio that the agencies sought to counsel. Like Namibia's private sector, Fitch was also critical of NIPA. In explaining Namibia's downgrade, the firm cited the "controversial provisions" within NIPA as "underscore[ing] the lingering policy risks" in the country, noting approvingly that the Act was likely to be significantly reworked and that this could have a favourable effect on Namibia's credit rating (quoted in Reuters, 2017).

Globally credit ratings agencies are playing an important part in shaping the policy choices of states, advocating a conservative approach to economic policy. In the case of Namibia, we can see their interventions to have contributed to the massive budget cuts that have left most of the industrial policy initiatives outlined in chapter 4 to be on hold, as well as to add further weight to calls for NIPA – a minor effort to increase the contribution of foreign investment to the national economy – to be fundamentally reformed.

A further example is the role that the EU has played in shaping Namibian industrial policy. Relations between the EU and Namibia over the past fifteen years have been centred around the free trade deals known as 'Economic Partnership Agreements' (EPAs) between the EU and African, Caribbean, and Pacific (ACP) countries. EPA negotiations were undertaken at the regional bloc level, with Namibia part of the long-winded negotiations between the EU and the Southern African Development Community (SADC) which eventually led to

---

[38] Namibia's public debt-to-GDP ratio increased from 16% in 2010 to 45% in 2018 (so admittedly from a very low starting base).

[39] See, for example, Brown (2015).

[40] Following the verdict, a team of Namibian Government Ministers futilely flew to London to meet with the agencies to contest the decision, testament to the influence of the agencies (Namibian Broadcasting Corporation, 2017).

the signing of an EU-SADC EPA in 2016. Whilst it has been claimed by the EU that EPAs will encourage industrialisation amongst ACP countries (European Commission, 2016), critics argue that EPAs will likely make industrial development much more challenging for these countries (Sanders, 2015).

In the late 2000s and early 2010s Namibia proved, despite pressure from its export industries such as meat, fish, and grapes (which rely on access to the EU markets), reluctant to sign the EPA. Minister of Trade and Industry Hage Geingob stated that the agreement would forfeit Namibia's right to use export taxes on raw materials to incentivise value addition and force the country to abandon infant industry protection and the country's horticultural marketing scheme (Melber, 2016).[41] In response to Namibia's hesitance, the EU trade negotiators "increased pressure on Namibia" by, for example, announcing in 2011 that if the SADC-EPA were not signed by 2014 then all preferential market access for SADC goods into the EU would come to an end, effectively crippling Namibia's food export industries (*ibid.*: 143).

Namibia, along with the rest of the SADC bloc, did eventually agree to sign the EPA. SADC had, however, successfully negotiated some policy space within the EPA, with SADC states permitted to deploy quantitative restrictions on EU imports, tariff protection (for eight years, with the possibility of extension), and the ability to apply export taxes (European Union, 2016). In the case of the EU-SADC EPA, Namibia was able to defend its right to deploy industrial policy, though not for want of trying, and manufacturing firms in Namibia will nevertheless likely struggle in the face of increased EU competition.

The EU has recently and in quite extraordinary ways exerted its authority over Namibian industrial policy by other means too. In December 2017, the EU published a list of 'non-cooperative jurisdictions for tax purposes' ('tax havens') as part of a bid to stamp down on the practice of firms offshoring profits. The original list comprised fifteen countries, most of which were those commonly cited as suspected tax havens. But a curious inclusion on the list was Namibia, a country which has never been accused of being a tax haven and which, by an understanding of a tax haven as being a jurisdiction that is purposefully used by international corporations to avoid paying taxes, is *not* a tax haven. As of June 2018, the list of non-cooperative jurisdictions has been reduced to seven, with Namibia still amongst its ranks (Council of the European Union, n.d.).

The reasons cited by the EU as to why Namibia was included on the list were that it is not signed up to certain international bodies that aim to maintain standards of tax regulation

---

[41]   In 2007 Namibia refused to sign an interim EPA, with the Prime Minister of Namibia calling the deal "imbalanced against African countries" (quoted in The Namibian, 2007), and the Deputy Minister of Trade and Industry stated that "we will continue negotiating on issues of concern to us like infant industry protection for our products and abolition of quantitative import restricts for EU goods into Namibia" (quoted in Weidlich, 2007).

and that Namibia has "harmful preferential tax regimes and did not commit to amending or abolishing them by 31 December 2018" (Council of the European Union, 2017: 10).[42] It transpired that the 'harmful preferential tax regimes' in question were Namibia's EPZ programme and its tax incentives for manufacturing firms. Minister of Finance Schlettwein initially suggested that Namibia would not give up its support for manufacturing firms just to be removed from the EU's list, stating that "it's wrong for Namibia as a sovereign state to be expected to make changes to its laws without taking its own interest into consideration" (quoted in Kaira, 2017).

However, the perceived damage to Namibia's reputation were it to remain on the EU's list, coupled with revenue constraints in Namibia, meant that in March 2018 Schlettwein, "bowing to pressure from the European Union", announced the termination of manufacturing incentives and the EPZ programme (Kahiurika, 2018). And whilst, as noted earlier in this chapter the Government reversed its decision on the EPZ Act due to pressure from the mining sector, general manufacturing tax incentives – the most significant piece of industrial policy deployed by the state in independent Namibia's history – is still intended to be withdrawn. Namibia may avoid a damaging reputation if it can successfully remove itself from the EU's list, but in return Namibia's ability to support manufacturing firms has been deeply eroded.

Conclusion: the absence of developmentalism in Namibia

The introduction to this research began by emphasising that for industrial policy to be successful requires high levels of commitment from the state to the achievement of structural transformation. It continued by stating that a country without such high levels of commitment would struggle to implement industrial policy because the pressures embedded within the country's system of accumulation would prove too great to overcome. This chapter has shown the workings of independent Namibia's system of accumulation and the manifold ways in which industrial policy has been thwarted by the distribution of power in Namibia and globally.

In my mind, these challenges are extremely difficult to overcome. The obstacles to industrial policy and development – be they the functioning of SWAPO's political system, the interests of Namibia's most influential economic actors, the actions of foreign firms, or the pressures exerted from international bodies – are multifaceted and inter-

---

[42] The international bodies are: the Global Forum on Transparency and Exchange of Information for Tax Purposes, the OECD Multilateral Convention on Mutual Administrative Assistance, and the anti-Base Erosion and Profit Shifting's minimum standards.

linked, creating and recreating a social order that it is difficult to rupture. And, as I have stated, to overcome "the mountains of routine and prejudice" present in a given system (Gerschenkron, 1962: 24) by successfully "generating and energizing human action" (Hirschman, 1958: 25) in the direction of development is crucially aided by the state really needing or wanting successful industrial policy to occur. In the case of Namibia, this commitment from the state is absent, and it is absent in large part because of how the system of accumulation in Namibia works. And I really mean 'works' – with independent Namibia having shown remarkable political, economic, and social stability, and the governing elites in a position of relative comfort.

The emergence of developmentalism is dependent in part on the very likelihood of developmental success (in a 'virtuous circle'). In my view, many of the obstacles identified above (such as the constant court cases against the use of IIP, the pressures from international credit rating agencies, or the consistent pantomime-uproar from the domestic private sector following more-or-less any policy action from the state) have crucially thwarted the emergence of increased developmentalism from the Namibian governing elites. Almost every direction that the state turns it faces organised resistance. It is true that a more committed state would be able to push back harder and more successfully override these conservative interests. But commitment in the first place, I argue, is becoming less likely to manifest itself because of how perilous the road to successful industrial policy and development is in Namibia.

The statement that 'Namibia has not industrialised because it has no significant industrial policy because the state is not committed to industrial development' is clearly unprovable. Commitment is so unquantifiable that it is impossible to scientifically test. I think it compelling, though, to reflect on the question of why Namibia decided to implement a re-energised industrial policy in the early 2010s, if all these pressures I have mentioned were so debilitating. As noted earlier in the chapter, part of the reason for the revival of industrial policy in Namibia was the global re-emergence of industrial policy at the time. As one member of staff at MITSMED told me, with a host of states and regional bodies launching industrial policy strategies at the time, "it would just be a bit embarrassing if we were left behind". This is clearly part of the explanation, but another crucial factor was explained to me by the Minister of Finance. When I asked him why there was a shift in Namibia's industrial policy the early 2010s, he responded:

> I think we realised that poverty... was not going away, it was persistent and perpetuated. And one could sense with the Arab Spring that we couldn't continue to live in a situation where the gap was widening, where those that 'have' continue to have more, and those that 'have not' perpetuate their poverty. Politically there grew impatience and pressure went up, and I think that this [issue of inequality] was becoming more

obvious when the novelty of being independent and politically free wore-off... [with] the realisation that 'wow we are not better off than we were before [independence]'.[43]

The Minister's response suggests that it was pressure that was driving the revival of industrial policy in Namibia, with the governing elites concerned that without marked economic progress the political stability of the region would prove to be a façade, as it had done in countries during the Arab Spring beginning in 2010. As has transpired, however, this perceived threat to the Namibian state was, whilst strong enough to help to induce the establishment of an active industrial policy framework and a recasting of the state's rhetoric towards economic development, not strong enough to lead to sustained and purposeful action from the state.

In this regard, the experience of Namibia can be seen to closely reflect that of South Africa. Here, since the mid-2000s the South African state has frequently self-identified as a developmental state – in what has been called by Satgar (2012: 39) a "declaratory developmental-state" – but has failed to follow its rhetoric with action, and accordingly "the general contours of neoliberal macro-economic management have not shifted" (*ibid.*: 38). Satgar's account stresses the influence of international bodies and contestation amongst the economic groups of South Africa in shaping and curtailing its forlorn commitment to state-led development, concluding that "[i]n short, the forces shaping the post-Apartheid state are not pushing it toward being a developmental state, despite the state's discourse" (*ibid.*: 39).[44] Clearly, the same is true of Namibia.

To conclude, this chapter has sought to provide insight into the political economy of industrial policy and development in independent Namibia. Drawing from interviews and primary documents, it has highlighted how power dynamics within the Namibian system of accumulation (a system which transcends state boundaries in its scope) works in such a way as to make it less likely that the state will become fully committed to an industrial development strategy because of how insurmountable the task appears and because of how effectively the prevailing system in Namibia works. This means that the cosmetic industrial policy issues (e.g. of poor management within MITSMED) persist. The chapter represents the most in-depth analysis of the politics of Namibia's industrial policy yet undertaken and an attempt to understand processes of industrial and economic development through a conceptualisation of the workings of the economic system, both at the national and international level.

---

[43]   Interview with Calle Schlettwein, Minister of Finance of Namibia. 23.3.2016.
[44]   Somewhat similar experiences have been identified in other countries, with Ban (2013: 298), for example, arguing that in Brazil the Government has "institutionalized a hybrid regime that layers economically liberal priorities originating in the Washington Consensus and more interventionist ones associated with neo-developmentalist thinking".

6 Conclusion

The ambition of this book has been to provide a thorough account of industrial policy, industrial development, and economic change in Namibia since 1900. It is the first work of its kind, uncovering the detail of manufacturing development in the country and interrogating the political economy dynamics of the sector's progress and changes in the economy at large. This has been achieved through extensive archival research, examination of government documents and secondary material, and the interviewing of close to one hundred people within the Namibian Government, the country's civil society, manufacturing sector, and the wider private sector.

I have argued that an important component of industrial policy success is how committed the governing elites are to the ambition of structural transformation and that, by extension, an important explanation of failure is that a given government is not wholly committed to the project of structural transformation. The integral point of analysis then becomes the reasons that a country is unable to adopt a 'developmental mindset', with two reasons identified in this research being how 'urgently' the achievement of structural transformation is perceived to be by a country's governing elites and how plausible the achievement of structural transformation is to begin with.

A further view taken has been that in understanding problems of industrial development it is essential to be cognisant of *international* power dynamics. More work must be done to understand how the transmission of ideologies, the make-up of international trade agreements, and the activities of foreign enterprises influence processes of structural transformation. Importantly, this is not just a question of identifying 'constraints' but is also a matter of understanding how the mindsets of governing elites are affected by these international phenomena. The interaction between the domestic and the international has been stressed.

With these conceptual points in mind, the work embarked on the assessment of Namibian industrial policy and development. Beginning with the 1900 to 1945 period in chapter 2, it documented the scant industrial development of the era, arguing that progress was most importantly hindered by the attitude of Namibia's governing elite and by trade relations with South Africa. Through the uncovering of trade data from 1920 to 1954, the work charted the changing of the Namibian economy. It also demonstrated the important role that the state was playing in said change – particularly aiding the karakul and dairy industries – supporting the view that the state must play a role in diversifying an economy and demonstrating that, were the Namibian state willing to support broad industrial development, it would have been able to do so.

The next period to be covered was 1946 to 1989, the final epoch of colonial rule in Namibia, in chapter 3. This era included the sole period of industrial boom in Namibia's history, from the late 1940s through to the 1960s, driven mainly, but not exclusively, by fish processing activities. It also chartered the demise of Namibia's dairy industry, the relative collapse of fish processing activities, and the emergence of meat processing from the late 1960s onwards. The lack of industrial policy deployed by the colonial state and the South African government in Namibia was emphasised, arguing that it was in the interest of South Africa to curtail industrial development in the country.

After over one hundred years of colonial rule Namibia achieved independence in 1990, and its fortunes in industrial progress from then until present day were the subject of chapter 4. Despite strong rhetorical commitment from the state to structural transformation in the 1990s, little was done to support firms. The most ambitious industrial policy was the EPZ Act of 1995, but the highly neoliberal approach to industrial development proved spectacularly unsuccessful, failing to encourage foreign investment. The 2010s witnessed a marked change in Namibian industrial policy, with the state proclaiming that, in contrast to its previous approach, it was now willing to embark on a project of state-led development. Nevertheless, as was shown, subsequent progress was disappointing, hamstrung by limited funding, a lack of coordination from the central Government, and issues within the state bureaucracy. All in all, the Namibian economy has changed very little since independence, and the manufacturing sector has been stagnant.

Finally, chapter 5 focused on the political economy of industrial policy and development in independent Namibia. It detailed how the nature of Namibia's system of accumulation served to undermine the emergence of a developmental mindset and progression in industrial policy. The nature of SWAPO's political system, the interests of Namibia's economic elites, the actions of South African states and companies, and international political economy factors such as the transmission of a neoliberal ideology by the likes of the World Bank and IMF and recent efforts from bodies such as international credit rating agencies to curtail state-intervention in the economy were highlighted.

In the introduction I stated that the key questions that the research wanted to answer were 'what industries have been able to develop in Namibia and why?' and 'has the Namibian state played a role in supporting industrial development and what explains its action or inaction?' As was argued in this research, the Namibian state has largely proved unwilling to deploy industrial policy because industrial development has never been an ambition of Namibia's economic elites and because the relative stability of country's system of accumulation has dissipated any developmental urgency. Industrial policy has been further limited by external influences, as was clearly the case during the colonial era and further in the independence era, where the actions of South Africa have continued to be of significance.

It has also been shown that the state has only proved willing to deploy targeted industrial policy when it has been of benefit of the country's prevailing elite to do so, as was the case with the dairy and then meat industries for the country's farmers during the 20th century, or when it was seen as a necessary means through which to preserve the prevailing political order, as was the case with the work of the FNDC in the 1970s and 1980s. Finally, the research demonstrated that the only manufacturing industries that have been able to develop in this context have been those producing high-volume, low-cost goods for the domestic market (such as soap, plastic packaging, paint, and beer) or firms who exploit their competitive advantage of being closer to the domestic market to differentiate themselves from foreign firms – this has been of particular relevance to firms in construction-related activities (e.g. window and door frames, metal products, and furniture).

Before drawing this research to a close, I would like to address one moral issue within the work which is particularly important to me, before highlighting some potential shortcomings in the piece.

On the first point, this research has supported the idea of 'developmentalism' and developmental states; of the need to have states actively involving themselves in the economy to encourage structural transformation. Kohli (2004) provides one of the most thought-through assessments of what developmental states have typically looked like.[1] He writes that they are characterised by "centralized and purposive authority structures that often penetrate deep into the society"; have "a close alliance with producer or capitalist groups" and typically deploy a "tight control of labor"; with a political approach that "has often been repressive and authoritarian" (*ibid.*: 11).[2] He notes that "for better or for worse, these states have... proved to be the most successful agents of deliberate state-led industrialization in peripheral countries" (*ibid.*: 11).

Kohli does not shy away from the often-painful reality of what these states have historically been like, and the failure to do this has frequently been an unsatisfactory omission from the development literature. For example, Mkandawire (2001: 310) stated that "the first few examples of development states were authoritarian. The new ones will have to

---

[1] Kohli (2004: 10) deliberately does not use the term 'developmental states' in his work, opting instead for "cohesive-capitalist states".

[2] His abrasive account goes as far as to say that in some instances these states have shared "some organizational and class characteristics with fascist states of interwar Europe and Japan" (Kohli, 2004: 11). In an earlier draft of the book, Kohli had actually used the term "neofascist states" rather than "cohesive-capitalist states" (*ibid.*: 10).

be democratic, and it is encouraging that the two most cited examples of such 'democratic developmental states' are both African – Botswana and Mauritius". It is safe to say that 'the first few' is an understatement and rather ignores the continuities between the various examples of developmental states in 19th and early 20th century Europe and North America and in East Asia in the late 20th century. Moreover, the idea of Botswana being either a democratic or a developmental state is contentious, particularly the latter.[3] Further, the oft-cited 'developmental states' of Africa today, Rwanda and Ethiopia, can be decried for their lack of political freedom, democracy, and respect of human rights.[4]

There appears to be a hope amongst writers who advocate for a more active role of the state that developmentalism can emerge without 'the nasty bits' evident in the history of successful state-led industrialisation. This is unsurprising, given that many of these writers are coming from a position where they see the injustices in the makeup of contemporary global capitalism and are seeking to in some way help to eradicate poverty and halt exploitation by fully-fledged capitalist states of those at the periphery. Or, as Selwyn (2016: 789) puts it, much of the developmental state approach's "popularity within development studies derives from its penetrating critique of … neoliberal axioms".

But is this possible? As Weiss and Hobson (1995: 250) state of developmentalism and democracy, "it would appear enormously difficult to combine the two before industrialization when the catch-up tasks of development are so very great. Not surprisingly, all second-wave industrialisers have made the transition under the auspices of an authoritarian regime". Amsden (1990: 18) similarly noted that "labour repression is the basis of late industrialization everywhere".

To the author, it is apparent that historically there has been no happy marriage between effective developmental strategy and immediate pro-poor, egalitarian policies within a democracy. The history of capitalist development, to paraphrase Hobbes, has been nasty, brutish and short, and, from the 19th century factories of Victorian England to the sweatshops of 21st China, industrial progress has occurred through the physical and emotional toils of the many for the benefit of the few. As Selwyn (2016: 790) has recently argued, the developmental state school, like the neoliberal school, views "workers as bearers of labour, to be managed, disciplined and exploited in order to yield economic surpluses for further investment."

As the author of this research, I must try to come to terms with these issues. Do I think that it is worth going through the pains of industrial development? Do I think that advanced capitalism is a worthy goal?

---

[3]   For a critique of the idea of Botswana as being democratic, see Good (2010). For a critique of the idea of Botswana as a 'developmental state", see Hillbom (2012).
[4]   For Ethiopia, see Clapham (2017); for Rwanda, see Mann & Berry (2016).

The position to which I resolved myself is that my answers to the above questions are both 'yes'. For me, all countries are already enmeshed within the global economic system, to varying degrees. This system involves the exploitation of labour and involves dominance and dispute between nations. It involves extreme poverty and inequality. But it is clear that the wealthiest countries in the world tend to have better systems of welfare, healthcare, less inequality, less violence, greater security, better treatment of women, and the like.[5] There is nothing necessarily ideal about it, but I think the advancement of capitalism (from a position of peripheral capitalism) is a good thing.

Moreover, I subscribe to the view that the establishment of 'democratic developmental states' is possible and what countries should aim to achieve (Kanyenze et al., 2017). Today, most countries of the world pursue industrial policy without the presence of what most commentators consider authoritarian or oppressive regimes, with Germany an exemplar of this. And, particularly in an age when automation will likely mean less people working in factories, the 'disciplining' of labour will become of diminished significance. In small countries like Namibia where, irrespective, labour-intensive manufacturing would be highly unlikely, successful industrial policy will not be about the subjugation of a citizenry but will be about the state actively fostering firms through supportive trade measures, financing, logistics, and investment in technological innovation. These policies can and should be achieved without oppression and in a democratic state.

On to the potential shortcomings of this work. Fine (2013) presented a good critic of the developmental state approach to studying economic development. His various points will not be repeated here, but suffice it to say that by including considerations of agricultural development, incorporating the impact of international factors, looking at earlier phases of industrial catch-up, looking beyond East Asia, not just seeking to critique neoliberalism, and providing a detailed case study of a country's 'systems of accumulation', most of Fine's criticisms have been avoided.[6] Nevertheless, I consider there to be two main potential shortcomings: too much analytic attention on manufacturing and the lack of obvious policy conclusions.

Did the research focus too much on manufacturing, when other sectors are also important to economic development? In defence, the research has always tried to be broad in its assessment of the economy – charting developments in mining, services, and particularly agriculture. And whilst the question of the relevance of the manufacturing sector to eco-

---

[5] For a presentation of the correlation between positive development indicators and export diversification in natural resource-rich countries, see Lebdioui (forthcoming).

[6] One that has not is the role of class, which has not featured in this research to any significant extent. This would no doubt disappoint Fine.

nomic development going into the mid-21st century is perhaps an open one, its importance in the 20th century, which is the subject of large parts of this research, is far less contentious. Moreover, my view is that manufacturing will continue to be important in fostering economic development in the future.

On the final issue, that this research does not lead to obvious policy conclusions, my view is that this is somewhat true, but not a critique. My ambition was to try to understand, rather than prescribe. That said, there are some possible policy prescriptions. Prospects of economic development advancing in low-income countries would be wholly improved were international organisations to firmly acknowledge the positive role that states can play in economic development. This would make it far harder for high-income countries to curtail policy space for low-income countries and, by increasing the 'space' for industrial development, increase the likelihood of more 'developmental' states emerging. Moreover, if state intervention to increase wealth in a country becomes what is expected from a citizenry, then greater pressure will be placed on states to be developmental, with increased urgency likely improving the prospects of advancement.

In 2016 Nobel Memorial Prize-winning economist Joseph Stiglitz visited Namibia, presenting to the Government and providing economic policy advice. Subsequently, Stiglitz co-authored an opinion piece with Anya Schiffrin which proclaimed that "Namibia shows that even countries that start with serious disadvantages – extremes of racism, colonialism, inequality, and underdevelopment – can chart a path toward shared prosperity. Its achievement deserves international recognition – and emulation" (Stiglitz & Schiffrin, 2016).

In many ways, Namibia does deserve to be praised for its economic and political stability and the comparatively strong protection of civil liberties. Nevertheless, progress, as acknowledged by most in the country and indicated in this research, has been relatively disappointing since independence. When I asked renowned Namibian journalist and anti-apartheid activist Gwen Lister for her views she responded thusly:

> I am in a little way disappointed for one reason. Because I believed if there is one country in Africa that could have made a success story, it was Namibia. And Nujoma told me that in 1981 when I interviewed him, he said 'I want Namibia to be the first success story in Africa', and those were his words, literally. And I said to myself, 'yeah, that's want I would like too'. For a country like ours... with a small population, if we cannot feed, house, clothe and educate those people, then it cannot happen anywhere. And that was my dream, and I think that is still what keeps me going. But I'm not going to see it, unfortunately it is not going to come true.[7]

---

[7]   Interview with Gwen Lister, founder of *The Namibian*. 22.3.2016.

As has been argued, there has been very little success in industrial policy and development in Namibia, for a host of very significant reasons. But this should not be read as indicating that there is no hope of substantive economic development in Namibia. So much depends on the attitude of the governing elite, and if civil society can help to entrench commitment to structural transformation from the state and draw attention to corrupt or wasteful activities, then change can happen. Change, moreover, can occur very quickly, as the sudden emergence of developmental states in the past is testament too. Success is possible; what is required is determination.

Maps

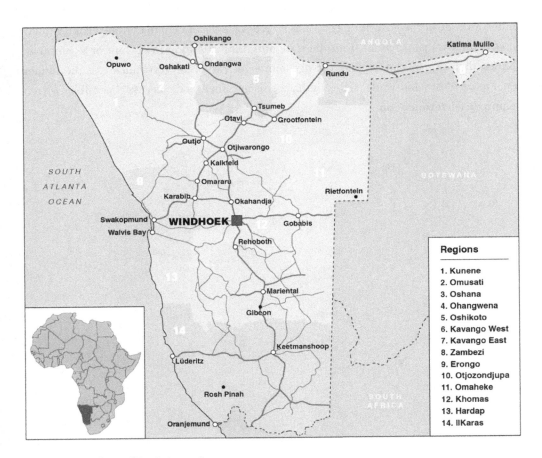

Map 1: Map of Namibia. © *James Pryor.*

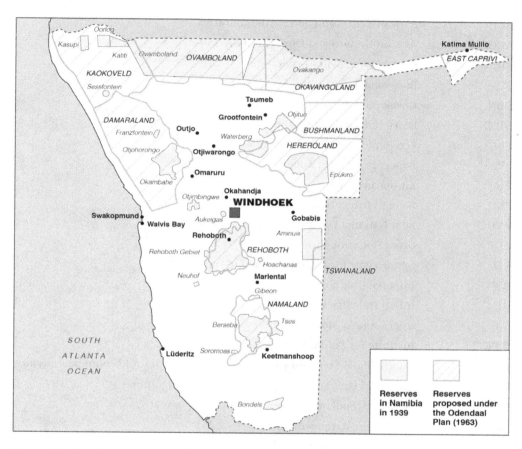

Map 2: The Namibian reserves under segregation and apartheid. Source: Wallace (2011),
© James Pryor.

List of Abbreviations

ACP	African, Caribbean and Pacific countries
AGOA	African Growth and Opportunity Act
BIC	Bantu Investment Corporation
BLS	Botswana, Lesotho and Swaziland
DBN	Development Bank of Namibia
DICB	Dairy Industry Control Board
EPA	Economic Partnership Agreement
EPZ	Export Processing Zones
EU	European Union
FDI	Foreign Direct Investment
FNDC	First National Development Corporation
GDP	Gross Domestic Product
GIZ	Gesellschaft für Internationale Zusammenarbeit
ICS	Imperial Cold Storage
IIP	Infant Industry Protection
IMF	International Monetary Fund
IPPR	Institute for Public Policy Research
ISIC	International Standard Industrial Classification of All Economic Activities
IUMP	Industrial Upgrading and Modernisation Programme
LSE	London School of Economics
MFA	Multi Fibre Arrangement
MITSMED	Ministry of Industrialization, Trade and SME Development
MSc	Master of Science
MTI	Ministry of Trade and Industry
MVA	Manufacturing Value Added
NDC	Namibia Development Corporation
NEPRU	Namibian Economic Policy Research Unit
NIC	Namibia Investment Centre
NIDA	Namibia Industrial Development Agency
NIE	New Institutional Economics
NIPA	Namibia Investment Promotion Act
NMA	Namibian Manufacturers Association

NPC	National Planning Commission
NTF	Namibia Trade Forum
ODC	Offshore Development Company
SAB	South African Breweries
SACU	Southern African Customs Union
SADC	Southern African Development Community
SME	Small and Medium-Sized Enterprise
SOE	State-Owned Enterprise
SWA	South West Africa
UN	United Nations
UNCTAD	United Nations Conference on Trade and Development
UNDP	United Nations Development Programme
UNECA	United Nations Economic Commission for Africa
UNIDO	United Nations Industrial Development Organization
UNIN	United Nations Institute for Namibia
WTO	World Trade Organization

List of Figures and Tables

Figures

Tables

Bibliography

Books, reports, and academic articles

Abebe, G. & Schaefer, F. 2016. "Review of Industrial Policies in Ethiopia: A Perspective from the Leather and Cut Flower Industries." In A. Noman & J. Stiglitz (eds.) *Industrial Policy and Economic Transformation in Africa*. Columbia University Press.

Acemoglu, D., Johnson, S., & Robinson, J.A. 2001. "The Colonial Origins of Comparative Development: An Empirical Investigation." *The American Economic Review* 91(5): 1369–1401.

Acemoglu, D., Johnson, S., & Robinson, J.A. 2004. "Institutions as the Fundamental Cause of Long-Run Growth." *NBER Working Paper* No.10481.

African Development Bank, United Nations Economic Commission for Africa, & the African Union Commission. 2017. *African Statistical Yearbook 2017*. Addis Ababa: ECA Printing and Publishing Unit.

Altenburg, T. 2011. "Industrial Policy in Development Countries: Overview and lessons from seven country cases." *German Development Institute* Discussion Paper 4/2011.

Altenburg, T. & Lütkenhorst, T. 2015. *Industrial Policy in Developing Countries: Failing Markets, Weak States*. Edward Elgar.

Amsden, A. 1989. *Asia's Next Giant: South Korea and Late Industrialization*. Oxford: Oxford University Press.

Amsden, A. 1990. "Third World Industrialization: 'Global Fordism' or a New Model?" *New Left Review* 1(182): 5–31.

Ashworth, W. 2017. *The Industrial Revolution: The State, Knowledge, and Global Trade*. London: Bloomsbury.

Austin, G. 2008. "The 'reversal of fortune' research and the compression of history: perspectives from African and comparative economic history." *Journal of International Development* 20(8): 996–1027.

Austin, G. & Broadberry, S. 2014. "Introduction: The renaissance of African economic history." *Economic History Review* 67(4): 893–906.

Austin, G., Frankema, E., & Jerven, M. 2017. "Patterns of Manufacturing Growth in Sub-Saharan Africa" in K.H. O'Rourke & J.G. Williamson (eds.) *The Spread of Modern Industry to the Periphery since 1871*, Oxford: Oxford University Press.

Baran, P. 1957. *The Political Economy of Growth*. New York: Monthly Review Press.

Behuria, P. 2017. "Learning from Role Models in Rwanda: Incoherent Emulation in the Construction of a Neoliberal Developmental State." *New Political Economy*.

Beilstein, J.C. 1982. "SWAPO's Political Economy and the Prospects for Development in Namibia After Independence." Paper to be presented at the conference on 'Namibia: Africa's Last Colony: Problems of Freedom and Development', University of Vermont, Burlington, April 5–6, 1982.

Bertelsmann Stiftung. 2014. *BTI 2014: Namibia Country Report*. Gütersloh: Bertelsmann Stiftung.

Bertelsmann Stiftung. 2016. *BTI 2016: Namibia Country Report.* Gütersloh: Bertelsmann Stiftung.

Bewersdorf, R. 1939. *Die Industrialisierung der Südafrikanischen Union und Deutsch-Südwestafrikas.* Berlin: Mier & Glasemann. Dissertation, University of Bonn.

Briguglio, L. 1998. "Small Country Size and Returns to Scale in Manufacturing." *World Development* 26(3): 507–515.

Brown, R. 2015. "The 2015/16 National Budget: Maxing out the credit card?" IPPR Democracy Report, Special Briefing No. 8, May 2015.

Brown, R. 2017. "The National Budget 2017–18: Prioritising Personnel." IPPR Democracy Report, Special Briefing No. 19, May 2017.

Bunting, B. 1972. "Namibia between the two wars: South Africa, the mandate and the League of Nations." Paper presented to the Namibia International Conference, Brussels.

Burlamaqui, L. Castro, A.C., & Chang, H-J. (eds.) 2000. *Institutions and the Role of the State.* Cheltenham, UK: Edward Elgar.

Cardoso, F. & Faletto, E. 1969. *Dependencia y desarrollo en América Latina: ensayo de interpretación sociológica.* México, Siglo Vientiuno Editores.

Cardoso, F. & Faletto, E. 1979. *Dependency and Development in Latin America.* Berkeley: University of California Press.

Chang, H-J. 2002. "Breaking the mould: an institutionalist political economy alternative to the neo-liberal theory of the market and the state." *Cambridge Journal of Economics* 26(5): 539–559.

Chang, H-J. 2003. *Kicking Away the Ladder: Development Strategy in Historical Perspective.* London: Anthem Press.

Chang, H-J. 2009. "Industrial Policy: Can we go beyond an unproductive confrontation? *World Bank: A plenary paper for ABCDE,* Seoul, South Korea, 22–24 June 2009.

Chang, H-J. 2011. "Institutions and economic development: theory, policy and history." *Journal of Institutional Economics* 7(4): 473–498.

Chang, H-J. & Evans, P. 2005. "The Role of Institutions in Economic Change." In G. Dymski & S. Da Paula (eds.) *Reimagining Growth.* London: Zed Press.

Chang, H-J. & Andreoni, A. 2016. "Industrial Policy in a Changing World: Basic Principles, Neglected Issues and New Challenges." *Cambridge Journal of Economics* 40 Years Conference.

Chang, H-J., Hauge, J., & Irfan, M. 2016. "Transformative Industrial Policy for Africa." Addis Ababa, Ethiopia: Economic Commission for Africa.

Chenery, H.B. & Taylor, L. 1968. "Development Patterns: Among Countries and Over Time." *The Review of Economics and Statistics,* 50(4): 391–416.

Christiansen, T. 2011. "Assessing Namibia's performance two decades after independence. Part I: Initial position, external support, regional comparison." *Journal of Namibian Studies* 10: 31–53

Christiansen, T. 2012. "Assessing Namibia's performance two decades after independence. Part II: Sectoral analysis." *Journal of Namibian Studies* 11: 29–61.

Cimoli, M., Dosi, G. & Stiglitz, J. (eds.) 2009. *Industrial Policy and Development: The Political Economy of Capabilities Accumulation.* Oxford: Oxford University Press.

Clapham, C. 2017. "The Ethiopian developmental state." *Third World Quarterly.*

Cleveland, T. 2014. *Stones of Contention: A History of Africa's Diamonds.* Ohio: Ohio University Press.

Coetzee, J.J. 2018. "The role of the private sector in tackling corruption." IPPR Briefing Paper. April 2018.

Collie, J. 1915. "Economic Position of D.S.W.A.: Report by Mr Collie." Namibia National Archives.

Collinson, S. (ed.) 2003. "Power, livelihoods, and conflict: case studies in political economy analysis for humanitarian action." *Overseas Development Institute* Humanitarian Policy Group Report No. 13.

Commonwealth Secretariat. 1994. "Namibia: Development of Small Scale and Informal Industries." Prepared by the Industrial Development Department, Export and Industrial Development Division. EIDD/1/ND/006. July 1994.

Cooper, I. 2012. *Parties, Factions and Votes: A comparative study of electoral politics in post-colonial Namibia.* University of Oxford: PhD research.

Council of the European Union. 2017. "The EU list of non-cooperative jurisdictions for tax purposes." Outcome of Proceedings from General Secretariat of the Council. 15429/17. Brussels, 5 December 2017.

Craig, D. & Porter, D. 2006. *Development Beyond Neoliberalism? Governance, poverty reduction and political economy.* London: Routledge.

Cronje, G. & Cronje, S. 1979. *The Workers of Namibia.* London: International Defence and Aid Fund for Southern Africa.

Curry, S. & Stoneman, C. 1993. "Problems of industrial development and market integration in Namibia." *Journal of Southern African Studies*, 19(1): 40–59.

Dieckmann, U. 2013: "Land, Boreholes and Fences: The Development of Commercial Livestock Farming in the Outjo District, Namibia." In Bollig et al. (eds.) *Pastoralism in Africa: Past, Present and Future.* Bergahn Books.

Dobell, L. 1998. *Swapo's Struggle for Namibia, 1960–1991: War by Other Means.* Basel: P. Schlettwein Publishing.

Dobler, G. 2014. *Traders and Trade in Colonial Ovamboland 1925–1990: Elite Formation and the Politics of Consumption under Indirect Rule and Apartheid.* Basel: Basler Afrika Bibliographien.

du Pisani, A. 1989. "Beyond the transgariep: South Africa in Namibia, 1915–1989." *Politikon* 16(1): 26–43.

Dundas, C. 1946. *South-West Africa: the factual background.* Johannesburg: The South African Institute of International Affairs.

Elkhoury, M. 2008. "Credit rating agencies and their potential impact on developing countries." UNCTAD *Discussion Papers* No.186. January 2008.

Erasmus, G. 2014. "Namibia and the Southern African Customs Union." In A. Bösl, A. du Pisani & D. Zaire (eds.) *Namibia's Foreign Relations.* Windhoek: Konrad Adenauer

Eriksen, T. & Moorsom, R. 1989. *The Political Economy of Namibia: An annotated critical bibliography.* Uppsala: Scandinavian Institute of African Studies in cooperation with United Nations Institute for Namibia and Norwegian Institute of International Affairs.

European Commission. 2016. "10 benefits of Economic Partnership Agreements (EPAs)." Directorate-General for Trade (European Commission). 28.11.2016.

European Union. 2016. "Economic Partnership Agreement between the European Union and its Members States, of the one part, and the SADC EPA States, of the other part." *Official Journal of the European Union* L 250/3. 16.9.2016.

Evans, P. 1995. *Embedded Autonomy: States and Industrial Transformation.* Princeton: Princeton University Press.

Ewing, A.F. 1968. *Industry in Africa.* London: Oxford University Press.

Feinstein, C. 2005. *An Economic History of South Africa: Conquest, Discrimination and Development.* Cambridge: Cambridge University Press.

Felipe, J. (ed.) 2015. *Development and Modern Industrial Policy in Practice: Issues and Country Experiences.* Edward Elgar Publishing.

Felipe, J., Mehta, A., & Rhee, C. 2018. "Manufacturing matters... but it's the jobs that count." *Cambridge Journal of Economics,* bex086.

Fine, B. 2013. "Beyond the developmental state: an introduction." In B. Fine, J. Saraswati, & D. Tavasci (eds.), *Beyond the developmental state: Industrial policy in the twenty-first century.* London: Pluto Press.

Flatters, F. & Elago, P.M. 2008. "Ramatex Namibia: Government Policies and the Investment Environment." US AID Southern Africa Global Competitiveness Hub, Contract No. 690-M-00-04-00309-00 (GS 10F-0277P).

Furtado, C. 1964 *Development and Underdevelopment.* Berkeley: University of California Press.

Gann, L.H. 1975. "Economic Development in Germany's African Empire, 1884–1914." In P. Duigan & L.H. Gann (eds.) *Colonialism in Africa 1870–1960 Volume 4: The Economics of Colonialism.* Cambridge: Cambridge University Press.

Geingob, H. 1992. "Namibia: One Year After Independence." In M.B. Schneider (ed.) *Namibia: Views and Perspectives Since Independence.* Windhoek: Konrad Adenauer-Stiftung & Namibia Institute for Democracy.

Gerschenkron, A. 1962. *Economic backwardness in historical perspective: a book of essays.* Cambridge, Mass: Belknap Press of Harvard University Press.

Gervasi, S. 1967. "The South West Economy." In R. Segal & R. First (eds.) *South West Africa: A travesty of trust.* London: Deutsch.

Gibb, R. 2006. "The New Southern African Customs Union Agreement: Dependence with Democracy." *Journal of Southern African Studies,* 32(3): 582–603.

Godana, T. & Odada, J.E. 2008. "A Case Study of Namibia." In B. Ndulu et al. (eds.) *The Political Economy of Economic Growth in Africa, 1960–2000. Volume 2: Country Case Studies.* Cambridge: Cambridge University Press.

Goldblatt, I. 1971. *History of South West Africa from the beginning of the nineteenth century.* Cape Town: Juta & Company Ltd.

Good, K. 2010. "The illusion of democracy in Botswana." In L. Diamond and M.F. Plattner (eds.) *Democratization in Africa: Progress and Retreat.* Baltimore: The John Hopkins University Press.

Good, K. & Hughes, S. 2002. "Globalization and Diversification: Two Case Studies in Southern Africa." *African Affairs* 101(402): 39–59.

Gray, H. 2013. "Industrial policy and the political settlement in Tanzania: aspects of continuity and change since independence." *Review of African Political Economy* 40(136): 185–201.

Green, R.H. 1970. "Political independence and the national economy: an essay on the political economy of decolonisation." In C. Allen & R.W. Johnson (eds.) *African Perspectives: Papers in the history, politics and economics of Africa presented to Thomas Hodgkin.* Cambridge: Cambridge University Press.

Green, R.H. 1979. "Namibia: A Political Economic Survey." *University of Sussex Institute of Development Studies,* DP No. 144.

Green, R.H. 1986. "The Liberation Struggle and the Economic Stagnation in Namibia." The Second Brussels International Conference on Namibia, Brussels, May 5th to May 7th, 1986.

Green, R.H. & Kiljunen, K. 1981. "The colonial economy: structures of growth and exploitation." In R.H. Green, M.L. Kiljunen, & K. Kiljunen (eds.) *Namibia: the last colony.* London: Longman.

Greenwald, B., & Stiglitz, J. 2013. "Learning and Industrial Policy: Implications for Africa." In J. Stiglitz et al. (eds) *The Industrial Policy Revolution II.* Basingstoke: Palgrave Macmillan.

Haggard, S. 2018. *Developmental States.* Cambridge: Cambridge University Press.

Hall, P. 1997. "The role of interests, institutions, and ideas in the comparative political economy of the industrialized nations" in Lichbach and Zuckerman (eds.) *Comparative Politics: Rationality, culture, and structure* (1997): 174–207

Hansohm, D. 1998. "Alternative paths for economic development in Namibia." Namibia Economic Policy Research Unit, Scientific paper for the research project 'Evaluating alternative paths for sustainable development in Botswana, Mozambique and Namibia'. February 1998.

Hansohm, D. 2000. "Industrialisation." In H. Melber (ed.) *Namibia: A Decade of Independence.* Namibia Economic Policy Research Unit Publication No.7.

Hansohm, D. 2007. "Research and Policy-Making: The Unique Experience of NEPRU in Namibia." In E.T. Ayuk & M.A. Marouani (eds.) *The Policy Paradox in Africa: Strengthening Links between Economic Research and Policymaking.* African World Press.

Hansohm, D. & Mupotola-Sibongo, M. 1998. "Overview of the Namibian Economy." Windhoek: Namibia Economic Policy Research Unit

Hanusch, M. & Vaaler, P.M. 2013. "Credit Rating Agencies in Emerging Democracies: Guardians of Fiscal Discipline?" World Bank Policy Research Working Paper 6379.

Hanusch, M., Hassan, S., Algu, Y., Soobyah, L., & Kranz, A. 2016. "The Ghost of a Rating Downgrade: What Happens to Borrowing Costs When a Government Loses its Investment Grade Credit Rating?" World Bank Group MFM Global Practice, Discussion Paper No.13. June 2016.

Haraguchi, N., Cheng, C.F.C., & Smeets, E. 2017. "The Importance of Manufacturing in Economic Development: Has This Changed?" *World Development* 93: 293–315.

Harrison, A.E., Lin, J.F., & Xu, L.C. 2014. "Explaining Africa's (Dis)advantage." *World Development* 63: 59–77.

Hartmann, P.W. 1988. "A statistical representation of the national accounts of South West Africa/Namibia for the period 1920 to 1987", in *Statistical/Economic Review: SWA/Namibia 1988,* South West Africa/Namibia Department of Finance.

Harvey, D. 2005. *A Brief History of Neoliberalism.* Oxford: Oxford University Press.

Hausmann, R. & Rodrik, D. 2006. 'Doomed to Choose – Industrial Policy as Predicament', mimeo., John F. Kennedy School of Government, Harvard University.

Henderson, H.J.R. 1960. "The Dairying Industry in South Africa." *Transactions and Papers (Institute of British Geographers)*, 28: 237–252.

Herrigel, O. 1971. *Studien zur Bevölkerungs- und Wirtschaftsentwicklung Südwestafrikas.* University of Basel: PhD research.

Hickel, J. 2016. "The true extent of global poverty and hunger: questioning the good news narrative of the Millennium Development Goals." In *Third World Quarterly* 37(5): 740–767.

Hillbom, E. 2012. "Botswana: A Development-Oriented Gate-Keeping State." *African Affairs* 111(442): 67–89.

Hirschman, A.O. 1958. *The Strategy of Economic Development.* New Haven: Yale University Press.

Hirschman, A.O. 1968. "The Political Economy of Import-Substituting Industrialization in Latin America." *The Quarterly Journal of Economics* 82(1): 1–32

Hobsbawm, E. 1962. *The Age of Revolution: Europe 1789–1848.* New York: Vintage Books.

Hopkins, A.G. "The New Economic History of Africa." *The Journal of African History* 50(2): 155–177.

Hopwood, G. 2007. *Guide to Namibian politics.* Windhoek: Namibian Institute for Democracy.

Hosono, A. 2016. "Industrial Strategy and Economic Transformation: Lessons from Five Outstanding Cases." In A. Noman & J. Stiglitz (eds.) *Industrial Policy and Economic Transformation in Africa.* Columbia University Press.

Hsu, J. 2017. "The developmental state of the twenty-first century: accounting for state and society." *Third World Quarterly.*

Ikpe, E. 2013. "Lessons for Nigeria from developmental states: The Role of Agriculture in Structural Transformation." In B. Fine, J. Saraswati, & D. Tavasci (eds.), *Beyond the developmental state: Industrial policy in the twenty-first century.* London: Pluto Press.

Ikpe, E. 2014. "The development planning era and developmental statehood: the pursuit of structural transformation in Nigeria." *Review of African Political Economy* 41(142): 545–560.

Innes, D. 1981. "South African capital and Namibia." In R.H. Green, M.L. Kiljunen, & K. Kiljunen (eds.) *Namibia: the last colony.* London: Longman.

Jauch, H. 2001. "Playing the Globalisation Game: The implications of economic liberalisation for Namibia." Research Report prepared by the Labour Resource and Research Institute (LaRRI). July 2001.

Jauch, H. 2006. "Africa's Clothing and Textile Industry: The Case of Ramatex in Namibia." In H. Jauch & R. Traub-Merz (eds.), *The Future of the Textile and Clothing Industry in Sub-Saharan Africa.* Bonn: Friedrich-Ebert-Stiftung.

Jauch, H. 2007. "Between politics and the shop floor: which way for Namibia's labour movement?" In H. Melber (ed.), *Transitions in Namibia: Which Changes for Whom?* Stockholm: Elanders Gotab AB.

Jauch, H. & Tjirera, E. 2017. "The Need for a Developmental State Intervention in Namibia." In G. Kanyenze et al. (eds.) *Towards Democratic Developmental States in Southern Africa.* Harare: Weaver Press.

Jerven, M. 2015. *Africa: Why economists get it wrong.* London: Zed Books.

Johnson, C. 1982. *MITI and the Japanese Miracle: The Growth of Industrial Policy, 1925–1975.* Stanford: Stanford University Press.

Jones, R.T. & Mackey, P.J. 2015. "An Overview of Copper Smelting in Southern Africa." 8th *Southern African Institute of Mining and Metallurgy* Southern African Base Metals Conference. Livingstone, Zambia. 6–8 July 2015.

Kaakunga, E. 1990. *Problems of Capitalist Development in Namibia: The Dialectics of Progress and Destruction.* Finland: Åbo Academy Press.

Kadhikwa, G. & V. Ndalikokule. 2007. "Assessing the Potential of the Manufacturing Sector in Namibia." *Bank of Namibia* Occasional Paper – 1/2007.

Kahuika, S., Stork, C., von Krosigk, V., & Shilimela, R. 2003. "Trade Assessment: Namibia and Angola." *NEPRU* Occasional Paper.

Kamarck, A.M. 1952. "The Economy and Development Plans of Southern Rhodesia." Economic development report no. E200. Washington D.C.: World Bank.

Kambonde, A., & Rena, R. 2014. "Foreign Direct Investment in the Retail Sector of Namibia: An Analysis." *J Economics* 5(1): 27–35.

Kamhulu, A.T. 2014. *Assessing the Usage of Infant Industry Protection Policy in Selected Manufacturing Industries of the Namibian Economy.* Polytechnic of Namibia Harold Pupkewitz Graduate School of Business: Master's research.

Kanyenze, G., Jauch, H., Kanengoni, A.D., Madzwamuse, M., & Muchena, D. (eds.) 2017. *Towards Democratic Developmental States in Southern Africa.* Harare: Weaver Press.

Khan, M. 2010. "Political Settlements and Governance of Growth-Enhancing Institutions." Unpublished manuscript, SOAS, London.

Kilby, P. 1975. "Manufacturing in Colonial Africa." In P. Duigan & L.H. Gann (eds.) *Colonialism in Africa 1870–1960 Volume 4: The Economics of Colonialism.* Cambridge: Cambridge University Press.

Klerck, G. 1997. "The prospects for radical social transformation." In G. Klerck et al. (eds), *Continuity and change: Labour relations in an independent Namibia.* Windhoek: Gamsberg Macmillan.

Klerck, G. 2008. "Industrial relations in Namibia since independence: Between neo-liberalism and neo-corporatism?" *Employee Relations* 30(4): 355–371.

Knowles, L. 1924. *The Economic Development of the British Overseas Empire, Volume I.* London: Routledge.

Knutsen, H.M. "Black Entrepreneurs, Local Embeddedness and Regional Economic Development in Northern Namibia." *The Journal of Modern African Studies* 41(4): 555–586.

Kohli, A. 2004. *State-directed development: Political power and industrialization in the Global periphery.* Cambridge: Cambridge University Press.

Kozul-Wright, R. & Rayment, P. 2007. *The Resistible Rise of Market Fundamentalism.* London: Zed Books.

Krogh, D. 1955. "Economic aspects of the karakul industry in South West Africa." *The South African Journal of Economics* 23(2): 99–113.

Krogh, D. 1960. "The national income and expenditure of South-West Africa (1920–1956). *The South African Journal of Economics* 28(2): 3–22.

Kropohl, S., & Fink, S. 2013. "Different Paths of Regional Integration: Trade Networks and Regional Integration: Trade Networks and Regional Institution-Building in Europe, Southeast Asia and Southern Africa." *Journal of Common Market Studies* 51(3): 472–488.

Lal, D. 1983. *The Poverty of 'Development Economics'.* London: The Institute of Economic Affairs.

Lall, S. 2000. "The Technological Structure and Performance of Developing Country Manufactured Exports, 1985–1998." *Oxford Development Studies* 28(3): 337–369.

Lau, B. & Reiner, P. 1993. *100 Years of Agricultural Development in colonial Namibia: a historical overview of visions and experiments.* Windhoek: Archeia.

Lebdioui, A. 2019. *Economic diversification in resource-rich countries: the role of industrial policy in Chile and Malaysia.* University of Cambridge: PhD research.

Lee, M. 2003. *The Political Economy of Regionalism in Southern Africa.* Cape Town: University of Cape Town Press.

Lee, M. 2014. *Africa's world trade: informal economies and globalization from below.* London: Zed Books.

Leftwich, A. 1995. "Bringing politics back in: Towards a model of the developmental state." *The Journal of Development Studies* 31(2): 400–427.

Leistner, E. 1980. *Namibia/SWA Prospectus.* Pretoria: Africa Institute of South Africa.

Lin, J. & Chang, H-J. 2009. 'Should industrial policy in developing countries conform to comparative advantage or defy it? - A debate between Justin Lin and Ha-Joon Chang, *Development Policy Review* 27(5): 483–592.

Lin, J. & Monga, C. 2013. "Comparative Advantage: The Silver Bullet of Industrial Policy." In Stiglitz et al. (eds.) *The Industrial Policy Revolution II.* Hampshire: Palgrave Macmillan.

Links, F. 2018. "Procurement Tracker Namibia." *IPPR*, Issue No. 1. July 2018.

Maasdorp, G. 1982. "The Southern African customs union – an assessment." *Journal of Contemporary African Studies* 2(1): 81–112.

Mann, L. & Berry, M. 2016. "Understanding the Political Motivations That Shape Rwanda's Emergent Developmental State." *New Political Economy* 21(1): 119–144.

Mbuende, K. 1986. *Namibia, the broken shield: Anatomy of imperialism and revolution.* Malmö: Liber.

McMillan, M., Rodrik, D., & Verduzco-Gallo, I. 2014. "Globalization, Structural Change, and Productivity Growth, with an Update on Africa." *World Development* 63: 11–32.

Melber, H. (ed.). 2000. *Namibia: A Decade of Independence 1990–2000.* Windhoek: Namibia Economic Policy Research Unit Publication No.7.

Melber, H. (ed.). 2007a. *Transitions in Namibia: Which Changes for Whom?* Stockholm: Elanders Gotab AB.

Melber, H. 2007b. "Poverty, politics, power and privilege: Namibia's black economic elite formation." In H. Melber (ed.), *Transitions in Namibia: Which Changes for Whom?* Stockholm: Elanders Gotab AB.

Melber, H. 2011. "Namibia: a trust betrayed – again?" *Review of African Political Economy* 38(127): 103–111.

Melber, H. 2014. *Understanding Namibia: The Trials of Independence.* UK: C.Hurst & Co. Publishers Ltd.

Melber, H. 2015. "Integration of the industrialisation agenda in the national development strategy: Lessons from Namibia." In F. Matambalya (ed.) *African Industrial Development and European Union Co-operation: Prospects for a reengineered partnership.* London: Routledge.

Melber, H. 2016. *A Decade of Namibia: Politics, Economy and Society, The Era Pohamba, 2004–2015.* Leiden; Boston: Brill.

Mkandawire, T. 2001. "Thinking about developmental states in Africa." *Cambridge Journal of Economics* 25: 289–313.

Mkandawire, T. 2010. "From maladjusted states to democratic developmental states in Africa". In O. Edigheji (ed.) *Constructing a Democratic Developmental State in South Africa: Potentials and Challenges.* Cape Town: HSRC Press.

Mkandawire, T. 2015. "Neopatrimonialism and the political economy of economic performance in Africa. Critical Reflections." *World Politics* 67(3): 563–612.

Moorsom, R. 1982. *Transforming a wasted land.* London: Catholic Institute for International Relations.

Moorsom, R. 1984. *Exploiting the sea.* London: Catholic Institute for International Relations.

Moorsom, R. 1990. *Namibia's Economy at Independence: Report on Potential Norwegian-Namibian Industrial Cooperation.* Bergen: Chr. Michelsen Institute, Department of Social Science and Development

Myrdal, G. 1968. *Asian Drama: An Inquiry into the Poverty of Nations.* New York: Twentieth Century Fund.

Newman, C., Page, J., Rand, J., Shimeles, A., Söderbom, M., & Tarp, F. 2016. "The Pursuit of Industry." In Newman et al. (eds.), *Manufacturing Transformation: Comparative Studies of Industrial Development in Africa and Emerging Asia.* A study prepared for the UN University World Institute for Development Economics Research. Oxford: Oxford University Press.

Noman, A. & Stiglitz, J. 2016. *Industrial Policy and Economic Transformation in Africa.* Columbia University Press.

North, D.C. 1990. *Institutions, Institutional Change, and Economic Performance.* New York: Cambridge University Press.

Oqubay, A. 2015. *Made in Africa. Industrial Policy in Ethiopia.* Oxford: Oxford University Press.

Ovadia, J. & Wolf, C. 2017. "Studying the developmental state: theory and method in research on industrial policy and state-led development in Africa." *Third World Quarterly.*

Page, J. 2009. "Africa's Growth Turnaround: From Fewer Mistakes to Sustained Growth." *Commission on Growth and Development*, Working Paper No.54.

Page, J. 2012. "Can Africa Industrialise?" *Journal of African Economies* 21 (AERC supplement 2): ii86-ii125.

Page, J. & Tarp, F. (eds.) 2017a. *The Practice of Industrial Policy: Government-Business Coordination in Africa and East Asia.* Oxford: Oxford University Press.

Page, J. & Tarp, F. 2017b. "Overview and Insights." In J. Page & F. Tarp (eds.) *The Practice of Industrial Policy: Government-Business Coordination in Africa and East Asia.* Oxford: Oxford University Press.

Palma, G. 2008. "De-industrialization, 'premature' de-industrialization and the Dutch Disease." In S.N. Durlauf and L.E. Blume (eds.), *The New Palgrave Dictionary of Economics.* New York: Palgrave Macmillan.

Paterson, B., Kirchner, C., & Ommer, R.E. 2013 "A Short History of the Namibian Hake Fishery – a Social-Economic Analysis." *Ecology and Society* 18(4): 66.

Perkins, D.H. & Syrquin, M. 1989. "Large countries: the influence of size." In H.B. Chenery & T.R. Srinivasan (eds.) *Handbook of Development Economics, Vol.II.*

Phimister, I. 1988. *An economic and social history of Zimbabwe 1890–1948: Capital accumulation and class struggle.* London and New York: Longman Press.

Phimister, I. 2000a. "The Origins and Development of Manufacturing in Southern Rhodesia, 1894–1939." In A. Mlambo et al. (eds.) *Zimbabwe: A History of Manufacturing 1890–1995* Harare: University of Zimbabwe.

Phimister, I. 2000b. "From Preference Towards Protection: Manufacturing in Southern Rhodesia, 1940–1965." In A. Mlambo et al. (eds.) *Zimbabwe: A History of Manufacturing 1890–1995* Harare: University of Zimbabwe.

Rawlinson, J. 1994. *The Meat Industry of Namibia, 1835–1994.* Gamsberg Macmillan.

Reinert, E. 2007. *How rich countries got rich... And why poor countries stay poor.* London: Constable.

Ricz, J. 2017. "The rise and fall (?) of a new developmental state in Brazil." *Society and Economy* 39: 85–108.

Rijneveld, A.W. 1977. "Economic Exploitation: The Case of Namibia." Report prepared at the request of SWAPO. Rotterdam, March 1977.

Robinson, J. 2009. "Industrial Policy and Development: A Political Economy Perspective." Paper prepared for the 2009 World Bank ABCDE conference, Seoul June 22–24 2009.

Rocha, I.L. 2018. "Manufacturing as driver of economic growth." *PSL Quarterly Review,* 71(285): 103–138.

Rodrik, D. 2004. "Industrial Policy for the Twenty-First Century." UNIDO Working paper.

Rodrik, D. 2006. "Understanding South Africa's Economic Puzzles." Center for International Development at Harvard University. CID Working Paper No.130. August 2006.

Rodrik, D. 2014. "An African growth miracle?" *NBER* Working Paper 20188.

Rodrik, D., McMillan, M., & Sepúlveda, C. 2016. "Structural Change, Fundamentals, and Growth" in M. McMillan, D. Rodrik, & C. Sepúlveda (eds.), *Structural Change, Fundamentals and Growth: A Framework and Case Studies.*

Rosendahl, C. 2010. "Industrial Policy in Namibia." *German Development Institute* Discussion Paper 5/2010.

Sanders, R. 2015. "The EU, Economic Partnership Agreements and Africa." *The Round Table: The Commonwealth Journal of International Affairs* 104(5): 563–571.

Satgar, V. 2012. "Beyond Marikana: The Post-Apartheid South African State." *African Spectrum* 47(2–3): 33–62.

Schade, K. 2016. "What are the benefits of a second cement plant in Namibia?" *Economic Association of Namibia.* July 2016.

Schade, K. 2017. "Economic progress since Independence." *Economic Association of Namibia.* Published in Windhoek Observer, Independence Day supplement.

Schneider, G. 2009. *Treasures of the diamond coast: A century of diamond mining in Namibia.* Windhoek: Macmillan Education Namibia.

Selwyn, B. 2016. "Elite development theory: a labour-centred critique." *Third World Quarterly* 37(5): 781–799.

Selwyn, P. 1975. *Industries in the Southern African Periphery: A Study of Industrial Development in Botswana, Lesotho, and Swaziland.* London: Croom Helm.

Sherbourne, R. 2016. *Guide to the Namibian Economy 2017.* Windhoek: IPPR.

Shimada, G. 2016. "The Economic Implications of a Comprehensive Approach to Learning on Industrial Policy: The Case of Ethiopia." In A. Noman & J. Stiglitz (eds.) *Industrial Policy and Economic Transformation in Africa.* Columbia University Press.

Siboleka, M., Nyamba, J.M., & Osterkamp, R. 2014. "Agriculture and Manufacturing Sector Growth in Namibia During the Period 1981 to 2012: A Granger Causality Test." *British Journal of Economics, Management & Trade* 4(11): 1700–1707.

Silvester, J. 1998. "Beasts, Boundaries & Buildings: The Survival & Creation of Pastoral Economics in Southern Namibia 1915–35." In Hayes et al. (eds.), *Namibia under South Africa Rule: Mobility & Containment 1915–46.*

Simon, D. 2003. "Regional Development-Environment Discourses, Policies and Practices in Post-Apartheid South Africa." In J. Grant & F. Söderbaum (eds.), *The New Regionalism in Africa.*

Smit, P.G. & Rushburne, J.L. 1971. "A survey of the fishing industry in South Africa and South West Africa." Statsinform, Nedbank Group, Survey No.4.

Smith, C. 1993. "Overview – The Second Industrial Development Decade for Africa – Country Report for Namibia". Prepared for the Ministry of Trade and Industry with support from UNDP and UNIDO.

SNL Metals & Mining. 2014. "Beneficiation Possibilities for Namibia's Minerals: For Joint Value Addition Committee."

Sparks, D. & Murray, R. 1985. "Namibia's Future: The Economy at Independence." The Economist Intelligence Unit Special Report No.197.

Stiglitz, J. & Lin, J. (eds.) 2013. *The Industrial Policy Revolution I: The Role of Government Beyond Ideology.* Palgrave Macmillan.

Stiglitz, J., Lin, J., & Patel, E. 2013a. *The Industrial Policy Revolution II: Africa in the 21st Century.* Palgrave Macmillan.

Stiglitz, J., Lin, J., & Monga, C. 2013b. "The Rejuvenation of Industrial Policy." World Bank Policy Research Working Paper 6628.

Streeten, P. 1993. "The Special Problems of Small Countries." *World Development* 21(2): 197–202.

Sunkel, O. 1969. "National Development Policy and External Dependence in Latin America." *The Journal of Development Studies* 6(1): 23–48.

Sutcliffe, R. 1967. "The Economic Relationship with South Africa." In R. Segal & R. First (eds.) *South West Africa: A travesty of trust.* London: Deutsch.

Swanson, M. 1967. "South West Africa in trust, 1915–1939." In Gifford & R. Louis (eds.) *Britain and Germany in Africa.* New Haven/ London: Yale University Press.

SWAPO. 1981. *To Be Born A Nation: The Liberation Struggle for Namibia.* Department of Information and Publicity, SWAPO of Namibia. London: Zed Press.

SWAPO. 1989. "SWAPO Election Manifesto." Available at: https://sadcblog.files.wordpress.com/2012/05/swapo-1989-manifesto-namibia.pdf [accessed 16.8.2018].

Szirmai, A. 2011. "Manufacturing and Economic Development." UNU-Wider *Working Paper No. 2011/75.*

Thomas, W. 1978. *Economic Development in Namibia: Towards Acceptable Development Strategies for Independent Namibia.* Munich: Kaiser-Grünewald.

Thomas, W. 1983. "Economic Prospects." In C. Saunders (ed.) *Perspectives on Namibia: Past and Present.* Centre of African Studies, University of Cape Town, Occasional Papers No.4/1983.

Thomas, W. 1985. "Prospects for industrial development in Namibia." In *RP Congress 1985, SWA Economy*.

Thurbon, E. 2016. *Developmental Mindset: The Revival of Financial Activism in South Korea*. Cornell University Press.

Thurbon, E. & Weiss, L. 2016. "The Developmental State in the Late Twentieth Century." In E. Reinert, J. Ghosh, & R. Kattel (eds.) *Handbook of Alternative Theories of Economic Development*. Cheltenham: Edward Elgar.

Toye, J.F.J. 1993. *Dilemmas of Development: Reflections on the Counter-Revolution in Development Economics*. Oxford: Blackwell.

Tregenna, F. 2008. "The Contributions of Manufacturing and Services to Employment Creation and Growth in South Africa." *South African Journal of Economics* 76(S2): 175–204.

Tribe, M. 2000. "A review of recent manufacturing sector development in sub-Saharan Africa." In H. Jalilian, M. Tribe, & J. Weiss (eds.) *Industrial Development and Policy in Africa: Issues of De-Industrialisation and Development Strategy*. Cheltenham, UK: Edward Elgar

Troadec, J.P., Clark, W.G, & Gulland, J.A. 1980. "A review of some pelagic fish stocks in other areas." *P-V. Réun. Cons. int. Explor. Mer* 177: 252–277.

UN General Assembly. 1966. "Question of South West Africa." Twenty-first Session, 27 October 1966. A/RES/2145.

UNCTAD. 2016. "Namibia: Trade Policy Framework." United Nations Publication, UNCTAD/DITC/TNCD/2016/2.

UNECA. 2014. "Dynamic Industrial Policy in Africa: Economic Report on Africa." Addis Ababa: United Nations Economic Commission for Africa.

UNIDO. 1984. "Industrial Development Programme for Independent Namibia: Preliminary Report." United Nations Industrial Development Organisation.

UNIDO. 1990. "Namibia: Industrial development at independence." United Nations Industrial Development Organisation Industrial Development Review Series.

UNIDO. 1994. "Namibia: New avenues for industrial development." United Nations Industrial Development Organisation Industrial Development Review Series.

UNIDO. 2017. "Industrial Development Report 2018: Demand for Manufacturing: Driving Inclusive and Sustainable Industrial Development." United Nations Industrial Development Organization.

UNIN. 1986. *Namibia: Perspectives for National Reconstruction and Development*. Lusaka: United Nations Institute for Namibia

United Nations. 1957. "Report of the Committee on South West Africa." General Assembly Official Records: Twelfth Session, Supplement No.12 (A/3636).

United Nations. 2008. "International Standard Industrial Classification of all Economic Activities (ISIC), Rev.4." UN Department of Economic and Social Affairs: Statistics Division. Statistical Papers Series M No.4/Rev.4. New York: United Nations.

van der Hoog, T. 2016. *Brewing Identity: Beer and the establishment of the Namibian nation*. African Studies Centre, Leiden University: Master's research.

van Rensburg, B. 1989. "South West Africa/Namibia: Post Independence Economic Implications for South Africa." Special study for the Association of Chambers of Commerce and Industry of South Africa.

Wade, R. 1990. *Governing the Market: Economic Theory and the Role of Government in East Asian Industrialization*. Princeton: Princeton University Press.

Wade, R. 2014. "Industrial Policy – better, not less". *UNCTAD Trade and Development Board Sixty-first session.* Geneva, 15–26 September 2016.

Wade, R. 2018. "The Developmental State: Dead or Alive?" *Development and Change* 49(2): 518–546.

Wallace, D.F. 2005. *Consider the Lobster and Other Essays.* New York: Little Brown.

Wallace, M. 2011. *A History of Namibia: From the Beginning to 1990.* London: Hurst & Company.

Weiss, L. & Hobson, J.M. 1995. *States and Economic Development: A Comparative Historical Analysis.* Cambridge: Polity Press.

Wellings, P. & Black, A. 1986. "Industrial Decentralisation in South Africa: Tool of Apartheid or Spontaneous Restructuring?" *GeoJournal* 12(2): 137–149.

White, L.J. 2008. "Antitrust Policy and Industrial Policy: A View from the U.S." REG-Markets Center, Working Paper 08–04.

Whitfield, L. & Buur, L. 2014. "The politics of industrial policy: ruling elites and their alliances." *Third World Quarterly,* 35,1: 126–144.

Whitfield, L., Therkildsen, O., Burr, L., & Kjær, A.M. 2015. *The Politics of African Industrial Policy: A Comparative Perspective.* Cambridge: Cambridge University Press.

Williams, M. (ed.). 2014. *The End of the Developmental State?* London: Routledge.

Winterfeldt, V. 2007. "Liberated economy? A case study of Ramatex Textiles in Namibia." In H. Melber (ed.), *Transitions in Namibia: Which Changes for Whom?* Stockholm: Elanders Gotab AB.

Witulski, U. 1985. "Namibia's Development Constraints." *Working paper.* Available at: http://www.villacarmen.de/reports/Namibias_development_constraints.pdf [accessed 15. 8.2018].

Wood, B. (ed.). 1988. *Namibia 1884–1984: Readings on Namibia's history and society.* Lusaka: United Nations Institute for Namibia.

World Travel Tourism Council. 2017. "Travel & Tourism: Economic Impact 2017 Namibia." Available at: https://www.wttc.org/-/media/files/reports/economic-impact-research/countries-2017/namibia2017.pdf [accessed 16.8.2018].

WTO. 2015. "Trade Policy Review: Southern African Customs Union (Namibia, Botswana, Swaziland, South Africa and Lesotho)". WT/TPR/S/324.

Zinn, P.D. 1985. "Industrial Growth in Namibia: Theoretical Perspectives and Empirical Evidence." Essay submitted in partial fulfilment of examination requirements for the degree of B.A. (Hons.) Economics. University of Cape Town.

Government documents (Namibia, South West Africa, and South Africa)

Administration of SWA. 1980. "Budget 1980/81." *On the Economic Front.* Windhoek: Department of Finance, June 1980.

Administration of SWA. 1981. "White Paper on the Activities of the Different Branches for 1981." *SWA Administration for Whites.*

Administration of SWA. 1982. "White Paper on the Activities of the Different Branches for 1981." *SWA Administration for Whites.*

Administration of SWA. 1983. "White Paper on the Activities of the Different Branches for 1981." *SWA Administration for Whites.*

Agricultural Policy Commission. 1949. "Report of the Long Term Agricultural Policy Commission." Windhoek: John Meinert Ltd.

Department of Governmental Affairs. 1987. "The National Development Strategy of South West Africa." Directorate: Development Co-ordination. Windhoek.

Development Bank of Namibia. 2017. "Transforming Namibia: Annual Report 2017." Available at: http://www.dbn.com.na/index.php/investors-relations/annual-reports [accessed 16.8.2018].

DICB. 1956. "Annual Report of the Dairy Industry Control Board for the year ended the 30th September, 1956." Windhoek.

Economic Advisory Committee. 1978. "The Economy of SWA/Namibia: Problems, Future Prospects, and Required Policy Measures." *Report of the Economic Advisory Committee of His Excellency the Administrator-General of SWA/Namibia, January 1978,* Department of Finance.

FNDC. 1983. "ENOK in Perspective." First National Development Corporation of SWA Ltd. Windhoek: John Meinert Press.

FNDC. 1985. "Seven Years of Economic Development in SWA by the FNDC." First National Development Corporation of SWA Ltd. Windhoek: John Meinert Press.

FNDC. 1986. "FNDC Annual Review 1985–86." First National Development Corporation of SWA Ltd. Windhoek: John Meinert Press.

FNDC. 1989. "Annual Report 1989." First National Development Corporation of SWA Ltd. Windhoek: John Meinert Press.

FNDC & Department of Economic Affairs. 1989. "Namibia: Development and Investment." Compiled by the First National Development Corporation and the Department of Economic Affairs.

High Court of Namibia. 2016. "South African Poultry Association & 5 others v The Minister of Trade and Industry and 3 Others." NAHCMD 199 (A 325/2015). 8 July 2016.

Hirsekorn, H. 1935. "Minority Report by Dr. Hirsekorn." In Union of South Africa, *Report of the commission on the economic and financial relations between the Union of South Africa and the mandated territory of South West Africa.* Pretoria: Government Printer.

Ministry of Labour/Central Bureau of Statistics. 1998. "The Namibia Labour Force Survey 1997: An Interim Report of Analysis." October 1998.

Ministry of Trade and Industry. 1993. *Namibia: Manufacturing Guide 1992/3.* Windhoek: Industrial and Technical Information Division, Ministry of Trade and Industry.

Ministry of Trade and Industry. 1994. "National Industrial Statistics: Report of Census of Manufacturing Establishments 1994/95." *Republic of Namibia.*

Ministry of Trade and Industry. 1996. *Business Guide to Namibia.* Namibia Investment Centre, Ministry of Trade and Industry.

Ministry of Trade and Industry. 1998. *A Guidebook for Manufacturers in Namibia.* Windhoek: The Industrial Development Directorate.

Ministry of Trade and Industry. 2000. "Annual Report 2000." Windhoek: Ministry of Trade and Industry.

Ministry of Trade and Industry. 2001. "Annual Report 2001." Windhoek: Ministry of Trade and Industry.

Ministry of Trade and Industry. 2009a. "Annual Report 2008/2009." Windhoek: Ministry of Trade and Industry.

Ministry of Trade and Industry. 2009b. "National Enterprise and Establishment Census 2009." Windhoek: Industrial Development, Ministry of Trade and Industry.

Ministry of Trade and Industry. 2010. "Action Plan – Projects (MTI 2010)." Positioning Namibia in the Global Economy, Volume II. Windhoek: Ministry of Trade and Industry.

Ministry of Trade and Industry. 2012a. "Namibia's Industrial Policy." *Republic of Namibia.*

Ministry of Trade and Industry. 2012b. "Annual Report 2012." Windhoek: Ministry of Trade and Industry.

Ministry of Trade and Industry. 2013. "Annual Report 2012/13: Growth at Home." Windhoek: Ministry of Trade and Industry.

Ministry of Trade and Industry. 2014. "Annual Report 2013/14: Growth at Home." Windhoek: Ministry of Trade and Industry.

Ministry of Trade and Industry. 2015. "Growth at Home: Namibia's Execution Strategy for Industrial Development." Windhoek: Ministry of Trade and Industry.

MITSMED. 2016. "Annual Report 2015/16: Growth at Home." Windhoek: Ministry of Industrialization, Trade and SME Development.

MITSMED. 2017a. "Annual Report 2016/17: Growth at Home." Windhoek: Ministry of Industrialization, Trade and SME Development.

MITSMED. 2017b. "Strategic Plan 2017–22." Windhoek: Ministry of Industrialization, Trade and SME Development.

Namibia Department of Economic Affairs. 1989. "Manufacturing Industry Survey 1989." *South West Africa Administration.*

Namibia Statistics Agency. 2013. "The Namibia Labour Force Survey Report 2012." Windhoek: Namibia Statistics Agency.

Namibia Statistics Agency. 2014. "The Namibia Labour Force Survey Report 2013." Windhoek: Namibia Statistics Agency.

Namibia Statistics Agency. 2015. "The Namibia Labour Force Survey Report 2014." Windhoek: Namibia Statistics Agency.

Namibia Statistics Agency. 2017. "The Namibia Labour Force Survey Report 2016." Windhoek: Namibia Statistics Agency.

Namibian Agronomic Board. 2016. "Annual report 2015/16, 1 April 2016 – 31 March 2016." No.29.

Ollikainen, T. 1991. "Study on Wood Consumption in Namibia." Windhoek: Directorate of Forestry, Government of Namibia.

Report of the Administrator. Various years, 1919–1946. "Report presented by the Government of the Union of South Africa to the Council of the League of Nations concerning the Administration of South West Africa." Cape Town/Pretoria: Government Printer.

Republic of Namibia. 1990a. *Foreign Investment Act.* Government Gazette 28 December 1990, No.129.

Republic of Namibia. 1990b. *The Constitution of the Republic of Namibia.* Government Gazette 21 March 1990, No.2.

Republic of Namibia. 1992. "White Paper on Industrial Development". Ministry of Trade and Industry.

Republic of Namibia. 1993a. "Estimate of Revenue and Expenditure for the Financial Year ending 31st March 1993." State Revenue Fund Presented to Parliament.

Republic of Namibia. 1993b. "Special Incentives for Manufacturing Enterprises." Ministry of Trade and Industry.

Republic of Namibia. 1993c. "Namibia Development Corporation Act 18 of 1993." Government Gazette 30 August 1993, No.702.

Republic of Namibia. 1995. "Promulgation of Export Processing Zones Act, 1995 (Act 9 of 1995), of the Parliament." Government Gazette of the Republic of Namibia, 18th April 1995.

Republic of Namibia. 1996. "National Accounts 1981–1996." *Central Statistics Office/ National Planning Commission.*

Republic of Namibia. 1998. "National Accounts 1983–1998." *National Bureau of Statistics/ National Planning Commission.*

Republic of Namibia. 2000. "National Accounts 1993–2000." Central Bureau of Statistics/ National Planning Commission.

Republic of Namibia. 2004. "Namibia Vision 2030: Policy Framework for Long-Term National Development." Office of the President. Windhoek: Namprint.

Republic of Namibia. 2006. "National Accounts 1996–2006." Central Bureau of Statistics/ National Planning Commission.

Republic of Namibia. 2008. "Estimate of Revenue and Expenditure for the Financial Year ending 31st March 2008." State Revenue Fund Presented to Parliament.

Republic of Namibia. 2011. "National Accounts 2000–2011." National Statists Agency.

Republic of Namibia. 2012a. "Estimate of Revenue and Expenditure for the Financial Year ending 31st March 2012." State Revenue Fund Presented to Parliament.

Republic of Namibia. 2012b. "National Accounts 2002–2012." National Statists Agency.

Republic of Namibia. 2013. "Namibia 2011: Population & Housing Census Main Report." Namibia Statistics Agency.

Republic of Namibia. 2015. "Estimates of Revenue, Income and Expenditure 01 April 2015 to 31 March 2018."

Republic of Namibia. 2016a. "Promulgation of Act of Parliament No. 9 of 2016: Namibia Investment Promotion Act, 2016." Government Gazette of the Republic of Namibia, 31st August 2016.

Republic of Namibia. 2016b. "Estimates of Revenue, Income and Expenditure 01 April 2016 to 31 March 2019."

Republic of Namibia. 2016c. "Export Levy Act 2 of 2016." Government Gazette 20 June 2016, No. 6042.

Republic of Namibia. 2016d. "Annual National Accounts 2016." Namibia Statistics Agency.

Republic of Namibia. 2017. "Preliminary Annual Nationals Accounts 2017." Namibia Statistics Agency. Windhoek.

Republic of Namibia. 2018. "Estimates of Revenue, Income and Expenditure 2018 to 31 March 2021."

Republic of Namibia. Various Years. "Annual National Accounts." Namibia Statistics Agency. Windhoek.

Republic of South Africa. 1964. "Report of the Commission of Enquiry into South West Africa Affairs 1962–1963." Pretoria/Cape Town: Government Printer.

Republic of South Africa. 1967. "South West Africa Survey 1967." *Department of Foreign Affairs.* Cape/Pretoria: Government Printer.

Republic of South Africa. 1968. "South-West Africa Constitution Act 39 of 1968." Pretoria/Cape Town: Government Printer.

Republic of South Africa. 1974. "South West Africa Survey 1974." *Department of Foreign Affairs.* Cape/Pretoria: Government Printer.

Republic of South Africa. 1978. "Executive Powers (Industries) Transfer Proclamation, AG 5 of 1978." Pretoria/Cape Town: Government Printer.

Republic of South Africa. 1980. "SWA Statistics in Brief 1980." *Department of Statistics.* Pretoria: Government Printer.

Schlettwein, C. 2015. "Statement by Hon. Calle Schlettwein, Minister of Trade and Industry, on the Growth at Home Strategy, Namibia's Execution Strategy for Industrialisation in the National Assembly, on Tuesday 17 February 2015." Republic of Namibia.

SWA Department of Finance. 1988. "Statistical/Economic Review: SWA/Namibia 1988." Windhoek.

SWA Department of Finance. 1990. "Statistical/economic review Namibia 1990." Windhoek.

Union of South Africa, 1915. *Memorandum of the Country known as German SWA.* Pretoria: Government Printer.

Union of South Africa, Department of Customs and Excise. Various Years (1921–1954). "Annual Statement of Trade and Shipping, Union of South Africa."

Union of South Africa. 1935. "Report of the commission on the economic and financial relations between the Union of South Africa and the mandated territory of South West Africa." Pretoria: Government Printer.

Union of South Africa. 1952. "Report of the Commission of Inquiry into the Financial Relations between the Union and South West Africa 1951." Pretoria: The Government Printer.

Newspaper and magazine articles

Amupadhi, T. 2004. "Pidico ghost walks again." *The Namibian,* 12.11.2004.

Bhagwati, J. 2010. "The Manufacturing Fallacy." *Project Syndicate.* Available at: https://www.project-syndicate.org/commentary/the-manufacturing-fallacy?barrier=accessreg [accessed 20.8.2018].

Brandt, E. 2017. "Recovering diamond market could result in more cutting and polishing factories." *New Era,* 24.2.2017.

Cemnet. 2018. "Cheetah Cement to commence operations in Namibia." Available at: https://www.cemnet.com/News/story/163184/cheetah-cement-to-commence-operations-in-namibia.html [accessed 16.8.2018].

Collins, G.G. 1971. "Future Trends in the Economy of South West Africa." In *South West Africa Annual 1971*, p. 71–77.

Davis, N. 1953. "A Peep Behind the £1,000,000 Pilchard Paradise in Walvis Bay" in *South West Africa Annual 1954*, p. 57–61

Duddy, J-M. 2011a. "Industrial policy wake-up call." *The Namibian*, 22.11.2011.

Duddy, J-M. 2011b. "Economics export briefs Cabinet on development." *The Namibian*, 25.11.2011.

Duddy, J-M. 2012. "Mammoth task awaits Schlettwein." *The Namibian*, 7.12.2012.

Grynberg, R. 2017. "Namibia's industrialisation policy is not succeeding – Why?" *The Namibian*, 1.9.2017.

Hamata, M. 2013. "Tenderpreneurs and nepotism selling out our soul." *Confidente*, 25.4.2013. Available at: http://www.confidente.com.na/2013/04/tenderpreneurs-and-nepotism-selling-out-our-soul/ [accessed 16.8.2018].

Hamutenya, M. 2017. "Namibia's lucrative grape industry – who really benefits?" *New Era*, 21.9.2017.

Insight Namibia. 2013. "Kicking over the traces." Available at: http://www.insight.com.na/kicking-over-the-traces/ [accessed 16.8.2018].

Insight Namibia. 2014a. "Book review: Economics: The User's Guide by Ha-Joon Chang." Available at: http://insightnamibiamagazine.blogspot.com/2014/11/book-review-economics-users-guide-by-ha.html [accessed 21.8.2018].

Insight Namibia. 2014b. "Clients not citizens." Available at: http://www.insight.com.na/clients-not-citizens/ [accessed 21.8.2018].

Insight Namibia. 2016a. "Cabinet Scorecards 2016." Available at: http://www.insight.com.na/cabinet-scorecards-2016/ [accessed 16.8.2018].

Insight Namibia. 2016b. "Waiting to Launch." Available at: http://www.insight.com.na/waiting-to-launch/ [accessed 16.8.2018].

Isaacs, D. 2008. "Ramatex's exit 'an embarrassment'" *The Namibian*, 11.3.2008.

Jauch, H. 2008. "The Ramatex Closure in Namibia: Hard Lessons To Be Learned." *The Namibian* 14th March 2008.

Kahiurika, N. 2017. "Fines for wildlife crimes too high – MPs." *The Namibian*, 7.8.2017.

Kahiurika, N. 2018. "Namibia to scrap preferential tax." *The Namibian*, 8.3.2018.

Kaira, C. 2016. "Arandis drum factory revived." *The Namibian*, 24.2.2016.

Kaira, C. 2017. "Namibia resists EU manufacturing incentives calls." *Windhoek Observer*, 8.12.2017.

Kamati, T.K. 2018. "The difference between entrepreneur and tenderpreneur." *New Era*, 8.6.2018.

Lardner-Burke. J.D. 1924. "The Union and South West." *Windhoek Advertiser*, 5.25.1924, p.2

Lister, G. 2016. "Political Perspective." *The Namibian*, 1.7.2016.

Melber, H. 2013. "Namibia and the Economic Partnership Agreement." *Pambazuka News*. Available at: https://www.pambazuka.org/governance/namibia-and-economic-partnership-agreement [accessed 16.8.2018]

Menges, W. 2012. "Setback for Govt on cement import tariffs." *The Namibian*. 3.9.2012.

Menges, W. 2014. "Court sets aside dairy import limits." *The Namibian*. 19.5.2014.

Menges, W. 2017. "Arrested Chinese businessman gets bails of N$1 million." *The Namibian*, 2.2.2017.

Menges, W. 2018. "Enquiry ordered into SME Bank collapse." *The Namibian*, 20.2.2018.

Minney, T. 1991. "Major battle for Citroen hits top gear." *The Namibian*. 8.7.1991.

Minney, T. 1992. "Citroen deal OFF." *The Namibian*. 24.3.1992.

Moody's. 2015. "Moody's affirms Namibia's Baa3 government bond rating; outlook stable." Available at: https://www.moodys.com/research/Moodys-affirms-Namibias-Baa3-government-bond-rating-outlook-stable–PR_341556 [accessed 16.8.2018].

Moody's. 2016. "Moody's changes outlook on Namibia's Baa3 rating to negative, affirms rating." Available at: https://www.moodys.com/research/Moodys-changes-outlook-on-Namibias-Baa3-rating-to-negative-affirms–PR_357255 [accessed 16.8.2018].

Nakale, A. 2018. "Revised Investment Promotion Act to be promulgated." *New Era*, 24.10.2018.

Nakashole, N. 2016. "Schlettwein says SOEs need serious reforms." *The Namibian*, 1.3.2016.

Nakashole, N. 2017. "Ngatjizeko talks up SME Bank achievements." *The Namibian*, 20.4.2017.

Namibia Economist. 2012. "Lender to small business withers." 21.9.2012. Available at: https://economist.com.na/2771/special-focus/lender-to-small-business-withers/ [accessed 16.8.2018].

Namibia Economist. 2017. "Is the economy healthy or is it not?" Posted by Daniel Steinmann. 3.2.2017. Available at: https://economist.com.na/22180/editors-desk/is-the-economy-healthy-or-is-it-not/ [accessed 21.8.2018].

Namibian Broadcasting Corporation. 2017. "Sparks fly as Moody's meet Namibian ministers in London." 9.8.2017. Available at: http://www.nbc.na/news/sparks-fly-moody%E2%80%99s-meet-namibian-ministers-london.12911 [accessed 16.8.2018].

Nembwaya, H. & Shivute, O. 2014. "Hilundwa and his best friend, Ya Toivo," *The Namibian* 22.8.2014.

New Era. 2017a. "Tax evasion rife among business – Schlettwein." 15.11.2017.

New Era. 2017b. "DPA honours dairy producers." 25.7.2017.

Reuters. 2017. "Fitch Downgrades Namibia to 'BB+'; Outlook Stable." 20.11.2017. Available at: https://www.reuters.com/article/fitch-downgrades-namibia-to-bb-outlook-s-idAF-Fit7CcD1f [accessed 16.8.2018].

Sasman, C. 2012. "State's role in economy debated." *The Namibian*. 15.11.2012.

Shikongo, A. 2018. "Will Swapo's Socialism Come to 'Mixed Economy' Namibia?" *The Namibian*, 21.8.2018.

Shipale, P.T. 2012. "Developmental state: The politics & economics of nation building." Available at: http://www.swapoparty.org/developmental_state.html [accessed 16.8.2018].

South West Africa Annual. 1946. "A Brief Survey of South West Africa's 'Unprecedented Financial Prosperity'", p.81–83.

South West Africa Annual. 1951. "A New Vital Industry Comes to S.W.A.", p.65. Windhoek: South West Africa Publications.

South West Africa Annual. 1973. "SWA Statistical Summary", p.123–129. Windhoek: South West Africa Publications.

South West Africa Annual. 1976. "Economic Development in the South West African Homelands: The Role of the Bantu Investment Corporation.", p.45–47. Windhoek: South West Africa Publications.

Stiglitz, J. & Schiffrin, A. 2016. "Learning from Namibia." *Project Syndicate.* Available at: https://www.project-syndicate.org/commentary/namibia-economic-social-success-story-by-joseph-e–stiglitz-and-anya-schiffrin-2016-06?barrier=accesspaylog [accessed 24.8.2018].

Swilling, R. 2017. "Chimney hunting in Namibian countryside." *Gondwana Collection Namibia.* Available at: https://www.gondwana-collection.com/news/article/2017/08/03/chimney-hunting-in-the-namibian-countryside/ [accessed 16.8.2018].

The Namibian. 2007. "PM disappointed over trade partnership." 11.12.2007.

The Patriot. 2017. "Namibia's tenderpreneurship dynasty on its knees." Available at: https://thepatriot.com.na/index.php/2017/05/26/namibias-tenderpreneurship-dynasty-on-its-knees/ [accessed 16.8.2018].

The Southern Times. 2018. "Namibia's infant industry protection in limbo." Available at: https://southerntimesafrica.com/site/news/namibias-infant-industry-protection-in-limbo [accessed 21.8.2018].

Weidlich, B. 2007. "Nam signs EU trade deal." *The Namibian,* 14.12.2007.

Windhoek Chamber of Commerce. 1924. "Petition from the Windhoek Chamber of Commerce to General Hertzog", published in the *Windhoek Advertiser,* 8.9.1924.

Windhoek Observer. "Relief for manufacturers." 16.3.2018.

Webpages

CIA. n.d. "The World Factbook: Country Comparison: Distribution of Family Income – Gini Index." Available at: https://www.cia.gov/library/publications/the-world-factbook/rankorder/2172rank.html [accessed 16.8.2018].

Cirrus. n.d. "Rowland Brown: Co-Founder." Available at: https://cirrus.com.na/team/ [accessed 21.8.2018].

Council of the European Union. n.d. "Taxation: EU list of non-cooperative jurisdictions." Available at: http://www.consilium.europa.eu/en/policies/eu-list-of-non-cooperative-jurisdictions/ [accessed 16.8.2018].

Cronjé & Co. n.d.1. "Investing in Namibia." Available at: http://www.cronjelaw.com/investing [accessed 16.8.2018].

Cronjé & Co. n.d.2. "Namibian Law." Available at: http://www.cronjelaw.com/namibian-law [accessed 16.8.2018].

Kraatz Engineering. n.d. "Proud History." Available at: http://kraatz.com.na/KraatzEngineering.php [accessed 14.8.2018].

UNDP. n.d. "Namibia: Human Development Indicators." Available at: http://hdr.undp.org/en/countries/profiles/NAM [accessed 16.8.2018].

Datasets

Namibia Statistics Agency. 2018. "National Accounts Time Series 1980–2016." Dataset available at: https://nsa.org.na/page/publications/ [accessed 13.2.2018].

UN Comtrade. 2018. *International Trade Statistics Database.* Dataset available at: https://comtrade.un.org/ [accessed 23.8.2018].

World Bank. 2018. *World Development Indicators.* Dataset available at: https://data.world-bank.org [accessed 23.8.2018].

Archival documents

National Archives of Namibia

NAN NAO 71 32/9, Native Customs and Practices: Manufacturing and Sale of Basket Ware. 20/8/1947 – 3/11/1954.

NAN NAO 78 32/9, Letter Rodent Inspector to Native Commissioner, 12 July 1948.

NAN NAO 103 68/3 (v1), Industries Ovamboland. Meat canning.

NAN NAO 103 68/3 (v3), Industries Ovamboland. Carpet making.

NAN SWAA 0277 A29/2, Industrial Censuses, 1919–1926.

NAN Correspondence IMW 62 A44/1/3/19, Establishment of a Diamond Cutting Industry in S.W.A. 1950–57

British Library

BL OGS.270 No. 1278, Official Gazette of South West Africa, 1947–1968.

Index

A

Agriculture 2f., 14f., 30f., 34, 43, 46f., 50, 58, 67, 81, 89, 114f., 125, 155

B

Beverages 3, 24, 43, 50, 58, 62, 77, 115, 120

C

Cement Production 37, 58, 77, 100, 108, 116, 120–123, 141f., 172, 179f.
Construction sector 63, 96, 124, 163
Copper mining 14, 22, 30f., 53, 69, 72, 99, 112, 115f., 120f., 145

D

Dairy production 3, 15, 21, 24, 30, 36, 38, 40–44, 52f., 56f., 59, 61f. 68, 71, 73–75, 82, 88, 134, 141f., 151–153, 180f.
Development Bank of Namibia (DBN) 102, 110, 160
Diamond mining 14, 22, 24, 30, 37, 55f., 89, 112
Diamonds, cutting and polishing 63f., 79, 99, 116, 121f.

E

Economic Partnership Agreements (EPA) 102, 146f., 160, 166
Export Processing Zones (EPZ) 96f., 99f., 102f., 143, 145, 148, 152, 160
Exports 2, 18, 22, 24, 31–36, 38–43, 45, 50, 54–61, 72, 74, 77, 79, 98, 112, 114f., 117, 119f., 123f., 135, 162

F

Farming 3, 12, 21–24, 27–29, 34f., 46f., 60, 75, 79, 86
Fish processing 41, 121
First National Development Corporation (FNDC) 75f., 80–82, 85, 95, 153, 160, 176
Food production 3, 21, 24f., 36–39, 43, 49f., 52, 58f., 62f., 66, 72, 76f., 88, 115, 120, 147
Foreign direct investment (FDI) 6, 94, 98f., 160
Fruit and vegetables 79, 116
Furniture production 3, 38, 45f., 49, 58, 63, 72, 81f., 124, 153

I

Imperial Cold Storage Company 30, 42, 60, 160
Imports 23, 32, 39, 44–46, 48, 50f., 99, 122, 147, 162
Industrial development 1–4, 8–11, 14f., 17, 19–21, 35, 43–45, 47–50, 52f., 56, 68, 70, 78–91, 94–96, 99–101, 103–105, 107, 111, 116f., 125–127, 130, 132–134, 136, 139, 141, 143, 147, 149–152, 154, 156, 165, 174
Industrial policy 1f., 4–10, 15f., 19f., 53, 78–80, 83, 85–87, 90, 94–97, 100–107, 109–111, 125–133, 136–138, 141–153, 155, 157, 170f., 175

Industrial revolution 3
Industrial Upgrading and Modernisation Programme (IUMP) 108, 160
Infant industry protection 102, 122, 141f., 149, 160

K

Karakul 34f.

M

Meat processing 36, 38, 41–43, 52f., 56, 59, 71, 76f., 79f., 82, 121f.
Ministry of Industrialization, Trade and SME Development 16, 105f., 108f., 111, 127, 132, 138, 141f., 149f., 160, 177
Ministry of Trade and Industry 93–96, 100f., 103, 106f., 118, 125, 136, 140f., 160, 177

N

Namibia Industrial Development Agency 107f., 160
Namibia Investment Promotion Act 106, 137f., 146, 160
Namibian Economic Policy Research Unit (NEPRU) 15, 95, 100, 136, 160, 167, 169
Namibia Trade Forum 135

O

Ohlthaver & List 36, 77, 122, 134
Ovamboland 22, 27, 37, 64, 81f., 94, 165, 183

P

Pasta production 15, 102, 116, 120, 122, 134, 141
President Nujoma 13, 91f., 97, 136, 156

R

Ramatex 97–99, 119, 166, 168, 175, 180

S

SACU 102
Services 2f., 14, 89, 112, 114
Southern African Customs Union (SACU) 44f., 47f., 83f., 93, 97, 128, 139–142, 161
Southern African Development Community (SADC) 142, 146f., 161, 166
Southern Rhodesia 19, 21, 44, 48–51, 58, 66, 162, 169, 172
Structural transformation 1f., 6–10, 17, 83, 86, 89, 91, 111, 127, 134, 148, 151–153, 157, 168
Swakopmund 25, 36, 62f., 72, 81, 135
SWAPO 12f., 67, 91–94, 103, 105, 128f., 131–133, 143, 148, 152, 163, 172f.

T

Tourism 86, 116

U

United Nations 2, 5, 12f., 54, 67, 113, 171

W

Printed in the United States
By Bookmasters